CHANNELS OF RESISTANCE

CHANNELS
OF RESISTANCE

Global Television and Local Empowerment

Edited by

Tony Dowmunt

BFI PUBLISHING

in association with

CHANNEL FOUR TELEVISION

First published in 1993 by the
British Film Institute
21 Stephen Street
London W1P 1PL

in association with
Channel Four Television
60 Charlotte Street
London W1P 2AX

This book is published to accompany the Channel Four
Television season entitled 'Channels of Resistance'.

British Library Cataloguing in Publication Data.
A catalogue record for this book is
available from the British Library

Dowmunt, Tony
  Channels of Resistance
  I. Title
  302.234   # 286609659

ISBN 0-85170-392-5
      0-85170-388-7 Pbk

Designed by Art and Design

Front cover photo: Campaign for Open Media
demonstration, *The Star*, September 1991
Back cover photo: Bulgarian woman
watching MTV, MTV Press archive, 1991

Typesetting by
Goodfellow & Egan, Cambridge
Printed in Great Britain by
Page Bros, Norwich, Norfolk

For Zosia

CONTENTS

ACKNOWLEDGMENTS

The idea for this book grew out of conversations with Alan Fountain, Senior Commissioning Editor for Independent Film and Video at Channel Four. I very much appreciate both his personal support for the book's publication and his Department's support for the area of television work that the book describes and advocates.

Tana Wollen from the BFI has been a prolific source of editorial wisdom, guidance and practical help to me as a first-time editor; I don't know what I would have done without her. Warm thanks too to Jane Foot for her support during the editing process, and again to her, Su Braden, Tom Perlmutter and my partners Andy Porter and Paul Morrison for their helpful comments on my introduction. I am grateful also to Anita Miller and Shona Blass for typing and retyping manuscripts.

NOTES ON CONTRIBUTORS

Tony Dowmunt is a director of Apt Film and Television, an independent production company with whom he has made (among other programmes) *Remote Control: Television and Democracy* and co-produced *Satellite Dreaming* – about Aboriginal television in Australia – both for Channel Four. From 1974 to 1989 he worked in the community-based workshop movement in London. He now teaches part-time at King Alfred's College, Winchester. He is the author of *Video with Young People* (Cassell, 1986).

Tom Perlmutter is a Canadian writer and film-maker. He researched, wrote and co-produced *Distress Signals*, a documentary about the globalisation of TV. He was Toronto editor of Canada's national film magazine, *Cinema Canada*, and has written extensively on film. He is currently completing an innovative documentary about Marconi and the birth of the wireless.

Julian Petley is Head of Communication and Information Studies at Brunel University. He has written for numerous publications on cinema and edits the sleeve-notes for Connoisseur Video.

Gabriella Romano has worked as a freelance journalist and as a television researcher. Since completing a postgraduate diploma in Communications Studies at Goldsmiths' College, University of London, she has directed a documentary for BBC2 and is currently writing and researching future projects.

Corinna Sturmer graduated in 1992 from Goldsmiths' College, University of London, where she studied Media, Communications and Sociology. Her essay in this book was the basis for her final dissertation. She now works as a researcher and production assistant for Roger Bolton Productions.

Roberto Mader is a Brazilian television and print journalist. He teaches at the Catholic University in Rio de Janeiro and has recently completed an MA in Communications Policy Studies at City University, London. He is the director of *Brazilian Snapshots*, a documentary for Channel Four.

Willie Currie is General Secretary of the Film and Allied Workers Organisation (FAWO) in South Africa.

Michael Markovitz is a broadcasting consultant based in Johannesburg and a member of the FAWO Broadcasting Commission.

Philip Batty works as a consultant and writer. He co-founded the Central Australian Aboriginal Media Association (CAAMA) in 1980 and has since been closely involved in the development of Aboriginal broadcasting. He has produced various television programmes, including *Nganampa Anwernekenhe, Sing Loud Play Strong* and *Benny and the Dreamers*. His publications include *Aboriginal Media Organisations* and *Aboriginal Television*.

Derek Tini Fox is Foundation Director of Mana Maori Media, a news and information agency specialising in Maori perspectives on current affairs. He has worked in broadcasting in Aotearoa (New Zealand) for the past twenty-five years as a producer, reporter and director on current affairs programmes. In 1982 he established *Te Karere*, a Maori TV news programme.

Mark Derby is an Auckland journalist with a special interest in mass media. He is the South Pacific correspondent for *Journal Expresso* of Lisbon and a director of Paradigm, a public-interest communications company.

Daoud Kuttab is a producer with Al Quds Television and political columnist for the Arabic daily *Al Quds* in Jerusalem. He is an adviser to Reuters on Palestinian affairs and, on media questions, to the Palestinian peace negotiations.

Su Braden is a freelance television producer/director. She has also worked for many years in community-based projects and is the author of *Artists and People* and *Committing Photography*. She worked as a consultant trainer producer for the Television Trust for the Environment in Africa from 1990 to 1992, and is currently course director of the Postgraduate Diploma/MA in Television for Development at King Alfred's College, Winchester.

Jon Dovey is currently in charge of public education at Watershed Media Centre in Bristol. He also lectures in Media Studies at the University of Plymouth. He has worked as an independent video producer for more than ten years and is a director of Gorilla Tapes.

Martin Lucas is a founding member of Paper Tiger Television and an independent producer and playwright. His work includes the film *Tighten Your Belts, Bite the Bullet*, the video *Camino Triste: the Hard Road of the Guatemalan Refugees*, and the play *The Pearl of the Orient*. A graduate of New York University Film School, he currently teaches at the School for Visual Arts, NYC.

Martha Wallner is a founding member of Deep Dish Satellite Television Network and a long-time media activist and producer. At Deep Dish she has co-ordinated several series and individual productions such as *Spigots for Bigots or Channels for Change*. She has recently completed her Masters in Communications at Hunter College, City University of New York.

INTRODUCTION

Tony Dowmunt

This is a book about the potential for difference, diversity and radical innovation in world television. Since Marshall McLuhan first suggested that TV was creating a 'global village',[1] it has become a commonplace assumption that television is shrinking the world, homogenising its cultures, evening out differences. The clear dominance by the US television industry of the world market for programmes has led to this process being seen as monolithic 'cultural imperialism'.

There is certainly evidence to support this. 'We are the town-crier in the global village,' asserts Ed Turner, Head of News at CNN, the US-based satellite news service that now spans the globe.[2] The discipline of the world market is tending more and more to exclude the local, the culturally specific, the politically oppositional; and it is part of the purpose of this book to show how in particular instances this exclusion occurs. But the 'monolith' is by no means unchallenged. It is also true that there are many vital currents of opposition to these homogenising tendencies, and our main ambition in the following pages is to document and analyse some of them.

The evidence of these essays challenges the picture of a single all-inclusive 'global village', suggesting instead a diversity of smaller 'villages'. Some are certainly more powerful and dominant, others are in some ways dominated; but they all contain distinct communities which relate to each other, and to the television available to them, in varied ways. There is no single, homogenised, global audience. A Polish teenager marvels over a Sinead O'Connor video on MTV Europe; 25,000 fans of a Brazilian *tele-novela* (soap opera) gather in a Rio stadium to salute the stars of the show; an ANC supporter in South Africa

1

sees previously jailed representatives of her party on national TV for the first time; and in the Australian outback an Aboriginal community watches *Miami Vice*, then switches over to a locally made video of traditional songs and dance. World television is a site of complex cultural mixing – sometimes harmonious, often conflicting – at global, national and local levels.

The factor which perhaps more than any other explodes the concept of a unified 'global village' is economic inequality. To be a member of this imagined electronic community you must presumably have access to a TV set; but in Africa and other areas of the 'South' the cost of a receiver is beyond the means of the average income, and television ownership in many countries in the world is confined to city-dwellers with a higher than average income.[3] The 1980 MacBride Report for UNESCO stated that 'in some forty countries only 10 per cent of household units have a receiver',[4] and UNESCO figures for 1981-2 reveal that 'Whereas in Europe, the number of television sets is about 275 per 1,000 inhabitants, this figure drops to 90 per 1,000 in Latin America and 11 per 1,000 in Africa.'[5]

These figures do not take into account communal (as opposed to domestic) viewing of TV, or more recent evidence which shows a yearly growth in the ownership of TV sets of 300 per cent in the 'developing' world, against 40 per cent in the 'developed' countries.[6] Even so, for those of us who do have access to sets, other kinds of inequality and difference come into play, particularly those determined by the forces of 'media imperialism':

> the process whereby the ownership, structure, distribution or content of the media in any one country are … subject to substantial external pressures from the media interests of any other country or countries without proportionate reciprocation of influence by the country so affected.[7]

This means that not only programmes, but the technologies of production, transmission and reception, the kinds of industrial organisation and patterns of ownership, and the working practices of those involved in making television, all replicate and sustain power imbalances in world media. The first few chapters in this book all address the issue of how this 'imperialist' process works in specific situations.

Tom Perlmutter's essay is both a report on MIP-TV, the world's largest television market-place, staged annually at Cannes, and an examination of how the economic forces displayed there are affecting the TV industry in Canada, where he lives. Canada offers probably the earliest example of the subordination of domestic television by the US, and as such prefigures what is now a worldwide tendency. But Perlmutter's analysis of the current situation in Canada qualifies the picture of media imperialism as a process in which the US entertainment industry will always be culturally dominant. The growing influence of Japanese capital, both within the US industry and globally, and the market pressure for universally digestible product, are encouraging the making of programmes that are not culturally specific in any sense.

Julian Petley and Gabriella Romano describe how the current processes of deregulation in Western Europe are changing television systems which until recently have been predominantly state-run or state-regulated, operating on a variety of 'public service' models – changing them in ways that can be thought of as 'Canadianisation'. What we are experiencing is not so much 'deregulation' as 're-regulation', according to the less visible but equally powerful laws of the global market-place, a market-place Petley and Romano show to be clearly dominated by entertainment programming from the USA, or based on American models. They show how the remaining 'public service' stations are changing their programming priorities in order to compete in this new situation.

Petley and Romano also raise the 'problem of the popular'. A number of critics have claimed that much of the antagonism to entertainment TV derives from class-based snobbery. This is certainly the main 'cultural' argument put forward by entrepreneurs who wish to benefit from deregulation: 'It's not for the few to dictate to the many what they should or shouldn't watch.'[8] They portray the market as an instrument of popular will – giving the people what they want. But while many of us may enjoy relaxing in front of *Blind Date* or an American soap, there is no evidence to suggest that that is all we want TV to offer. In fact the UK Broadcasting Research Unit reported in 1986 that 93 per cent of people surveyed thought that TV should 'inform' as well as entertain, and 84 per cent thought that it should also 'educate'.[9] It is now fashionable in the TV industry to suggest that poll results like this are obtained because people answer as they think they 'ought to', rather than owning up to their actual opinions. Even if this were partly true, the attitudes expressed remain significant and the percentages indicate that an exclusive diet of entertainment would, at least in the UK, go against the popular will. Paradoxically, it seems that replacing middle- or low-rating programmes with top-rating shows disenfranchises the majority of viewers. Seen in this light, the growing world dominance of exclusively entertainment-led TV, as described by Petley and Romano and others in this book, appears increasingly totalitarian; in the sense that, as a system, it does not tolerate, in fact it annihilates, all alternatives.

Corinna Sturmer's chapter about MTV Europe (the European subsidiary of the American Music Television satellite/cable channel) is, in contrast, relatively optimistic about the survival of European identities in the face of MTV's particular brand of media imperialism. Much of what she says hinges on the crisis of 'nationhood', touched on by Petley and Romano when they ask, of Italy, 'Is it merely a coincidence that the Western European country which has gone farthest down the deregulated road should also be the one whose unity is most seriously in doubt?' MTV Europe attempts to promote a unity of 'European Youth' in preference to national identities which have become, for many of the channel's young audiences, stale and repressive. But Sturmer also demonstrates that MTV's European ideal is only infrequently achieved; its audiences respond to it in very different ways, and these differences are often defined by their national origins. For instance, young Italians appear more resistant to MTV colonisation than, say, young Swedes. Sturmer points out, however, that this has more to do with particular cultural circumstances (the existence of a strong popular music tradition in Italy, together with a national music video cable channel) than with any abstract, atavistic notions of national identity, which are certainly dissolving as the cultural and political borders of 'Europe' shift.

MTV Europe clearly demonstrates a number of the contradictions at work within 'media imperialism'. Although part of a global and growing empire owned by a US conglomerate, and with a transmission model (satellite and cable) and an aesthetic approach developed in America, the station is nevertheless heavily inflected by local cultural conditions. It has self-consciously sought a European rather than an American identity, but is also finding that to maintain and extend its audience it may need to serve quite specific (rather than pan-European) musical tastes in national or regional cultural blocs. But whether its wholly commercial nature will allow MTV Europe to be genuinely expressive of a wide range of European youth cultures (including those that are socially and economically marginal) remains an open question.

The same local/global contradictions are evident in other parts of the MTV empire. In Brazil, for instance, the government insisted that the channel play 50 per cent Brazilian music when it started transmitting in

1990. This may in part be attributable to the size and strength of the Brazilian television industry, the development of which is the subject of Roberto Mader's chapter. He shows how this almost entirely commercial system was transformed from the scattered distribution of a range of regional stations into a satellite-based nationwide network dominated by one company, Globo, now the world's fourth largest network (after the North American CBS, NBC and ABC).

This achievement again qualifies the picture of the world's media empires being run exclusively from the USA (or from the North generally), but there are other ways in which Globo exemplifies US media imperialism. Mader details the influence of US advertising agencies on TV in Brazil, and the involvement of US capital and technical and administrative expertise in the growth of Globo. So, although now indigenously owned and operated and with its own nationally specific forms (*tele-novelas*, for instance), there is still a way in which the Brazilian system is a North American import. Globo, in turn, is now engaged in exporting its own programming and expertise, building its own empire.

What is significant – and sinister – in the case of Globo is how effectively it was able to achieve a virtual monopoly within the deregulated environment of Brazilian TV, and how it was then able to protect and promote the interests of the military dictatorships whose reigns 'coincided' with its expansion. This punctures the free-marketeers' argument that the absence of state intervention in deregulated television systems is some sort of guarantee of political freedom. In fact those interested in democratic expression in Brazil are fighting for television to be 'regulated' – for the adoption of many of the rules and ideals currently being abandoned in Europe.

In South Africa, the democratic movement involved in the struggle to dismantle apartheid is also advocating regulatory structures for national television. Willie Currie and Michael Markovitz show how this is a war on two distinct fronts. On the one hand progressive groups are trying to wrest power away from the Boer Broederbond interests that have dominated TV until now; on the other, they are trying to win for the emerging non-racial, democratic state powers to regulate the South African television industry and thereby prevent it falling completely under the influence of the global market and the American industry. This involves proposing an inclusive national public service model (again, of the kind under threat in Europe), to deal with the fragmentation dictated by apartheid, under which the South African Broadcasting Corporation (SABC) ran three racially segregated channels.

Zimbabwe TV crew shooting Ziva Kawakaba *in a village outside Harare*

Meanwhile the strategy of the current State President, De Klerk, is working in the opposite direction. He has divided the SABC into separate business units, apparently in readiness for selling off after the proposed deregulation of the broadcast sector. Currie and Markovitz believe that this fragmentation process, transferring 'control over broadcasting from the political to the economic sphere', corresponds to De Klerk's overall strategy in the negotiations for a new South Africa, in which he is seeking to give power to semi-autonomous regions in an attempt to curb the influence of any future majority government. Judging by the record of M-Net, a burgeoning commercial broadcaster in South Africa, deregulation is unlikely to benefit South Africa's majority. M-Net continually disregards its 'local content' obligations, and a large proportion of its meagre local programming is in Afrikaans. Its overall purpose is clearly to satisfy the richer (mainly white) sections of the audience.

Currie and Markovitz's advocacy of a strong, national broadcast sector, adequately regulated and resourced, also makes sense when viewed alongside the situation in neighbouring Zimbabwe. ZTV can only afford to produce about twelve hours of indigenous drama a year, albeit incredibly cheaply with the actors also doing day jobs and providing their own costumes. Drama series like *Ziva Kawakaba* (*Know Your Roots*) are very popular with the majority black audience, but the advertisers know that they are going to get better value for money from imported programmes that appeal to the more affluent white or middle-class black audiences. And ZTV know that they can acquire an episode of *Miami Vice*, say, for the special 'Third World' rate of $500 – a fraction of the already minimal budget of an episode of *Ziva Kawakaba*.[10]

Of course there are those (like Sturmer in her analysis of MTV Europe) who question the 'demonology' inherent in the 'media imperialism' concept, pointing out that all external media influences are not always 'bad' and oppressive. For many young Swedes or Poles, MTV is a cultural lifeline; and in the 1980s in South Africa foreign documentaries smuggled in on video were a vital source of information for the democratic movement. During the political turmoil in Thailand in 1991, videos of BBC World Service coverage of the rioting, recorded off satellite in a Bangkok bar, were widely circulated as an alternative to the censored national TV.[11] In the UK, Channel Four's programme *South* commissions work from programme-makers from the South and 'developing' countries, enabling them to be critical of their countries' regimes.

Economic arguments are also used to question the 'media imperialism' thesis. Richard Collins, for instance, argues that

> there is no particular economic reason why a nation-state should seek autarchy in the production of information goods any more than Switzerland should seek to be self-sufficient in seafish, Britain in bananas, or Egypt in forest products. In the production of other commodities an international division of labour takes place, why not with information goods?[12]

The answer to his question is that there is no easy equivalence between self-sufficiency in products and in information. There are no 'natural' barriers, analogous to Switzerland's lack of coastline, which prevent cultures from producing their own information. A key sentence in the constitution of Te Manu Aute, the organisation of Maori Communicators in New Zealand reads:

> Every culture has a right and a responsibility to present its own culture to its own people. That responsibility is so fundamental it cannot be left in the hands of outsiders, nor be usurped by them.[13]

This feeling is echoed around the world where people experience their cultures threatened by powerful external pressures, and with increasing frequency these peoples are using video and television as tools with which to assert themselves and fight back. Just a few examples:

– in Catalonia, a part of Spain with a regional identity increasingly strongly expressed since the death of Franco, there are about a hundred community TV stations;[14]

– the film and video workshop movement in the UK received its impetus in part from the regional (or national) aspirations of Scotland, Wales, Northern Ireland and the North-East, and from the demands of black film and video makers;

– in Papua New Guinea in the late 1980s the then Prime Minister, Paias Wingti, fought for indigenously controlled media and against the introduction of TV into the island by Australian magnates Alan Bond and Kerry Packer, saying 'We are being asked to sacrifice our cultural heritage for passing material gain. No money can buy back our languages once they are gone';[15]

– in the Caribbean island of St Lucia, which boasts seventeen TV channels, of which only two are local (and they show 90 per cent re-broadcast material from international satellites), Soufrière Community TV makes its own local programmes and strips the ads off the satellite material before re-broadcasting it; and the Folk Research Centre makes programmes about traditional dance and culture, so that 'when now they [St Lucians] look at CNN or some other actors ... they can say "Hey, we can be there too."'[16]

The same thirst for cultural self-expression is evident in the work of indigenous people's organisations around the world; the Inuit in the Canadian Arctic, the Indian peoples in Brazil and Bolivia, Maori in New Zealand, Aboriginal people in Australia and Native American Indians are all engaging with video and television in a variety of ways. The essays by Philip Batty and Derek Tini Fox offer accounts of indigenous people's practice in Australia and New Zealand.

Philip Batty presents a stark contrast between two very different strategies for Aboriginal television: the local model of Ernabella Video and Television, based in the Pitjanjatjarra community, and Imparja TV, an Aboriginal-owned commercial satellite station covering the whole of central Australia. He explores why the former succeeds and why the latter is apparently failing to serve the cultural needs of Aboriginal people which both stations were originally set up to meet. His conclusions are illuminating for anyone interested in workable alternatives to mainstream global TV.

8

The Pitjanjatjarra have been able to engage with television in Ernabella very much on their own terms. They use appropriate and affordable production and transmission technology, based on their own lands where they are in a majority, and have remained relatively self-financing, which affords them independence from both government funding constraints and commercial pressures. The Central Australian Aboriginal Media Association (CAAMA), who set up Imparja, were on the other hand greatly influenced by these pressures. Government policy determined that they had to apply for a commercial licence to transmit to a vast (and only about 40 per cent Aboriginal) area, and so Imparja has ended up as a reasonably typical commercial TV station existing in the international market-place – it just happens to be Aboriginal-owned. During the whole of 1991 Imparja broadcast only 6.5 hours of Aboriginal programming in Aboriginal languages, even though language maintenance was one of the prime reasons CAAMA had established it in the first place. In contrast, the Inuit Broadcasting Corporation in northern Canada have been running their own satellite station for the last twelve years, basically supported by government money. Despite inadequate resources, constant budget squeezes and political arguments with their funding masters, they have survived and continue to broadcast an innovative schedule of Inuit programming, much of it in Inuktituk, the Inuit language.

Derek Tini Fox explores some of these issues from the perspective of a professional Maori broadcaster. Where Batty's analysis of the Australian situation suggests that 'local is best', Fox draws a different conclusion from his experience. The position of Maori people in New Zealand differs from that of Aboriginal people in Australia, in that they form a larger percentage of the population, and despite continued discrimination are currently negotiating with their former colonisers from a position of relative strength. Maori people are arguing for a substantial stake in the national public broadcasting system, on the basis of the Treaty of Waitangi, signed in 1840 between the British crown and the Chiefs of Aotearoa (New Zealand) and guaranteeing Maori people authority over their resources. Though there is a movement in support of local, tribal TV stations (stimulated by the rapid growth of tribal radio), Fox wants the government to fund a national Maori TV station, which could screen material originated locally but would also be sufficiently well resourced to compete for a wide national audience. The lesson from Australia may be that if such a national station were forced by government to take on a commercial structure, its cultural objectives would be unlikely to survive. The strength of tribal radio in Aotearoa, and of CAAMA's radio station 8KIN mentioned by Batty, also suggests that there are circumstances in which the economic, technical and institutional complications of television production make it an inappropriate medium for cultural activists when compared with the cheapness and simplicity of radio.

Fox concludes with a description of Mana Maori Media, a Maori news service which he has helped to establish and which is currently starting to change the white bias of news provision in Aotearoa. He also sees its potential as a communications channel with other indigenous peoples, and as a way to influence the international news agenda more generally, from a Maori perspective. It is an interesting prototype in a world where

> the overwhelming majority of world news flows from the developed to the developing countries, and is generated by four large transnational news agencies – AP, UPI, AFP and Reuters. Moreover the West dominates the use of satellites, the electromagnetic spectrum controlling the use of airwaves, telecommunications, micro-electronics, remote sensing capabilities, direct satellite broadcasting, and computer-related transmission.[17]

Even to begin to affect Western-dominated information channels in this situation will clearly be a long and complex struggle, beginning with isolated experiments through which international alliances may start to be formed. Daoud Kuttab describes one such experiment in his account of a programme he produced, partly for the UK's Channel Four. *Palestinian Diaries* was an indigenous response to the impoverished international coverage of the *intifada* in the occupied territories, which included plenty of footage of stone-throwing youths but little insight into the realities of daily life for Palestinians. The customary limitations of international news-gathering, such as a lack of local knowledge on the part of foreign crews, and news values which prioritise sensationalism and stereotyping over understanding, were compounded in this case by curfews and filming restrictions. The producers of *Palestinian Diaries* dealt with these problems by making use of small domestic video cameras (camcorders) which they put into the hands of specially trained 'non-professionals' from less well publicised areas in the occupied territories. The resulting programme is a collage of three 'video diaries'.

There has been a long tradition of this way of using video, initiated by the Canadian National Film Board's 'Challenge for Change' programme in the late 1960s, when portable video cameras first became available. This technology's main characteristics – relative cheapness, ease of use, and the instant playback facility – made it accessible to 'non-professionals' and ideal for community-based work. For many media workers worldwide, portable video continues to suggest an alternative philosophy of television production: 'Mass media tends to obliterate identity. Video tends to rediscover identity and consolidate it.'[18] Neville Jayaweera, former Director General of Sri Lanka TV, is here referring to work such as that of Video SEWA in Ahmedabad, India. SEWA is the Self-Employed Women's Association, an organisation of more than 24,000 street vendors, small-scale producers and labourers, some of whose members have been trained in video production with American aid funding. They use video to communicate with their (often illiterate) membership, and to organise:

> One of its video programmes about a dispute between small-scale vegetable vendors and the city was shown to a municipal leader and contributed to an equitable resolution. This municipal leader had never really listened to these women before and probably never would have if not via videotape. The vegetable vendors themselves would not have spoken freely and forcefully to a city official but could do so to the impersonal video camera.[19]

Though this kind of grass roots media activity provides an exciting and democratic model for the development of indigenous documentary production, it is unfortunately true that this work has very little effect on how the television systems of 'developing' countries are run. This is more often determined by 'media imperialist' pressures, as shown by the contrast of Africa 'adopting' European state-run models, and Latin American systems being more influenced by the commercial ethos of the US.[20] Much rarer is any attempt to start from scratch, to model TV systems around indigenous needs and aspirations, or on a concept of 'development' that promotes autonomy and self-reliance.

The work that Su Braden describes indicates how this approach might be encouraged. In her account of her involvement in a series of programmes about Uganda's wetlands, co-funded by Uganda Television and environmental agencies, she suggests a model of TV production that is neither Reithian and paternalistic nor dependent on market pres-

11

sures. Her Ugandan co-workers have now set up a 'Television for Development' unit and are being commissioned to produce programmes for local and international development agencies, who in the past would have been more likely to use producers from 'developed' countries. The unit provides an opportunity for Ugandans to represent themselves, to challenge the domination by the North of the market for images of the South, and may well prove to be a model for other African countries confronted by the same dilemmas.

The final two chapters look at examples of resistance on the fringes of mainstream TV, but in the developed 'North', where the need for democratic and responsive television is as great as anywhere else. In the UK much of the struggle to satisfy this need has been focused over the last twenty years on 'access' television, which seeks to give a voice to sections of society that have been ignored or misrepresented on television. Jon Dovey explores the contradiction that 'access' programming currently appears to be thriving while the public service broadcasting system which gave it birth is under severe threat. He shows how these programmes have carved a niche for themselves in the competitive schedules of the 90s by developing new forms of 'individually authored' production, in some cases relying heavily on the use of camcorders. He also shows how the political context of 'access' has changed over its twenty-year history, from a broadcasting environment dominated by the twin monoliths of the BBC and ITV networks addressing a relatively undifferentiated mass audience, to the present situation in which Channel Four, cable, satellite, and videocassette distribution compete with the BBC and ITV for a diverse and fragmented community of audiences. Dovey sees in this new environment both opportunities and threats for the development of democratic television.

The importance of the camcorder as a tool for democratic TV, identified by both Dovey and Daoud Kuttab, is becoming increasingly evident throughout the world. It is a continuing cause for optimism that the same transnational electronics industry that feeds the growth of mainstream global TV also produces the means by which it can be challenged and resisted. Neville Jayaweera points out that TV

is like a two-headed monster, fuelled by the same technology. You see, the same technology unfortunately is putting power in the hands of mass media to wrap up the whole globe in one *Dallas* culture, through satellites and switching techniques, and uplinks and downlinks. But the same technology jumps across to the other side and says, 'Now you can use me to counter that force. I place in your hands power to counter that global tendency.'[21]

Martin Lucas and Martha Wallner's account of the Gulf Crisis TV Project perfectly exemplifies this 'two-headedness': the Project used camcorders, cable and satellites to spread a subversive message of opposition to the Gulf War, which achieved wide national and international distribution. But they stress that the main reason for the success of the project was not the availability of the technology itself, but the networking and political organisation that enabled it to be exploited. They point in particular to their links with over 300 public access stations in the US, who both transmitted the Gulf Project shows and provided much of the footage for them. The project was remarkable for the ways in which this network blurred the division between producers and consumers and achieved a global reach from local roots. Lucas and Wallner conclude by pointing to the international significance for media activists of this kind of 'horizontal networking' in our increasingly commercial and restrictive world TV system.

The chapters in the book are arranged so that their geographical focus ranges from the global and national to the local; the earlier sections look at wider situations and issues, the later ones at specific aspects of national TV systems or at particular projects. In this way we hope that the local initiatives described are put in a clear transnational context, which is shown in turn to exert particular pressures on what is possible locally.

This dialectic between the global and the local is also at the heart of most of the chapters. However, the book is not a survey: we have not attempted to cover the world exhaustively, but to include work and issues which illuminate the main themes. The most glaring omission is any treatment of developments in Eastern Europe. The role of television in the Romanian revolution or in the continuing political changes in Russia, for instance, highlights fascinating instances of changing media power relationships. It is already clear that as these countries open themselves up to market forces and transnational capital, their television systems are increasingly exposed to the global media economy and the same pressures we see elsewhere in both the North and South – pushed from the frying pan of state control into the fire of market discipline, but also generating their own indigenous opportunities for resistance along the way. As Corinna Sturmer shows in her essay on MTV, for Eastern

13

Europeans 'Western culture' has had symbolic value as a resistance to totalitarianism, demonstrating again that what for one community may be media imperialism may for another be a liberating force.

Most of the contributors to this book are involved in some way in television production. So the book presents, in the main, the experiences and analyses of activists and practitioners. This differentiates our approach from much current academic work in media studies, which prioritises an exploration of the experiences and pleasures audiences have of mainstream, dominant media; it is as if the overwhelming fact of this dominance inhibits many academics from imagining or thinking about alternatives. This is well typified by John Fiske's work, which plays down the importance of radical television production:

> ... television can and does participate to an extent in offering progressive, if not radical, meanings. But I would argue that television's political effectivity and its progressive potential lie rather in its ability to devolve the power to make meanings rather than in any alternative meanings it may offer.[22]

It is 'the freedom of the viewer to make socially pertinent meanings and pleasures out of television',[23] rather than what is actually produced for showing on television, that is significant for Fiske; and to support his argument he cites, among other examples, Eric Michaels's account of Australian Aboriginal viewers enjoying *Rambo* on video.[24] But there is an irony here. While Michaels's work certainly contains many references to the very different ways in which Walpiri people read, and derive pleasure from, white/North American films and TV shows (different, that is, from audiences in the cultures that originated them), the main body of his work is about the video and TV production of the Walpiri Media Association; it describes the decision of these people to represent themselves, to gain power in similar ways to the Pitjanjatjarra people described in Philip Batty's essay, by controlling the means of TV production as well as its reception.[25]

How all of us receive and use dominant television forms is clearly an important concern. But the fact of this dominance does not stop us from imagining, developing and analysing alternatives. That is why this book describes how groups all over the world, in institutional and technological situations not of their own making, have begun to resist this domination in diverse and creative ways. Some of these groups are already in contact, and other networks will grow in the next few years.

Although the economic and political pressures on the global television system are strong, they are not totally determining. We can dare to imagine, and start to create, something different.

NOTES

1. Marshall McLuhan and Bruce Powers, *The Global Village: Transformations in World Life and Media in the 21st Century* (New York: Oxford University Press, 1989).
2. From an interview in the TV documentary *Distress Signals* (Toronto: Orbit Films, 1990).
3. Tapio Varis, 'Trends in International Television Flow', in Cynthia Schneider and Brian Wallis (eds.), *Global Television* (New York: Wedge Press, 1988), p. 105.
4. Quoted in Sean Cubitt, *Timeshift: On Video Culture* (London: Routledge, 1991), p. 10.
5. Quoted in Armand Mattelart, Xavier Delcourt and Michèle Mattelart, *International Image Markets* (London: Comedia, 1984), p. 23.
6. UNESCO World Communications Report (Paris: UNESCO, 1989).
7. Oliver Boyd-Barrett, 'Media Imperialism', in James Curran (ed.), *Mass Communication and Society* (London: Matthew Arnold, 1977), p. 117.
8. Eddie Shah, quoted in the TV documentary *Remote Control* (London: Apt Film and Television for Channel Four, April 1990).
9. David Morrison, *Invisible Citizens* (London: John Libbey, 1986), p. 30.
10. I am indebted to Tom Perlmutter for this information on Zimbabwe.
11. Philip Wood (unpublished research, UK, 1992).
12. Richard Collins, 'Wall-to-Wall Dallas: The US–UK Trade in Television', in Schneider and Wallis, *Global Television*, p. 80.
13. Quoted in Barry Barclay, *Our Own Image* (Auckland: Longman Paul, 1990), p. 7.
14. Miquel de Moragas Spa and Maria Corominas, 'Spain, Catalonia: Media and democratic participation in local communication', in Nick Jankowski, Ole Prehn and James Stappers (eds.), *The People's Voice* (London: John Libbey, 1992), p. 192.
15. Quoted by Phil Shingler, *Pacific Stories* (unpublished research, UK, 1989).
16. Monsignor Patrick Anthony of the Folk Research Centre, interviewed in Banyan TV's documentary *And The Dish Ran Away With The Spoon* (BBC2, 21 May 1992).
17. Francis N. Wete, 'The New World Information Order and the US Press', in Schneider and Wallis, *Global Television*, p. 139.
18. Interviewed in *The Media Show* (Channel Four, 1990).
19. Sara Stuart, 'Video in the Village', in *Development Communication Report* (New York: Spring 1986), p. 7.
20. Mattelart, Delcourt and Mattelart, *International Image Markets*, p. 24.
21. Interviewed in *The Media Show*, 1990.
22. John Fiske, 'Moments of Television', in Ellen Seiter, Hans Borcher, Gabriele Kreutzner, Eva-Maria Warth (eds.), *Remote Control* (London: Routledge, 1991), p. 73.
23. Ibid., p. 60.
24. Ibid., p. 61.
25. Eric Michaels, *Bad Aboriginal Art: Tradition, Media and Cultural Futures* (Minneapolis: Minnesota University Press, 1993).

DISTRESS SIGNALS
A Canadian Story – An International Lesson

Tom Perlmutter

Since the birth of broadcasting in the early 1920s, Canada has been a unique experimental laboratory for both the organisation of electronic media (public v. private) and the regulation of the flow of programming (local v. American). For over seventy years Canada has struggled to maintain a balance between the fervently held conviction that information flows must be totally open and a desire to rescue at least some portion of the spectrum for a Canadian vision of the world. It is a struggle that has ended in more defeats than victories, if by defeat we understand the erosion of a distinctively Canadian broadcasting system which reflects a Canadian point of view – whether in drama, news or documentary – and which supports a Canadian production industry technically, financially and artistically.

For the world, and for Europe in particular, Canada is often regarded as the critical case study of the effects of deregulation. Throughout its history Canada has struggled with the overwhelming presence of the United States. Deregulation and new technologies have now opened the possibility that 'we could all become each other's neighbours ... we may all become Canadians now.'[1] Often what others saw in Canada terrified them. Canadian broadcasting history is a history of good intentions, noble rhetoric and for the most part abject failure in creating a distinctive national television broadcasting system. As Anthony Smith noted, 'No country is more completely committed to the practice of free flow in its culture and no country is more completely its victim.'[2]

The Canadian dilemma was the dilemma of a country bordering the world's dominant media giant and its principal trading partner, the United States. Technically, it was almost impossible to erect a national frontier between Canadian television and American broadcasters. Throughout the 1950s, a distinctive physical characteristic of the Canadian landscape within 150 miles of the United States, where 80 per cent of the Canadian population lives, was the proliferation of rooftop aerials for the reception of American TV signals. The only hope for a technical barrier would have been to adopt a European standard at the start of television broadcasting. This was considered and rejected because it was assumed that to fill airtime most programmes would have to come from the United States, and that there would be a political backlash if Canadians were denied access to American programmes. There may also have been considerable pressure from Washington to ensure that the Canadian television market would remain as open and lucrative to American producers as the movie market had always been.

Within a short time the Canadian airwaves, like Canadian cinema screens before, were dominated by American programming. The Canadian response was contradictory and ineffective, despite standing legislation that enshrined the obligation of the national public broadcasting system to serve Canadians with Canadian programming. That legislation was the result of a battle fought and won in the 1920s. By the end of that decade much of Canada was inundated with American radio signals emitted from powerful transmitters. Nationalists quickly understood that foreign radio was undermining Canada's sense of itself. Led by Alan Plaunt and Graham Spry, they formed the Canadian Radio League with the battle-cry 'The state or The States', and lobbied for a national broadcasting system.

In 1928 a bank president headed a Royal Commission on the subject. This eminently conservative businessman reported that 'There has been unanimity on one fundamental question – Canadian radio listeners want Canadian broadcasting.'[3] The Commission recommended a national, publicly owned system to achieve a genuinely Canadian broadcasting system. Within four years the Canadian Broadcasting Corporation (CBC) was born. Equally importantly, Canadian diplomats worked at the international level to ensure an equitable distribution of the radio spectrum among all nations of the world and a limitation on transmitting power.

Twenty years later, the economics of television once again changed the balance of power. Despite a national, publicly owned broadcasting system and despite a fair allocation of the spectrum, Canadians quickly began to lose control of their airwaves. Buying American programming was substantially cheaper than producing Canadian programming. In addition, CBC did not have a secure funding base. It depended on a yearly allocation from parliament and on advertising revenues. The major advertisers, often branch plants of American companies, were less willing to risk their funds on Canadian programming than on tried and tested American productions.

Despite limited and uncertain resources and the pressure to buy American, the CBC managed to produce a body of Canadian work through the 1950s. But the economic pressure became an economic imperative when Ottawa decided to experiment with a moderate form of deregulation: the licensing of a private sector broadcasting system. The Royal Commission established to investigate the feasibility of a private system understood very clearly what deregulation meant for national broadcasting. More than thirty-five years later its conclusions are as relevant to a deregulating Europe as they were to Canada then.

In 1957, the Fowler Royal Commission on Broadcasting reported that 'We cannot choose between a Canadian broadcasting system controlled by the state and a Canadian competitive system in private hands. The choice is between a Canadian state-controlled system with some flow of programmes east and west across Canada, with some Canadian content and the development of a Canadian sense of identity, at a substantial public cost, and a privately owned system which the forces of economics will necessarily make predominantly dependent on imported American programmes.'[4] The government ignored Fowler, and in 1961 private television was licensed in Canada, to the detriment of Canadian broadcasting. Within four years Fowler reported that the private networks' 'undertakings [to produce Canadian programming] given to obtain the grant of a public asset have largely been ignored.'[5] Twenty-two years later another government task force on the sorry state of Canadian broadcasting saw no improvement. 'The contribution of private broadcasters to Canadian programming has been less than impressive over the past twenty-five years.'[6] In the end the cost was borne by Canadians in the form of a lost sense of purpose and national identity and in the constitutional crises which have beset the country since the early 1980s. The CBC had been given a legislative mandate to act as a unifying force in Canadian life; it was never given the means to fulfil that mandate.

Having opened broadcasting's Pandora's box, Ottawa subsequently tried to contain the damage by regulatory means. Regulated deregulation would balance the demands of public policy with the private market-place. A promise of public performance would result in a private licence. The promises proliferated through the 1970s and 1980s, as did private broadcasters. Once on air, the promises evaporated with the simple explanation that to fulfil them would result in unacceptable economic hardship. In all cases the regulatory agency concurred. It was a classic case of a regulatory agency being captured by those it was established to regulate. The agency had become an instrument of the regulated.

Now, the whole question of regulation is becoming a moot point. Regulation is based on the notion of the airwaves as a scarce public resource, but new satellite, fibre optic and compression technologies promise an unlimited spectrum. Blend in the convergence of computers and telecommunication systems, and the airwaves, so technological enthusiasts claim, will be open to all. The necessity for a specific national public broadcasting system with a public interest remit, it is argued, will be obviated by this democratisation of the airwaves. The national voice will exist in the summation of the multitude of individual Canadian voices seen and heard by whoever wishes to tune in. Broadcasting (narrow or wide) will be as simple as picking up a tele-phone. Already, in the United States, the Federal Communications Commission has approved the entry of telecommunications companies into the market to carry broadcast signals.

The argument seems to ignore the commercial reality. In the long run it matters little whether cable or telephone interests win the battle to carry broadcasting into the next millennium. In either case the common carrier will have to bear the enormous capital costs of installing the new fibre optic/compression technology over a range of services, whether primetime television or home shopping, and make these services mar-ketable to the consumer. Public interest will wilt in the market heat.

In Canada, each experiment in deregulation and the introduction of new technology has been heralded with the promise of choice and diversity, a victory for Canadians; but has actually resulted in a dimin-ishing of choice because commercial dictates become the only determi-nants of what should or should not exist in the broadcasting universe. Key words and phrases like 'deregulation', 'offering viewers greater choice', 'let consumers decide' mask the choking of a different tradition: a tradition of broadcasting as a public good and a public service.

Ironically, what has been uniquely a Canadian phenomenon, the result of its proximity to the United States, has over the last few years become increasingly familiar to Europeans. In Britain, one of Margaret

Thatcher's last acts as Prime Minister was the gutting of a universally acclaimed broadcasting system in the name of the market-place, deregulation and freedom of choice. Rupert Murdoch's BSkyB channel has swallowed its satellite competitors and is slowly increasing its audience reach with a diet of cheap American programming. To one degree or another France, Germany, Italy, Belgium and other Western, and now Eastern, European countries have experienced similar upheavals in the structure of their broadcasting industry.

The ideology of a free market providing free and varied broadcasting choices has served only as a thin smokescreen for the reality of concentration of the ownership of production and distribution on a global scale. As one media analyst put it, 'It's not just that bigger is better. Bigger is survival.'[7] When *Time* merged with Warners in 1989, *The Times* noted that 'Both parties admitted the merger was a response to the emergence of other international media groups', like German-owned Bertelsmann.[8] Robert Maxwell's downfall probably lay in his attempt to leap single-handedly into the global big league. On that scale Maxwell didn't have the bucks. Even hallowed American giants like MCA and Columbia have bowed to the inevitable and sought shelter in Japanese arms. These conglomerates are fighting for control of a significant portion of the world market. It is the kind of fight that requires enormous capital investment in production, distribution and marketing. The costs of production have escalated to the point where the American market alone is no longer sufficient to cover them. For the first time, companies like Warner Bros are looking to foreign markets in Europe and Asia to provide them with between a third and a half of their total revenue by the end of the 90s.

American product may still generate the revenues, but under the pressure of more and more foreign ownership and the need to please a widely varying foreign market as well as the American one, even American programming is being squeezed to conform to a homogeneous, globalised standard of mega-star mega-action of the kind provided by Arnold Schwarzenegger and Sylvester Stallone. The global market-place is becoming the sole and unremitting arbiter of the culturally permissible. Nowhere is this more evident than at MIP-TV, the world's largest television show market.

In an annual rite of spring, 7,000 TV executives from ninety countries converge on Cannes for a six-day shopping spree. By the early 1990s four billion dollars worth of TV product was being bought and sold annually at MIP. The bulk of the trade is in American or American-inspired programming. MIP is the reality of the new world order in broadcasting. A European TV executive admonishes a symposium on the future of broadcasting that 'If Europe wants to play the game of commercial TV it must use the right equipment: programming that audiences want to watch.'[9] The translation of 'give the audiences what they want' is 'give the advertisers what they need.' That the two do not necessarily coincide is unquestioned.

An Italian TV executive pinpoints a prime characteristic of the new television order: 'quantity, quantity, quantity.'[10] The proliferation of signals has created a giant appetite for programming, but all those broadcasters are competing for a limited pool of funds. The result is the need to fill those hours with cheap programming. The Americans and their new Japanese financial backers have been only too happy to fill the gap with 'universal' programming that can travel across language and cultural barriers. At MIP, Mel Harris, president of the Paramount Television Group, extends a welcome to creators from around the world to come to Los Angeles to learn the 'universal language' of programming. He gives an example of what that language might be: 'If a Canadian writer from Ottawa sits down and writes a good episode of *Star Trek*, I consider that to be as Canadian as if he had written some short story about the experiences of trying to locate the North Western Passage.'[11] Harris elucidates the meaning of 'universal' by asking, rhetorically, 'What country is *Star Trek* from? It's not from any country. Similarly *Mission Impossible* is from nowhere. It has no base. It doesn't reflect any point of view.'[12] 'Universal' thus means out of nothing, without context and without signification. And being from nowhere, these programmes are exportable everywhere.

At MIP, there is much talk of creativity, talent, new programmes, but the real activity there, its subtext, is not creation but erasure. MIP erases boundaries: national boundaries, cultural boundaries that exclude and boundaries that define. MIP is a giant soup ladle stirring all the ingredients into a uniform paste. The 7,000 delegates then disperse, taking with them the recipe for that international soup, hoping they can replicate it for local audiences everywhere. And no country has been more assiduous in trying to learn the MIP lesson than Canada.

Having failed in their experiments with regulated deregulation of broadcasting, the Canadian government turned to a supply-side solution to the problems of an Americanised Canadian broadcasting system. A stagnating government film agency, the Canadian Film Development Corporation, was refurbished with a new budget (from $4.5 million annually to $65 million, funded by a tax on cable), a new name (Telefilm Canada), and a new mandate: to kickstart a Canadian television production industry which would provide products for local and international audiences.

This change of direction in government policy coincided with the changing nature of world television, and particularly its increasing globalisation. International co-productions became a fundamental platform in this new industrial policy. Year after year the Trade Forum at Toronto's Festival of Festivals became boot camp for producers, initiating them into the mysteries of co-productions.

The establishment of Telefilm Canada represented a fundamental restructuring of Canadian audio-visual production and a way round the continuing frustration of the Canadian government in the face of the US distribution behemoth. Unable to prevent US domination of cinema screens, the government turned its attention to a sector which it did control – broadcasting – and set up the new Broadcast Fund with a new policy. This policy, however, announced the primacy of private production and its integration into the global market-place.

A reading of the Telefilm Canada annual reports underscores the extent to which this thinking had been assimilated into its workings. In his first report as Chairman, Ed Prevost noted that 'The Broadcast Fund came at a crucial time in the evolution of the Canadian production industry. Quality of production was increasing, methods of financing were becoming more sophisticated and there was a growing awareness of both the necessity and the potential of international dealings.'[13] Discussing Telefilm's marketing strategy, Prevost remarked, 'While the Corporation's marketing strategy focused, in its initial phase, on contacting and informing the business and broadcast sectors in Canada, the importance of foreign financiers and foreign markets was also stressed.'[14] That emphasis did not let up in the following years, as the Minister of Communications pushed to expand co-production treaties which would enable globalised product to be considered Canadian. Subsequent annual reports would have a section on international relations, expatiating with pride on the growth of such treaties. The first annual report pointed to three, the most recent to sixteen.

In 1986 the Caplan-Sauvageau task force on broadcasting noted that 'There has been and will be steadily increasing pressure on independent producers and, as a result, on Telefilm to tailor the projects that receive support better to satisfy foreign broadcasters. At the same time there will be more pressure to ignore anything but mainstream Canadian productions.'[15] The report quoted from a study it had commissioned which indicated that there 'had been reason for concern that Telefilm had been over-emphasising rate of return considerations and under-emphasising cultural significance.'[16] More than six years later those conclusions are just as apt. Of course, the irony here is that Telefilm has not succeeded in turning much of a profit either. Its rate of return is estimated at about 4 per cent. As an instrument of industrial policy, Telefilm's emphasis has consistently been on dealing with producers rather than film-makers, and increasingly producers who have shown their ability to exist in the international market-place. In the 1988-89 annual report executive director Pierre DesRoches noted that 'The Corporation will give priority to producers who have been successful in obtaining financing, have produced works of international calibre, and have achieved a certain degree of financial success.'[17]

The policy shift within the Department of Communications co-incided with a significant erosion of traditional Canadian film and tele-vision production, which was public sector-based and concerned almost exclusively with an essentially non-commercial home market. In 1984, CBC suffered the first of its major budgetary cutbacks of $80 million and hundreds of jobs lost. At the same time increasing pressure was put on the Corporation to contract out programming to the private sector in the name of diversity and efficiency, but the major subtext was a glob-alised, market-driven production industry. Meanwhile the National Film Board, the other main traditional producer of Canadian program-ming, was subjected to continuing scrutiny and budget cutbacks. The notion of the social function of film had completely lost its force, over-taken by the industrial needs of an information society. Within a year of the establishment of the Broadcast Fund, Telefilm reported proudly that 'The four foreign offices of the National Film Board of Canada were transferred to Telefilm Canada to help the private sector penetrate inter-national markets more effectively, as well as to facilitate co-productions and co-ventures.'[18]

Over the years a small group of well-connected producers have lob-bied to establish a Canadian version of the American studio system. They have argued that the Canadian pie was too small for more than the dozen major production houses which have monopolised the lion's share of funding from Telefilm. The larger television production houses like Alliance, Atlantis, Nelvana and Primedia are also vertically integrat-ing into distribution. In fact, on the international co-production scale there is a distinct merging of distribution and production. MIP these days is as much about forming international co-production partnerships as about the selling of national TV programmes internationally.

The response from the creative community, as opposed to the production industry, has been an anguished one. In a panel on 'Culture versus Money' at the 1989 Vancouver Film Festival, Quebec actor and director Micheline Lanctot had this to say about the funding system:

> Why then, as creators, are we systematically opposed by a barrage of readers at all stages of the decision process who talk to us about primetime requirements, the need for a mass market approach, the utmost necessity of the Perfect Story as a guarantee of excellence? In Canada entertainment is no more profitable than culture. By playing one against the other, our government has constructed an economic house of cards that holds creativity hostage to government funding while maintaining the illusion of profitability. In fact, we're all on welfare, as Gilles Carle used to say, producers even more so for Telefilm – producers are being increasingly treated as accountants, at best as managers of state monies.[19]

Mary Walsh, actor and leading member of Codco, a Newfoundland comedy troupe which has had a nationally acclaimed TV show on CBC for five years, also feels that government broadcasting policy is bankrupt. She blames it on the attempt to emulate the American production model.

> We don't have the population base to have the money to produce the kind of shows that they produce. We've always looked up to them, tried to emulate them. So we try to produce the shows that they're supposedly good at producing – sitcoms, game shows, the things that they churn out with about fifty times the amount of cash that we have to spend with a market all ready for it. And we fail at it. So it's like Canada was a younger sister who was really good at something but was constantly trying to be a cheerleader like her older sister. And a really lousy cheerleader, and then thought that we were no good because we weren't a cheerleader but were obviously really good at other things.[20]

It's those other things, the things Canadians are really good at, that are hard to fund because they may be too local, because they won't travel, won't sell well at MIP. Often, too, it's hard to find local airtime for such shows despite the fact that in some parts of the country there are well over fifty channels to choose from. Canada's national broadcasting system, for example, has no regular slot for independent documentaries. This is a particular shame when one considers the history, the talent and the expertise Canadian film-makers have in documentary production. For Mary Walsh the solution is simple:

> Somebody's got to be willing to say here's the bucks, we'll do it. If we fail, well, then we can go back to buying *Dallas* for $50. What have we really lost except to say that we believe that we have something that is important? So you might as well go the whole hog and provide primetime Canadian viewing. It's bound to get better the more you do it. We're not retarded. There's nothing intrinsically wrong with us. We don't lack imagination or creativity. It will just grow. But you've got to jump off the cart and do it.[21]

There are, of course, flashes across the Canadian airwaves of that imagination and creativity, not least in the work of Codco. But the question for local programming is continuity and support – and local programming involves the whole infrastructure. It means support for the writers, the actors, the crews. It is only through consistently producing Canadian shows that Canada can develop its distinctive programming.

In the global market-place, where the spectrum continues to expand at an exponential rate, the hope for local programming may lie in its ability to differentiate itself from a homogeneous, globalised product. But to survive, particularly as governments face severe deficit pressures, local programming will have to revolutionise the production process. American programming is wedded to a particular means of production relying on large, expensive crews. It has been suggested that Canada can steal a march on its southern neighbour by taking advantage of computerised production technologies and new means of production (such as Hi-8) to produce inexpensive programming of a quality that matches American programming. Even more boldly, Canada can take full advantage of the extended spectrum to produce programming that is interactive and extends across multiple signals, allowing an audience unprecedented entry into a story at whatever level of detail they wish to engage with it. If Canada can get it together to find the right match of production process and broadcast technology, it may well provide the model for a renewed and vigorous local broadcasting.

NOTES

1. David Webster, 'Direct Broadcast Satellites: Proximity, Sovereignty and National Identity', *Foreign Affairs*, vol. 62 no. 5, Summer 1984, p. 1161.
2. Anthony Smith, *The Geopolitics of Information: How Western Culture Dominates the World* (London: Faber and Faber, 1980), p. 54.
3. Canada, Royal Commission on Radio Broadcasting (Aird Commission), *Report* (Ottawa: King's Printer, 1929), p. 6.
4. Canada, Royal Commission on Broadcasting (Fowler Commission), *Report* (Ottawa: Queen's Printer, 1957), p. 10.
5. Canada, Committee on Broadcasting (Fowler Committee), *Report* (Ottawa: Queen's Printer, 1965), p. 107.
6. Canada, *Report of the Task Force on Broadcasting Policy* (Caplan-Sauvageau Report) (Ottawa: Ministry of Supply and Services, 1986), p. 417.
7. Quoted in Marc Gunther, 'Time Deal Affects the Little Guy', *Toronto Star*, 20 June 1989.
8. Philip Robinson, 'Warner and Time Agree $15bn tie-up', *The Times*, 6 March 1989, p. 25.
9. Author's notes, MIP-TV seminar, 'Television Europe: The Challenge of 1992', Cannes, 23 April 1989.
10. Ibid.
11. Interview in the documentary *Distress Signals* (Toronto: Orbit Films, 1990).
12. Ibid.
13. Telefilm Canada, *Annual Report, 1983–1984* (Montreal, 1984), p. 4.
14. Ibid.
15. Caplan-Sauvageau Report, p. 370.
16. Ibid.
17. Telefilm Canada, *Annual Report, 1988–1989* (Montreal, 1989), p. 7.
18. Telefilm Canada, *Annual Report, 1984–1985* (Montreal, 1985), p. 4.
19. Micheline Lanctot, 'Culture Versus Money', *Bulletin of Independent Film and Video Alliance* (Montreal: IFVA-AVCI, December 1989), p. 12.
20. Interview in *Distress Signals*.
21. Ibid.

AFTER THE DELUGE

Public Service Television in Western Europe

Julian Petley and Gabriella Romano

The purpose of this chapter is to examine the changes current in the broadcasting environments in various EC countries in order to begin to assess their effects on national cultures and on the identity of Europe itself. This amounts to a survey of how new private, commercial television stations have affected some of the existing public service channels.

Of course, all broadcasting is commercial in that even public service channels are at least partly motivated by economic interests. In the UK, the BBC channels are constantly locked in a ratings battle with ITV and Channel Four, and these channels as previously regulated by the ITA/IBA fell within the public service sector as decisively as the BBC. ITV, as regulated by the new 'light touch' ITC, will now clearly be rather less of a public service animal than it was, but Channel Four's famous remit is enshrined in the 1990 Broadcasting Act. 'Commercial' in this context really means broadcasters with no public service remit whatsoever, which leaves BSkyB as Britain's first truly commercial broadcaster, the first and only British equivalent of the RTL and Berlusconi operations in continental Europe.

Unfortunately, public service broadcasting ideals in the UK have become identified with the practices of the BBC, and so, in the hour of its greatest need, public service broadcasting has found few friends or defenders in what one might expect to be its natural constituency. As Nicholas Garnham has said, the image of public service broadcasting is 'centralised, bureaucratic, inefficient, arrogantly insensitive to the people's needs, politically subservient to the holders of state power and so on.'[1] In particular, he argues that over the past twenty years or so the BBC has totally failed to respond to calls made to it both by the public and by broadcasting workers to forge a more participatory, collaborative and democratic relationship which might truly serve the public by expressing their political and cultural diversity rather than serve the state and associated power elites by transmitting an elitist, authoritarian or manipulative political and cultural message.[2]

And, *pace* Garnham, we would argue that much the same can be said about the ITA/IBA and the way in which it regulated ITV and Channel Four.

And yet, for all its faults, British television over the past thirty years has made available a *far* wider range of representations to a far wider range of people than has the press, 'quality' or popular. In our opinion, public service broadcasting needs to be redefined and reconceptualised, not abandoned in despair and impatience. Media moguls such as Murdoch, Bertelsmann and Berlusconi are likely to prove even more intractable and less accountable than the BBC/ITC mandarins, and the hidden hand of the market an even greater stumbling block to radical innovative programmes than the stifling consensual ideology which has traditionally underpinned public service broadcasting in the UK.

Public service broadcasting principles are not laid down in tablets of stone, and the practices vary from one country to another. However, it is possible to isolate certain considerations which are relevant to the kinds of programmes that are the focus of this volume. Amongst the eight public service broadcasting principles outlined by the Broadcasting Research Unit in 1985, we find

> universality of appeal: television programmes should cater for all interests and tastes. Minorities, especially disadvantaged minorities, should receive particular provision. Broadcasters should recognise their relationship to the sense of national identity and community.[3]

In addition regional, linguistic, political, cultural and aesthetic pluralism in broadcasting should mean that all the diverse groupings which constitute society find scheduled programmes which reflect their tastes, interests and values and, equally important, encounter programmes which

> stretch their minds and horizons; awaken them to less familiar ideas and tastes in culture, the arts and sciences; and perhaps even challenge some of their uncritically accepted assumptions about life, morality and society.[4]

One of the problems with purely commercial TV is that it shifts the emphasis from what Jay Blumler calls a principled pluralism to a pragmatic one. That is, it appeals to more than one section of the audience and broadcasts a range of programmes, but both audiences and programmes are considered solely in financial terms, as attractions for advertisers. Furthermore, commercial television tends to shift its reliance on national programmes to ones which are more internationally available. Viewers run the risk of becoming more familiar with the sights and sounds of the backlots of Los Angeles than with representations of their own society and its concerns; and indigenous television production industries become ever weaker, thus setting up a vicious circle whose sole beneficiary is the multinational media conglomerates. Finally, purely commercial television can be said to threaten what Blumler calls 'the integrity of civic communication'.

In the UK, this value is enshrined in television's obligation to be fair, impartial and balanced in party political terms, and in the ban on political advertising on television. In the past, the ITV companies were obliged to broadcast a proportion of current affairs programmes in primetime. In many other EC countries, similar stipulations are complemented by safeguards concerning cross-media ownership and the growth of media monopolies. But as Blumler points out, these values could all be threatened, not simply by the growth of commercial television but by the effect of that growth on the public broadcasters:

> The priorities of providers and viewers alike could shift from information toward entertainment. News bulletins could concentrate on presentation of the most dramatic and arresting events, short-changing analysis and discussion. Current affairs programmes could lose their cachet, and their producers could cater more for viewers' spectator interests than their citizen roles. Political competition could increasingly be presented through horse-race models and chess-like scenarios. Slogans, images and racy soundbites might take precedence over substance, information and dialogue.[5]

It is worth considering these assertions in the light of changes which have been taking place in Western Europe. The 1980s saw major changes in European broadcasting. It has been estimated that between 1980 and 1987 broadcasting hours increased by some 125 per cent. Large numbers of new channels, most of them outside the public service framework, appeared on the scene, distributed both terrestrially and by satellite and cable. The main features of the new, commercially led systems have been usefully summarised by Jeremy Tunstall and Michael Palmer as

> competition for audiences between a substantial number of channels; direct inter-channel competition for advertising; aggressively competitive programme scheduling; a sharp decline in serious programming in peak hours; aggressive competition for popular talent, leading to star salary inflation; wholesale resort to imported programming; extension of the broadcasting day to include most of the twenty-four hours; aggressive scheduling of repeat programming (including daily 'stripping' of series originally shown weekly).[6]

It was estimated by various authors before the 'commercial deluge' that the ratio of 'serious' to 'popular' programmes on public service stations was on average 55 to 45 per cent, whereas commercial broadcasters put out an average of 60 to 70 per cent 'popular' programmes. However, in a recent study covering fifty-three European television stations from 14 to 27 January 1991, the Euromedia Research Group found that no public service broadcasting channel broadcast as much as 55 per cent 'serious' programmes, defined here as comprising information, culture and education.[7] Only the German and Norwegian public service channels reached a figure of 50 per cent, followed by the Belgian, British, Swedish and Swiss stations at around 49 per cent. (It should be noted, apropos our earlier remarks, that the Euromedia study includes the UK's ITV and Channel Four under the 'commercial' heading, and excludes BSkyB altogether.) At the other end of the scale the public service channels in Austria broadcast only 34 per cent 'serious' programmes, in Finland 36 per cent, in Italy 37 per cent, in Spain 38 per cent and in Ireland 39 per cent. This situation signals a change from 1988, when a Euromedia study of twenty channels over roughly the same number of days showed the public service stations broadcasting at least 55 per cent 'serious' programmes. The Euromedia Research Group have no hesitation in laying the blame for this state of affairs at the door of the new national and transnational commercial stations, some of whose output comprises as much as 90 per cent 'popular' programming in primetime (in Germany, Italy and Norway, for instance).

The Euromedia study also shows how the commercial channels rely more heavily than the public channels on imports. In Germany, for example, the public service channels import only 15 per cent of their programmes whilst the commercial channels import 51 per cent, in the Netherlands the public service channels import 21 per cent and the commercial channels 54 per cent, and in Norway public service broadcasting scores only 24 per cent in imports against the commercial sector's 61 per cent. Significantly, there is a relatively low (19 per cent) proportion of imports on UK 'commercial' channels – a clear indication of the successful operation of the IBA's import quota in the former ITV system.

It comes as no surprise to discover that a large proportion of imports is made up of feature films, and that most of these come from the United States. Eighty per cent of the films shown on the fifty-three stations studied were imported, and 53 per cent of these were American in origin. It is also no secret that the new commercial stations make movies, especially recent Hollywood releases, one of their strongest selling points. The Euromedia figures confirm that the commercial stations broadcast more North American movies than the public ones – in particular the Norwegian TV Norge with 100 per cent, the Swedish TV3 with 81 per cent, the French M6 and La Cinq with 78 and 73 per cent respectively, and Italia 1 with 75 per cent. Also revealing is the fact that the percentage of American movies broadcast has risen from 46 per cent in 1988 to 53 per cent in 1991, whilst the programming of domestic movies has actually decreased by almost 10 per cent. Thus the appetite for more films, far from stimulating the European domestic industries, has simply led to an ever increasing flood of imports.

A similar picture appears in respect of series. Here 83 per cent are imported, and only the UK programmes a majority of domestic series. Like the French, the British import few series from elsewhere in Europe, preferring American and Australian series. At the other end of the scale, only one per cent of the series broadcast by the German commercial stations is domestically produced! Ninety-seven per cent of series broadcast by RTL Plus are North American, and 84 per cent of those on Sat-1. An interesting exception to this trend is Italy, where the Berlusconi channels programme 67 per cent North American series, whilst for the public channels the figure is a remarkable 90 per cent. Austria, French-speaking Belgium, Ireland, Switzerland and the commercial stations of Norway and Sweden all rely heavily on US imports, but the public service stations of countries such as Denmark, Finland, Norway and the Netherlands buy more of their series from within Europe. Among the non-US imports Australian ones are prominent; indeed, more series are imported from Australia than from other

European countries, with the exception of the UK. Again, a comparison with the 1988 study is instructive, with US imports rising from 36 to 56 per cent, and domestically produced series dropping from 37 to 17 per cent.

The effects of commercial competition on public service broadcasting in France are clearly illustrated by the results of the Chirac government's decision in 1987 to sell off TF1. This was the first state television network in Europe to be privatised, and in some quarters it was regarded as the equivalent of selling Versailles. Even though it retained certain programming obligations and was subject to limitations on the amount of advertising it could carry, TF1 marked its passage from the public to the private sphere by taking up an aggressively populist stance, and set the pace for others to follow. The average cost of the French television rights to a feature film doubled within a year, and a race began to recruit star names, which cost the various channels some 300m francs – witness the vast salaries paid to the presenter Christine Ockrent, and to Stéphane Collaro, the inventor of *Cocoricoboy* and *Le Bébête Show* (a variation on the *Spitting Image* format). The network also began fierce competitive bidding with A2 and La Cinq for the rights to sports events and star-studded extravaganzas, which pushed up their prices. In its first year as a private enterprise, TF1 dropped all its documentary and educational programmes (which had previously accounted for 15 per cent of its output), the number of game shows screened per week jumped from five to sixteen, the amount of light entertainment doubled, feature films quadrupled, there was a 400 per cent increase in the number of US imports, and a marked increase in the production of French mini-series on the North American model. The statutory obligation to broadcast at least 50 per cent French-originated features and documentaries was openly flouted, in spite of heavy fines: in 1987 TF1 managed only 39 per cent, although this compares favourably with the commercial channels La Cinq at 32 per cent and M6 at under 20 per cent.[8]

Two of the main casualties of the privatisation of TF1 were the remaining public channels, A2 and FR3, which began to compete with TF1 for audiences and, in the case of A2, about half of whose budget comes from advertising, for advertisers as well. Both channels lost over half their audience at one point, and FR3 responded to the challenge by increasing its light entertainment by 16 per cent in primetime and its 'soap' quota from 5 per cent to 20 per cent in one year, and by cutting news and current affairs programmes by more than a third.[9] This is particularly serious in the present context, since FR3 is France's only regional network, with twelve regional offices and twenty-five different local channels which are required to cater for specific regional demands. It is also the only French channel to have correspondents in every French region.

In Germany, the two major public service broadcasters, ZDF and the regionally based ARD, are faced with strong competition from RTL Plus, Sat-1, Pro 7 and Tele 5. In 1987 RTL Plus' schedule consisted of 58 per cent movies, 42 per cent imported entertainment and only 14 per cent factual programmes.[10] In 1988 it outbid the public channels for the rights to German football league games, and in 1989 to the Wimbledon tennis tournament. A study by the Institute of Applied Communication Research at the University of Göttingen discovered that light entertainment programmes account for 82 per cent of RTL Plus' 'quota relevant' output and that 60 per cent of programmes on private channels are bought in.[11] This in spite of the statutory principle that 'the majority share of every full-length TV programme shall consist of station-produced and commissioned broadcasts including co-productions.'

Sat-1, which was founded in 1985, is less populist than RTL Plus, but 64 per cent of its programmes in 1987 consisted of light entertainment from the United States. PRO 7 was founded in 1989 by Thomas Kirch and has the advantage of being able to draw on films from the Leo Kirch Library, which it supplements with American-produced crime series and TV movies. The Göttingen study discovered that 98 per cent of its material was bought in and, as a result, its local franchise in Bremen was withdrawn. Like its namesakes in France and Spain, Tele 5, in which Berlusconi holds a 21 per cent stake, survives on a diet of soaps, bought-in series and chat shows. The Göttingen study shows that 43 per cent of its output is fiction, and 45 per cent is made up of music programmes.

From 1984 onwards competition from the private channels has led both ARD and ZDF to buy up the rights to an increasing number of Hollywood films, and prices for these (and for sporting events) have trebled since 1986. In 1986 ARD lost 20 per cent of its early evening audience to the private channels, by which time 40 per cent of its schedule was already devoted to movies in a bid to keep and attract audiences. Similarly, ZDF has increased the number of US soaps in its schedules, and has indulged in some head-hunting from ARD. The newly competitive relationship between the two public service broadcasters is also illustrated by the fact that their schedules are no longer co-ordinated, ZDF now beginning its primetime programmes earlier than ARD.

On the basis of these figures it would be all too easy to set up a polarity which opposes 'bad' programming (North American, commercial, popular, fiction) to 'good' (indigenous, public service, serious, factual). Indeed, the Euromedia Research Group's work tends in this direction. But as Ien Ang has pointed out:

> The institutional categorisation of televisual discourse, which constructs an opposition between the serious (= what really matters) and the popular (= easy pleasures), obscures the fact that, from the point of view of the audiences, 'information' can also be pleasurable. The problem is that in televisual discourse 'informative' programmes, especially when they are about 'serious' politics and culture, are too often constructed as the important – and thus unpleasurable – which the viewers are supposed to watch because it is 'good for them'.[12]

But the problem with the prioritising of audience pleasures in much current research is that it can so easily slide over into what William Seaman calls 'pointless populism'[13] and James Curran 'the new revisionism',[14] reassuringly turning our attention away from the seismic structural changes currently shaking the European broadcasting environment, or seductively suggesting that these do not really matter and may even indeed have positive consequences for 'progressive' opinion. Where no one discourse is seen to be dominant, the impermeability of audiences to media influences is actually exaggerated and allows the media to be analysed in isolation from wider societal power relationships – paradoxically, at a time of intense concentration of media ownership and (in the UK at least) massive centralisation of political power.

The question of popular pleasures has become unproductively dichotomised, as Judith Williamson points out:

> Surely we can try to understand what pleasures are had from mass culture and how personal and social needs feed into these pleasures without therefore jumping to the conclusion that they are a 'good thing'? And can we no longer imagine different forms in which those needs might be met?[15]

In this light, the history of broadcasting in the Netherlands is especially interesting, since the manner in which Dutch radio and television were originally organised represented a particularly thoroughgoing attempt to regulate diversity and heterogeneity into the system – qualities which have since been threatened by two rather different forms of commercial penetration.

It is impossible to understand broadcasting in the Netherlands without reference to the 'pillarisation' of Dutch society. As Kees Brants explains:

> ... social movements, educational and communication systems, voluntary associations and political parties were organised along the lines of religious and ideological cleavages. The Netherlands has long been one of the most typical examples of segmented pluralism: it is pluralist in its recognition of diversity of religious, socio-economic, and political affiliations; it is 'segmented' in its institutionalisation of most other forms of association along the lines of politico-religious cleavages.[16]

Originally only those broadcasting organisations with firm links to the major politico-religious streams in society were allowed on the air. The allocation of broadcasting time operates on a three-tier system based on membership levels. To become a member, a person either takes a subscription to the programme guide of the respective organisation or pays an annual membership fee. Class A broadcasters have to have over 450,000 members, and there are six of these: VARA (Socialist), KRO (Catholic), NCRV (Protestant), and the entertainment-oriented AVRO, TROS and VOO. Each receives around twelve hours television airtime per week. Class B broadcasters have between 300,000 and 450,000 members and receive seven hours weekly airtime; these are VPRO (liberal/progressive) and EO (fundamentalist). At present there are no broadcasters in Class C, the category with between 150,000 and 300,000 members.

By law all corporations are obliged to present a reasonable ratio of culture (20 per cent), entertainment (25 per cent), information (25 per cent) and education (5 per cent). Advertising was introduced in the 1969 Broadcasting Act, and for national broadcasting there are now three sources of finance: a licence fee (65 per cent), advertising (35 per cent) and membership dues.[17]

Until the mid-1960s most of the broadcasting organisations represented distinct politico-religious interests. However, like every other Western society in that decade, Holland underwent significant social changes, which had the effect of 'depillarising' Dutch society. As Kees Brants puts it:

> Religion lost its unifying and integrating function: the pillars lost their flock. The organisations, associations and political parties became less segmented and more pluralistic, while interactions between members of the pillars increased rapidly. [18]

Television both contributed to the secularisation/depillarisation process and was itself significantly affected by it. According to Brants, 'While the parties had to search for floating voters, the media had to aim for new consumers. ... The diversity is no longer based on beliefs but merely on commercial considerations.' [19] Accordingly, the 1969 Broadcasting Act opened up the system to new licensees provided that they aimed at 'satisfying cultural, religious or spiritual needs felt among the population' and added to the system's diversity. The real beneficiaries of this were the former television pirate station TROS and, later, the former radio pirate station VOO (Veronica), both of which followed a determinedly populist programme policy and grew rapidly in members and audience shares. The flavour of TROS can be judged by the remarks of its first chairman: 'The essence is to give the people the programmes they want to see. So, no politics. I say to the viewers: we are here for you, not for ourselves. The viewer is the boss.' [20] Of course, it was never simply a matter of 'no politics'; like many populist organisations TROS leans to the right, and was strongly supported in its early years by the *Telegraaf* newspaper, the Dutch equivalent of the German paper *Bild*.

TROS depended heavily on a diet of North American movies, serials and quizzes. It got round its legal obligation to broadcast a 'comprehensive' programme with heavy doses of wildlife films and leisure items, which it counted as 'information'. Its current affairs programmes were more like news shows, consisting of short items which mixed hard news with lighter elements, drama with documentary, and the serious with the offbeat. Originally, current affairs programmes had been the flagships of the broadcasting organisations: they may have been partisan, but at least the viewers knew where they stood, and the tone was resolutely responsible and serious-minded. Now news became part of the entertainment package, a crucial part of the organisations' marketing strategies.

In 1971 TROS had over 250,000 members, by 1974, 400,000. In 1977 TROS, VOO and AVRO had 51 per cent of all broadcasting membership and by 1985, 55 per cent. As elsewhere, the other broadcasting organisations were forced to follow in the footsteps of the former pirates, and the term 'Trossification' was coined to describe television's pursuit of the mass market and its turn towards commercialism. The very openness and democracy of the Dutch broadcasting system was part of the problem, compelling the other broadcasting organisations to compete with TROS in a bid to keep up their own all-important membership figures.

It became increasingly difficult to harmonise the broadcasting policies of all the various organisations as regulated competition turned into an increasingly anarchic free for all. The more conventional broadcasters were torn between chasing the highest possible ratings and accentuating their own specific identities: which was the best way of attracting new members and hanging on to existing ones? Current affairs programmes were increasingly pushed to the margins, and lost their critical function. As Herman Wigbold described it:

> Informative programmes in the 1960s took the initiative, focusing on internal and external dialogue. Information in the 1970s has been defensive, focused on maintaining the group. Programmes are designed to give their own supporters just enough to prevent them from running away but not enough to irritate outsiders. Television has completely lost its agenda-setting function. [21]

The Dutch system is particularly interesting in the present context because VARA, the Socialist broadcasting organisation, has traditionally seen itself in quite explicitly 'progressive' terms. However, as in any left-wing organisation there have been disagreements over how VARA should best fulfil its 'progressive' mission. Thus in the 1970s broadcasters within the Werkgroep Socialistische VARA wanted to use television as a tool for political mobilisation and emancipation, producing radical populist documentaries like *Van Onderen*, a series dealing with the exploitation of industrial labour under contemporary capitalism. This view was opposed by a less militant, less overtly 'political' view which saw VARA's mission as being

> to spread Enlightenment ideals such as rationality, tolerance and human dignity among the people (working class or otherwise).... Furthermore, it is stated that VARA should perform this task by transmitting programmes that are accessible and appealing to a large

audience. To make full use of the potential of broadcast television as a *mass* medium it should not only be progressive, but popular.[22]

Hardly surprisingly, given the success of TROS, this latter view has tended to prevail. Popular programmes are seen as necessary to beat TROS and the others at their own game. Furthermore, it is hoped that by offering people popular entertainment programmes they will be drawn to the organisation, and to the ideological stance taken by its 'serious' (i.e. current affairs) programmes, VARA's so-called 'identity carriers'. According to Ien Ang, this means that VARA's brand of institutionalised progressivism is marked by a 'troubled fusion of paternalism and populism', each characterising the audience very differently. The populist conception sees television as delivering an *audience* to advertisers, whilst the paternalist view regards it as delivering VARA's stated ideals to a *public* which needs to be instructed and enlightened.

Seen from this perspective, what has happened in the Netherlands is that the public has begun to behave like an audience and decided that it no longer wishes to watch television from the 'correct' ideological position and with the 'right' balance between the 'serious' and the 'popular'. 'Trossification' can be seen as a consequence of the Dutch broadcasting system's essentially paternalistic relationship with its audience, which fails to take account of attitudes to viewing. As Ang has pointed out, it may be that TROS's success is based on a discontent with the moralising surveillance and denial of popular tastes by the traditional organisations. In other words, through TROS the 'silent majority' spoke. More specifically, it was a refusal by popular audiences to be put in a position in which serious information is recognised as the most valuable part of televisual discourse and entertainment is tolerated as a diversion as long as it gives 'enjoyment' and not 'fun'.[23]

This account of Dutch television neatly illustrates some of the points raised at the start of this chapter. For the populist, of course, there is no problem; it is simply a matter of 'giving the people what they want'. But what of those concerned with a politics of resistance? The 'semiotic democrats' may not have much to worry about, since they can always point to the possibilities of all sorts of oppositional readings, the 'subversive' power of pleasure, and so on. Others would argue, correctly in our view, that resistance must not confine itself solely to the 'serious', public service aspect of broadcasting and should certainly not lose sight of the importance of the pleasurable. Others again might say that it does not really matter what TROS and its like get up to as long as the other organisations keep to their original remit, albeit in modified form. This, we believe, is profoundly mistaken, and one of our main purposes here is to point out that what happens in the deregulated sector massively affects what happens in the regulated or public service sector which, whatever its problems and shortcomings, has historically provided a site for oppositional work, and which still seems to offer more hopeful possibilities for such work than a media environment dominated by moguls in the Murdoch, Berlusconi, Bertelsmann mould.

In 1976, the Italian Constitutional Court declared that the state broadcasting monopoly hitherto enjoyed by RAI was valid only at the national level. Henceforth local, private, deregulated television stations would be permitted. This is why, as Denis McQuail puts it, 'Italy provides the closest model in Europe to the American system and has, consequently, been regarded as an example of what might happen if public service frameworks were to be abandoned.'[24]

At first, this move was widely welcomed. RAI's prestige had never been especially high, and many regarded the organisation as politically compromised. Rather than seeing private television as a competitor for advertising, the press themselves entered the broadcasting field. Left-wing political groups saw an opportunity to set up a whole network of alternative broadcasting, infused with political content. And intellectuals hoped for a cultural explosion on TV. These hopes were soon dashed. At first there was a mushroom growth of some 600 companies, some of which were indeed engaged in oppositional and resistance work; but by the end of 1979, 80 per cent of all advertising revenues were flowing into three private 'networks'. This was in breach of the spirit of the law, which forbade national private networks; however, numerous companies forged links with each other and 'synchronised' their output. Programmes were delivered to stations on videocassettes by fleets of couriers, and then transmitted *almost* simultaneously in different parts of the country.

The three main networks were Rete 4, Italia 1 and Canale 5. This last was owned by building and property magnate Silvio Berlusconi, who took over Italia 1 in 1983 and Rete 4 in 1984. It is between RAI, with its three channels, and Berlusconi's Fininvest that the main competition in Italian TV now takes place, although there are still a few hundred small and medium-sized independent, private, local television stations, reliant mainly on cheap imported programmes, light, tabloid-style news and 'current affairs' shows and, in the worst cases, advertisements posing as programmes. There are also, in this group, Catholic channels which run talk shows on religious and moral issues.

In May 1983 the private television stations notched up a market share of 53.3 per cent, beating RAI for the first time. From 1981 to 1983 RAI's market share dropped from 61 per cent to 44 per cent. However, in the late 1980s it made something of a recovery; according to figures quoted by the Euromedia Research Group, the primetime audience ratings for RAI rose from 45 per cent in 1987 to 52 per cent in 1990, whilst the Fininvest channels' shares dropped from 44.9 per cent to 36.3 per cent. [25]

As the following figures for 1988 from the Euromedia Group demonstrate (see Table I), there soon developed a huge disparity in the different types of programme broadcast by RAI and Fininvest.

TABLE I

Programme Type	RAI (%)	Fininvest (%)
Entertainment	45.7	76.1
Cultural	16.8	3.3
Educational	4.5	0.2
Information (News and Sport)	26.8	3.4
Advertising	2.5	13.7
Other	3.7	3.3

The differences in output between RAI and Fininvest need no further stress. What does need to be investigated, however, is the effect on RAI of the competition from Berlusconi.

Firstly, the competition forced RAI to expand its programme day. In 1974 RAI broadcast 5,000 hours of television, in 1990 23,000. In itself this may be no bad thing, but it has to be remembered that, to start with at least, this expansion of the schedules took place without any proportional increase in budget and at a time when inflation was eating into the licence fee. Furthermore RAI, unlike its competitors, had to limit its advertising slots to 5 per cent of total transmission time and could place advertisements only between, not within, programmes. This resulted in RAI making savings in programme costs by relying more heavily on imports and cutting down on expensive 'quality' programming. The restrictions on the placing of advertisements also led RAI to introduce more short programmes as a way of increasing the number of advertisements broadcast; indeed, some programmes were so short that some critics regarded them as breaks between advertisements.

Hand in hand with the expansion of broadcasting hours have come changes in scheduling practices. The output of the private networks was characterised from the start by expensive daytime programming, consisting of soaps, sitcoms, cartoons etc., arranged in virtually identical daily sequences. This procedure, known as the *palinsesto orizzontale*, is clearly aimed at hooking audiences to particular programmes and thereby to the station which broadcasts them, as well as making daytime viewing a regular habit. It is also designed to help them find their way through the ever-increasing and bewildering amount of material available on TV.

RAI was not slow to follow in the private networks' footsteps, provoking the criticism that it was pushing its channel towards homogeneity and safe predictability and privileging easily packaged light entertainment forms. Such packages, by offering an uninterrupted flow of undemanding material, encouraged the viewer to spend an entire morning or afternoon with one particular channel, and RAI took this idea a step further by offering a new mode of programming – the *contenitore* ('container' or 'hold-all', as Eco has called it). Basically a mix of genres, the TV *contenitore* normally contains sports news, games, quizzes, guest interviewees and phone-ins; it is broadcast live from a studio (thereby emphasising RAI's advantage over the private networks which, until 1990, were allowed to transmit only recorded material), is hosted by a well-known presenter and lasts several hours. Its chief attractions are the star quality of the guests, the popularity of the presenter and the buzz engendered by the live element – the sense of collective participation, the acknowledged presence of the whole paraphernalia of TV production, the unpredictable chemistry between the participants, and so on.

Critics of the *contenitore* argue that its emphasis on light entertainment has resulted in a dubious form of 'infotainment' which uncritically mixes serious news with gossip, reality with fiction and politics with performance, and that it is contributing to the demise of the broadcast 'expert' in that the format allows everyone to express an opinion about everything, irrespective of what they actually know. Again, the *contenitore* raises the 'problem of the popular'. It could be argued that the form has its democratic, pleasurable, demystificatory aspects, and seems to have broken with the often starchy and elitist mode of presentation of traditional talk shows.

41

Whether this kind of generically mixed programme provides a useful model for revitalising traditionally 'serious' current affairs programming remains a matter of debate. Does it make discussion of complex contemporary issues more approachable, engaging and interesting to sections of the audience, or does it simply present a hopelessly fragmented view of the world, diluting and rendering banal all the issues it raises by tackling them superficially? And what hopes for the 'ordinary' participant if the ratings demand the presence of stars and personalities in ever greater numbers?

Competition has also caused an increase in the importing of programmes by all the channels. In 1980 Italy was the largest importer of Japanese programmes, and in 1982 of programmes from the US. Although RAI was required by law to draw 50 per cent of its programming from domestic sources, it signed an agreement with NBC not simply for the supply of programmes but also for advice on matters such as scheduling, following the example of the commercial stations' deals with CBS and ABC. Thus, as well as the importing of programmes themselves from the US there was also a 'massive borrowing of American industrial practices'.[26] In 1982, 21,000 programmes were imported at a cost of 200 billion lire – a 100 per cent increase on 1981, and four times as much as in 1980. By 1983, 80 per cent of films transmitted on Italian television were of foreign origin. By the late 1980s US imports had begun to fall in number, but the gap has been at least partly filled by imports from elsewhere in Europe and by home-produced imitations of North American successes. For example, Canale 5 has programmed long daily sequences of Italian versions of *Family Feud*, *The Dating Game*, *Blockbusters*, *The Price is Right*, *The Newlywed Game* and *Hollywood Squares*. In 1987, RAI and all the private networks still spent £62.5m on cinema films and TV movies made in Hollywood, and only 38 per cent of Canale 5's output was made in-house, with 49 per cent bought in and the rest made up by advertising. On Rete 4 the home-produced element was lower still. In 1988 only 23 per cent of the Fininvest channels' programming was home-produced, compared to RAI's 74 per cent. As Donald Sassoon has remarked:

> A country with a major artistic and cultural tradition which has made a significant contribution to the cinema has a broadcasting system which is increasingly like a huge network of terminals transmitting programmes produced in and around Los Angeles.[27]

Of course North American television produces all sorts of material which is capable of all sorts of progressive readings, and European channels churn out a good deal of conformist dross. Notions of a 'common European identity' are very problematic, and in the last analysis is there any real difference between the original American *Dating Game* and its Italian re-tread? Perhaps not in purely textual terms, but it should be remembered that the Italian version is made in Italy and thus helps keep alive a production base that is at least capable of producing other, more 'progressive' programmes. Nor should it be forgotten that the absorption and naturalisation of forms imported/imposed from outside is one of the major manifestations of media imperialism, and brings other consequences in its wake.

After Berlusconi, there has been a vast increase in the amount of informational material available on Italian television. Far from being an indication of an increase in 'quality' television, this in fact points to a growth of what in America is referred to as 'infotainment' and in Britain as 'tabloid TV'. News is an area in which RAI has something of an advantage over the private networks, which, as mentioned earlier, were until recently not allowed to broadcast live. Thus at the start of Italian television there were only two news bulletins per day on RAI, whereas by the late 1980s there were twenty-five, with RAI making these regular bulletins a distinctive selling point. News therefore acquires a corporate strategic function, playing a key role in the networks' image-making and becoming an increasingly market-oriented television genre. The way in which news has developed on Italian TV, both public and private, reflects a wider shift from broadcasting to narrowcasting as specific market sectors are targeted. Furthermore, the nature of news programmes has itself changed, with a greater stress on reconstruction and other dramatic and often sensational devices, along with a distinct 'star system' of highly paid presenters with known ratings appeal.

This kind of *TV-realità* – or *TV-spazzatura* (TV-garbage) as it is known by some of its critics – has become the subject of considerable controversy. On the one hand a crime reconstruction series like *Telefono giallo* has had the merit of drawing attention to serious miscarriages of justice, only (echoes of the UK) to find itself pulled from the schedules under pressure from the authorities. On the other hand, there is the spectacle of a drug addict shooting up 20,000 lire worth of heroin on Canale 5 before millions of viewers – all in the cause of a diatribe against drug addiction, naturally – which caused the Vatican to thunder that the programme was 'a further escalation of the death of pity and an ever more morbid portrayal of human suffering'.[28] Not to be outdone, RAI has *Un Giorno in Pretura*, transmissions of particularly emotive court cases turned into voyeuristic television by the unashamed use of every dramatic device in the book. As the presenter of *Telefono giallo*, Corrado Augias, put it: 'The era of pacific, conciliatory television is over and there has begun instead a new era of television which is inquisitive and distressing.'[29] Whether this results in genuinely investigative journalism, or prurient scandal-mongering on the inimitable model of the British tabloid press, remains to be seen.

The arrival in Italy of the unregulated private channels, then, has created a climate in which chasing the ratings is the order of the day to an unprecedented degree. This in turn has led to a situation in which it becomes very difficult for RAI to maintain the standards of public service broadcasting. One example of this is the 'star factor' which now attaches itself to certain presenters. Stories about their vast salaries (which of course help to push up programme costs) and their flittings from channel to channel are now of themselves highly newsworthy. Indeed, the Italian press dubbed 20 March 1987 'Black Friday', all because Pippo Baudo and Rafaella Carrà had left RAI for Berlusconi. Meanwhile, down-market private channels like Italia 7 depress standards still further with quiz shows like *Il Colpo grosso*, home of the famous 'stripping housewives' who now (unfairly) seem to have become synonymous with Italian TV in general.

In this broadcasting environment the fate of RAI 3, the supposedly cultural, regional channel, is particularly instructive. RAI 3's genesis lay in the decentralisation programme initiated by the Christian Democrats as a response to the political unrest of the late 1960s; the channel was to be regionally oriented and therefore more in tune with local needs and demands than the other two RAI channels. It was also felt, in the early days of private broadcasting before Berlusconi moved in, that playing the local card would be an effective means of beating the new arrivals at their own game. The initiative was also supported by the Socialists and Communists. The latter had made significant gains in the local elections of 1975 and the Party had begun to think of itself in less purely oppositional terms. It also abandoned its traditional hostility to television and began to accept that it might have beneficial and positive social uses. Communist-dominated regional councils even expressed a desire to be represented at RAI headquarters (traditionally dominated by the Christian Democrats) at a decision-making level.

RAI 3 began broadcasting on 15 December 1979, with 60 per cent of its output being produced in the regions. It was not meant to be in competition with RAI 1 and 2 but, rather in the manner of Channel Four in the UK, to act in a complementary fashion by providing a distinctly different service. Each evening's programmes focused on a specific area: Mondays and Tuesdays were devoted to current affairs, Wednesdays to films, Thursdays to music (with special emphasis on opera and classical music in general), Fridays to theatre and Saturdays to high-quality TV drama. Films were presented not simply as escapist entertainment but also as a means of extending viewers' understanding of social and historical problems. Sports were taken equally seriously (with a notable emphasis on minority sports), and current affairs programmes were distinguished by the unusually high number of 'vox pops' and the relatively restricted use of interviews with politicians and other officials. The small amount of advertising was positively welcomed as a mark of the channel's 'alternative' status.

As RAI 3 developed, the number of programmes devoted to social subjects decreased in order to give more space to cultural issues. Similarly, 'vox pops' began to give way to interviews with 'experts' of one kind or another. As a consequence there was less genuine debate, and RAI 3 began to gain a reputation as a channel on which opinions were delivered by distinguished but hard-to-understand intellectuals in an increasingly radiophonic manner. Others complained that, although RAI 3 treated subjects new to Italian television, it did so in the traditional visual language of what Eco termed 'Paleo-TV'. One example of this might be the 'Signorina Buonasera' phenomenon: the reliance on the tried and trusted device of the on-screen announcer to present the programmes of the day. Although RAI 3 did experiment with new ways of presenting the announcers (for example in black and white and framed between coloured inverted commas), it didn't dare to dispense with them altogether.

One of the problems which RAI 3 faced was that its arrival excited great hopes for innovation which were never completely fulfilled (and may indeed have been unrealistic in the first place), thus alienating many potential allies. Furthermore, from the start the channel was starved of proper funding because RAI 1 and 2 had monopolised so much of RAI's resources in the growing battle with Berlusconi. It tried to turn this to its advantage by wearing its small budget as a badge of its 'alternative' status.

More recently, the channel has shown a much greater interest in the sport and light entertainment field, and has even launched a couple of highly successful *contenitori*. There is now a greater stress on the more popular sports, and a corresponding lack of attention to minority interests and to the question of sport as a social phenomenon. At the same time it has to be admitted that between March 1987 and 1988 the channel's viewing figures nearly trebled, by 1989 it had acquired nearly 10 per cent of the early evening audience, and by 1990 it was level pegging with RAI 2. As the station's new head, Angelo Guglielmi, commented in 1988:

> When I started, TV3 was like a school textbook. Today it is a crisp daily newspaper. We put aside the classical concerts, the books, the theatre, because we did not want to cater for minorities, and we went out to try to hook the overall audience.[30]

For example, in 1986 RAI 3 devoted 267 hours to classical music and dance, in 1987, 118; hours devoted to theatre production fell from 123 in 1986 to 49 in 1987, seven in 1988, and none at all in 1989. Meanwhile investigative journalism dropped from 299 hours in 1986 to 247 in 1987. On the other hand, arts magazine programmes actually increased from 210 hours in 1986 to 396 in 1987, whilst light entertainment rose from 586 hours in 1987 to 648 in 1988 and roughly the same figure in 1989.

At the moment RAI 3 is undergoing something of an identity crisis. Cultural and educational programmes still constitute a strong part of its identity, and attract an audience that would otherwise watch little television given the almost total absence of such programmes on other channels. 'Infotainment' and *contenitori* have succeeded in boosting audiences and reinvigorating the channel's image, and there has been a determined attempt to produce 'alternative' forms of popular programming. At the same time, certain kinds of programming have undoubtedly suffered in these changes, notably documentaries, expensive dramas and minority taste programmes, resulting in a reduction of viewer choice.

Whatever the future direction of RAI 3, it does seem clear that the arrival of private, deregulated television in Italy has done nothing positive for decentralisation, political pluralism, freedom of information and all the other causes which so many of its original supporters espoused. Instead, it has led to a formidable concentration of power in the private media sector and, far from improving the public service model of television, it has actually weakened and subverted it, pushing RAI into chas-

46

ing ratings, marginalising cultural and educational programming, and edging the two national networks towards competition and homogeneity of output instead of a diverse complementarity. As Giuseppe Richeri concludes, market forces have been allowed to run riot to the extent that

> The leading position is now held by the stations whose only function is that of being distribution points for standard programmes, mainly brought from abroad and lacking any informative, educational or original cultural value and without any relationship to true local requirements. What is more, the existence of these stations has certainly not helped to change the organisational and production model of public television, but has set in motion a process of denaturalising the very functions which public television should, by definition, guarantee.[31]

Bearing in mind Jay Blumler's remarks about commercial television threatening the 'integrity of civic communication', and the role of public service broadcasting in helping to construct and maintain a sense of national and social identity, is it merely a coincidence that the Western European country which has gone furthest and fastest down the deregulated road should also be the one whose unity is most seriously in doubt? It is too easy to see the current Italian political situation as the expression merely of disillusionment and impatience with an ossified party system. What we are witnessing here is rather, as Martin Woollacott has observed, a

> rejection of historic projects of unification and development, projects so central that the rejection constitutes a kind of repudiation of history itself. ... Voters are regressing toward a politics based on the defence of local privilege and a determination to loosen, or cut, ties with poorer classes and poorer regions. They are turning against history and against the myths and aspirations which make nations work.[32]

Public service broadcasting has played a key role in the elaboration of these projects, myths and aspirations, in Italy as elsewhere in Europe, and a crisis in that broadcasting system raises issues which stretch far beyond the presence or absence of certain kinds of programmes in the schedules, to trouble the very concept of nationhood itself.

NOTES

1. Nicholas Garnham, 'Public Service Versus the Market', in *Screen*, vol. 24 no. 1, January–February 1983, p. 21. See also Ian Connell's reply, 'Commercial Broadcasting and the British Left', in *Screen*, vol. 24 no. 6, November–December 1983, pp. 70–80.
2. Garnham, 'Public Service Versus the Market', pp 24–5.
3. Broadcasting Research Unit, 'The Public Service Idea in British Broadcasting: Main Principles' (London, 1985).
4. Jay G. Blumler, 'Public Service Broadcasting Before the Commercial Deluge', in Blumler (ed.), *Television and the Public Interest: Vulnerable Values in West European Broadcasting* (London: Sage, 1992), p. 11.
5. Jay G. Blumler, 'Vulnerable Values at Stake', in Blumler (ed.), *Television and the Public Interest*, p. 36.
6. Jeremy Tunstall and Michael Palmer, *Media Moguls* (London: Routledge, 1991), p. 43.
7. Els De Bens, Mary Kelly and Marit Bakke, 'Television Content: Dallasification of Culture?', in Karen Siune and Wolfgang Truetzschler (eds.), *Dynamics of Media Politics: Broadcast and Electronic Media in Western Europe* (London: Sage, 1992), pp. 75–100.
8. Jill Forbes, 'France: Modernisation Across the Spectrum', in Geoffrey Nowell-Smith (ed.), *The European Experience* (London: British Film Institute, 1989), pp. 23–36.
9. Carol Haslam, 'The International Television Industry', in James Firebrace (ed.), *Losing the Picture: the Future for Television's Coverage of Global Issues* (London: Third World and Environment Broadcasting Project, 1990), pp. 58–62.
10. Haslam, 'The International Television Industry'.
11. Quoted in Wolfgang Koschnik, 'Escape from the Euro-trash', in *TV World's* Guide to Germany, 1991, p. 24.
12. Ien Ang, 'The Battle Between Television and its Audiences: the Politics of Watching Television', in Phillip Drummond and Richard Paterson (eds.), *Television in Transition* (London: British Film Institute, 1985), p. 263.
13. William R. Seaman, 'Active Audience Theory: Pointless Populism', in *Media Culture and Society*, vol. 14 no. 2, April 1992, pp. 301–11.
14. James Curran, 'The New Revisionism in Mass Communication Research: a Reappraisal', in *The European Journal of Communication*, vol. 5, 1990, pp. 135–64.
15. Judith Williamson, 'The Problems of Being Popular', *New Socialist*, no. 41, September 1986, p. 14.
16. Kees Brants, 'Broadcasting in the Netherlands: from Pillar to Post', in *West European Politics*, vol. 8 no. 2, April 1985, p. 105.
17. For further clarification of the Dutch system see 'The Netherlands' in The Euromedia Research Group, *The Media in Western Europe* (London: Sage, 1992), pp. 152–66.
18. Brants, 'Broadcasting in the Netherlands', pp. 108–9.
19. Ibid., p. 110.
20. Quoted in Herman Wigbold, 'The Shaky Pillars of Hilversum', in Anthony Smith (ed.), *Television and Political Life* (London: Macmillan, 1979), p. 223.
21. Ibid., p. 230.
22. Ien Ang, 'The Vicissitudes of Progressive Television', *New Formations*, no. 2, Summer 1987, p. 95.
23. Ang, 'The Battle Between Television and its Audiences', pp. 261–2.

24. Denis McQuail and Karen Siune (eds.), *New Media Politics: Comparative Perspectives in Western Europe* (London: Sage, 1976), p. 158.
25. 'Italy', in The Euromedia Research Group, *The Media in Western Europe*, pp. 136–7, 141.
26. Tunstall and Palmer, *Media Moguls*, p. 18.
27. Donald Sassoon, 'Italy: the Advent of Private Broadcasting', in Raymond Kuhn (ed.), *The Politics of Broadcasting* (London: Croom Helm, 1985), p. 144.
28. Quoted in Ed Vulliamy, 'Italian Fantasy Factory', *Guardian*, 20 March 1989, p. 25.
29. Ibid.
30. Quoted in D. Doglio, 'Cinderella Culture', *TV World*, September 1988, p. 17.
31. Giuseppe Richeri, 'Television from Service to Business: European Tendencies and the Italian Case', in Drummond and Paterson (eds.), *Television in Transition*, p. 29.
32. Martin Woollacott, 'Europe's Politics of Discontent', *Guardian*, 20 June 1992.

MTV's EUROPE

An Imaginary Continent?

Corinna Sturmer

It came, We watched, It conquered. At midnight on August 1st 1981, a fledgling American cable-television service signed on with: 'Ladies and Gentlemen, ROCK AND ROLL.'[1]

I grew up in Coburg, once the centre of the duchy of Sachsen Coburg Gotha and at the heart of Germany. In the 1970s it was trapped by the East German barbed-wire fence on three sides. For us young people who thought of ourselves as living in the armpit of Europe, escape from this isolation meant sipping a cup of *café au lait*, listening to Siouxsie and the Banshees or PIL, smoking Spanish cigarettes, ordering an ice-cream in Italian – the flavours of distance, of holidays, of the exotic. Our silent rebellion. Had MTV Europe existed then, would it have fed our yearning for this imaginary continent?

Music Television (MTV) was the brainchild of Robert Pittman. With the proliferation of television channels in the United States, his idea was to capitalise on the initially free programming provided by pop videos (today MTV has to pay to air them), and to finance the enterprise through advertising revenue and sponsorship. The aim was to catch the attention of a narrow demographic sector: channel-hopping 16–34 year-olds, statistically the most TV-resistant age group, through theme-programming and narrowcasting.[2]

Music Television is the first ever commercial channel devoted to presenting a non-stop diet of music video. Its style is inimitable, unpatented but definitive; restless cameras, frantic editing, kaleidoscopic compression and blazing colours. Presenters' chitchat, commer cials, news and 'idents' all blend seamlessly into the animated image stream. This highly innovative televisual form of the 80s was to become one of the most important forces in the music industry and in youth life-style. It has been criticised as 'fetishistic materialism and political passivity',[3] as 'more effective than pornography',[4] or as 'fast food for the eyes of a new generation of illiterates'.[5] But a close examination of MTV in a European context reveals a more contradictory picture.

Is the imaginary Europe of MTV a product of the irresistible attraction of popular 'low' consumer culture, a consequence of American cultural imperialism? Are we being spoon-fed 'Europudding'? Is MTV the new lingua franca of European popular culture, diluting local styles and sounds in its flow, or does it open avenues of opposition for Europe's youth resisting either oppressive national identities or the values and life-styles of an older generation? Does it open up spaces for new and different identities to emerge across Europe?

What is Europe? European history is characterised more by warfare than by solidarity, and even today Europe seems to define itself predominantly by what it rejects. The borderlines of inclusion and exclusion are in constant flux: between Europe and Islam, between Europe and the Third World, between Europe and the US, Black and White, North and South, and along its eastern borders. And now, as satellite and cable and the facilitated importation of foreign (mainly US) media products further erode national public service television monopolies, any solid sense of national or European identity begins to melt. MTV provides some of the heat.

MTV's conquest of the globe has been rapid and extensive. When it was launched in August 1981 to 1.5 million North American subscribers, the network was so patchy that its New York employees had to move to a New Jersey pub to watch it; but by 1991 MTV was available in 201 million households across seventy-seven countries in five continents, including MTV Australia, established in 1987, and MTV Brazil, set up in October 1990. MTV Asia was launched in Hong Kong in September 1991 to transmit to thirty-one Asian countries. These branches produce a number of their own shows, and until recently MTV Brazil was obliged by government to play 50 per cent Brazilian music, broadcast in Portuguese. However, MTV strives to remain an American form worldwide and to maintain its recognisable style. 'MTV is an American concept. We can't lose that. That's what holds us together,' explains Brent Hanson, Director of Programming and Production at MTV Europe.[6]

Europe has been plugged into the MTV global network since August 1987, with production offices and studios located in Camden, London. Europe-wide distribution takes place via Astra satellite and cable subscription. MTV Europe is still financially dependent on its US proprietor Viacom since 'it is not quite profitable yet'.[7] It receives 90 per cent of its revenue through advertising, with 10 per cent coming from the sponsorship of individual shows by multinational companies, such as *The Coca Cola Report* and *Braun European Top 20*. According to Brian Diamond, Executive Producer, programming decisions are made largely independently of MTV US and about 80 per cent of MTV's European programming is produced in-house.[8] Except for non-English lyrics and the few German or Scandinavian commercials, it is broadcast in English.

MTVE's explosive growth rate matches that of MTV's in the rest of the world. By May 1992 MTVE had achieved network figures of almost 37 million households in comparison to 14 million in the previous year and 3 million in 1988. It has gained a potential reach of 44 per cent of all European households. Its transmission area comprises twenty-eight countries from Iceland to Israel, Portugal to Moscow, with Liechtenstein and the CIS being the most recent acquisitions. By March 1992 the production staff in London had grown from thirteen to 120.

MTV's lifeblood is maintained by creating and capitalising on horizontal transnational integration of narrow consumer groups through niche programming, narrowcasting and transnational marketing and advertising. With the emergence of the MTV generation, it might seem as if national culture is ruptured along the age faultline, with '16-year-olds having more in common with kids in other countries than with their parents'.[9] The key problem for MTVE is that European youth is not a homogeneous entity, and its aim must therefore be to combine global marketing with targeting regional consumers. Global culture is composed of a diversity of the local, and to stay at the forefront of music and life-style MTVE must respond to this reality. It must aspire, just like Coca Cola, to be not a 'multinational' but a 'multilocal'.[10] The best example of this is Ray Cokes's new video request show *Most Wanted*, the only live Europe-wide TV show. One of Cokes's prizes was a Brian Adams concert in a prizewinner's living room in Germany. Another time he arranged transnational telephone conversations for his viewers via the Camden studios. The letters and phone calls from all over Europe indicate that Cokes manages to address people personally, to enter and interlink local European front rooms.

To speak of MTV as 'European' might at first sight seem ludicrous. Europe has an ambivalent relationship to the US and to American cultural imports, and therefore to MTV. MTVE is trying to forge a new common language that is not 'American'. American is 'anti-Europe', a paradigm for the traditionless and the materialistic, and yet it is Europe's alter ego, an exaggerated reflection of what Europe fears it will be or what it has already become.[11] As Denis Brogan puts it, 'The Americans are telling us something about ourselves.'[12]

Significant taste differences between Europe and the US are reflected in the channel's content and style. MTVE's programming, which predominantly features Pop, Dance, Rock and Indie, is increasingly distinct from MTV US, where Hard Rock, Rap and Metal are higher on the agenda. For example, Jon Bon Jovi is considered mainstream in the US but Heavy Metal in Europe, while The Wonderstuff or EMF, mainstream in Britain, are classified 'alternative' in the US. MTV US offers less variety of music and it is more light entertainment-oriented. MTV Australia and MTV Europe have developed as important feeds back to the US, having for example brought Enigma, Sinead O'Connor and Snap to the attention of the music market there.

According to Brian Diamond, the MTVE playlist times are on average composed of 5–22 per cent continental European music and 20–40 per cent British music. MTVE claims that of its staff of more than 120, composed of fourteen nationalities, fewer than 10 per cent are American. But it must be said that these include the Chief Executive and Managing Director, the Executive Producer, the Directors of Research, Advertising Sales, Marketing/Network Development and the Creative Director. Diamond emphasises, 'We are very careful not to come across as too American. The problem is more being too British!'[13]

The channel's attempted European flavour and content is best documented in informational shows such as *MTV News* and *The Coca Cola Report*, composed of European news features and concert information. They are the only Pan-European source of information on what's rocking. Others are *MTV Braun European Top 20* and the monthly magazine programme *The Pulse*, packed with snippets of European fashion trends and events in the arts world. 'Europeanism' is also reflected in the choice of presenters, who are, according to Brent Hanson, 'the lifeline of the channel, the "real" person in the cartoon environment'. Apart from Pip Dann from New Zealand, all presenters mirror the North European target audience – Swedish, British, German or Dutch. 'I don't want any radio jocks,' Hanson says. 'You must see yourself a little bit in there.'[14]

Since MTVE constantly needs to 'reinvent' itself, to lead and reflect, create and capitalise on a European market, it is vital that it provides a breeding ground for national and local music – always appropriate to the MTV picture of course. Shows such as *Rock Block*, *XPO*, *Partyzone* and *Postmodern* provide a forum for the less mainstream or unestablished bands to be exposed or broken. A further platform for new music is provided by playlist categories, a scheme adapted from radio. The playlist has seven categories which determine how frequently acts are put on the air. A-list videos have five or six screenings per day while C-list singles have two. The first big video of a band might go into the breakers category, aired four times per day. The playlist caters for up and coming acts through the *Buzz Bin*, which means several consecutive screenings, always introduced by DJs. For example Nirvana, a Seattle band, was completely unknown, except for a few 1991 summer festivals and a screening on *120 Minutes*, when the video of *Smells Like Teen Spirit* was put on the *Buzz Bin* in November 1991. It soon charted all over Europe. 'Nirvana had all the ingredients for being a *Buzz Bin* band. They're brand new, got a good look, a great sound, a buzzing cool video,' explains Lauren Levine, of MTV programming.[15] Roxette or the Creeps from Sweden, French band Niagra (the first band to have a concert sponsored by MTV), Eros Ramanzotti from Italy and many others would not deny MTV's part in their international success.

Bernhard Betzen, the Manager and Booking Agent of the French band Mano Negra, who scored the greatest French export hit in 1990, credits MTV with being 'more adventurous than European Radio'.[16] On their last album, *Puta's Fever*, the band fuses French, Spanish and English musical styles – rockabilly, rock, flamenco, rap, salsa, reggae, country, funk. The result is 'Patchanka', and typifies MTVE's vision of truly 'European' music. They perform in French, Spanish and English and use Latin performers or the Arabic dance wail of Sidi H'Bibi to add visual spice to the panoramic quality of their album and video. 'A "wildin" 1990 Trans-Euro Express'.[17] MTV started playing Mano Negra's first video, *Mala Vida*, in 1988 even before they were on a major label or had secured a European release with *Puta's Fever*. Betzen argues that it was not radio exposure but the extensive airing of the *King Kong Five* video which boosted them to number 4 in Holland. Unlike the American genre-based stations, increasingly adopted in the UK, North European radio tends to be mainstream and conservative because of competition for audience ratings. Its unique position as 24-hour and pan-European gives MTV competitive edge in countries like Germany, which does not even have a national radio station.

Top: Bulgarian woman watching MTV, MTV Press archive, 1991
Bottom: East German soldiers on Berlin Wall, MTV Press archive, 1989

MTVE's Euro-cocktail is rooted in what emerged as a new pop era in the 70s, 'Europop'. It is best exemplified by the 'cleanliness', 'whiteness' and superficiality of ABBA, or the style and performance of Chic, the Bee Gees, Boney M and Donna Summer. Europop, for Simon Frith, is characterised by its different aesthetic from American rock and roll, which

> remains rooted (viz Bruce Springsteen and U2, the most America-fixated, tradition-conscious rock acts of our time) in authenticity, in the notion of a fixed code of musical and emotional truths. Europop ... rests on both a confusion of musical categories and, more importantly, on a sense of rootless self-invention.[18]

While Rock videos can get away with a harder feel and lower budgets because of the generally rough edge of the music, for Europop stylised and extravagant videos complement its music perfectly. This obsession with visual gloss explains the importance of MTV for European music culture.

The Stockholm-based trio Army of Lovers – composed of the Dutch-Swedish keyboard boffin Alexander Bard, a camp Parisian fashion victim Jean-Pierre Barda and a big-breasted Michaela de la Cour – take the concepts of Europop to the extreme. The band make no apologies for their blatantly attention-seeking videos, which are as important as their music, a collage of up-to-date rhythms and ethnic sounds. Barda explains: 'We are not musicians but pop stars and proud to mime.'[19] Their cartoon character existence is linked to Europe's flamboyant gay club and fashion scene, with the fan club 'Lovers of Army' devotedly escorting the band on tour in preposterous costumes. Despite the international mix of band members and their striking plasticity, they seek to preserve their unique 'authenticity'. Bard argues that to sustain their inimitable style they rejected the offer of being remodelled by London producers, like fellow Scandinavian bands A-ha and Roxette. 'What would Kraftwerk be if they hadn't stayed in Düsseldorf, or Yello if they hadn't stayed in Zurich?'[20] Does national origin still matter for bands like the black Franco-German disco duo Milli Vanilli or Milan-based Black Box? Who can tell that Ten Sharp of Technotronic are from Holland? All sing in English and blend seamlessly into the non-place-bound elastic MTV stream, as do Gypsy King's flamenco sound (the band is actually French) and Nina Hagen's inimitable mixture of German and English. The resulting collage – cultural enrichment or *Einheitsbrei* – is MTVE's distinctive quality.

Despite its stated cultural ideals, MTV must be understood as a business whose existence and growth is wholly dependent on its market success. There is space for only a few experiments like Nirvana. Increase in revenue does allow for an increase in Euro-based production, such as news items and concert coverage, but the more MTV expands, the more it moves into the music and advertising industries' spotlights, the more its playlist positions are demanded and the greater the pressure to produce internationally available and accessible material. A large proportion of its playlist categories conforms to the European Top 40, and it plays these in heavy rotation. Therefore, to understand the diversities of the 'imaginary continent' one must also look at the conditions under which MTV is consumed.

MTVE's Europe, which ranges from Israel to Norway and takes in the varying musical histories of Britain and Greenland, is much more diverse than it might seem at first sight. The appreciation of and response to MTVE varies dramatically. For example, this imaginary continent can be divided into 'taste-zones' – North European rock versus South European romantic ballad sound, or Britain versus the Continent. In his description of musical trends, Brian Diamond gives a clue to MTV's in-house perception of what really belongs in MTV's Europe. 'We are so aware of how Europe works. The UK is usually right on top of it, Holland follows after that. Then you might see Scandinavia jump in. And Germany is usually last in the picture.'[21]

In its choice of music, programmes and presenters, MTVE seeks to reflect the North European market, which constitutes the main target audience for its advertisers and sponsors. Tastes are generally becoming more homogeneous, thanks to MTV's trend-setting impact and to synchronised release patterns by record companies throughout Europe. MTV's Europe can also be categorised according to consumer spending power: Western versus Eastern Europe and North versus South. The concentration of audience research also shapes MTVE's in-house perception of Europe. With the exception of focus group research in 1991, and a special survey in 1992 in Italy, MTV receives no audience feedback outside of Scandinavia, the UK, Germany and the Benelux countries.

Sweden is probably the most faithful European MTV country. The channel is so popular that when MTV threatened to go off the air during a licence fee dispute, Martin Timell, a famous youth presenter, called this prospect a 'cultural catastrophe'.[22] In a country where 1.7 million of the 3.6 million households can receive MTV,[23] the channel is a dominant source of popular youth culture. Sweden has always been receptive to British and American imports, with little local resistance. The Swedish public service stations Kanal 1 and TV2, and even the more youth-oriented third terrestrial channel TV4, are not adequate alternatives to the seductions of MTV. Sweden's vast production of internationally accessible music with English lyrics, often on MTVE's heavy rotations, is unmatched by any other country. Jean-Pierre Barda explains Army of Lovers' success: 'We are of the country of Volvo cars and safety belts, suicide rates, Ingmar Bergman films and boring tennis players.... We are a reaction against the boredom, just like Greta Garbo and Gloria Swanson.'[24] Which also partly explains the popularity of MTV: voluntary exile for bored Swedish youth.

The newest member in the MTVE continent, Italy, plugged in since late 1991, is already the third largest MTVE territory in terms of its potential reach of 4.6 million homes, predominantly in the north of the country. Still, viewing figures are low. This is apparently due to Italy's strong sense of local identity and culture and the relatively low comprehension of English. There are further problems. Italy has an abundance of popular radio stations playing a large amount of indigenous music. Videomusic, a domestic TV music channel, is a real competitor to MTVE. They share the same channel-hopping audience but Videomusic plays a high percentage of Italian music and videos, and is broadcast round the clock, while MTVE can only be received for six hours during the afternoon. This is an inconvenient slot for its prime audience. Forty-two per cent of non-viewers are unaware that MTVE exists, and the channel does not spare viewers the most 'wordy' programmes such as the *Coke Report*, news and film reviews. Despite its lower visual production quality, 27 per cent of MTVE's viewers actually prefer Videomusic.

To support its launch in Italy, MTVE initially gave considerable prominence to Italian acts. But programming 'national' music is problematic for MTV. Some music remains too indigenous to cross over to other countries. Other music is hampered by long-standing rivalries – between Norway and Sweden or Germany and Holland, for example. The network seeks to avoid what Diamond calls 'patronising' or 'ghettoising' national music, partly to preserve its own credibility and international accessibility.[25] For example, MTV refuses to create a Dutch or German music show, although there is plenty of demand and it could be lucrative in terms of advertising revenue. In recent months the German market has mushroomed in both reach and viewing figures (with 12.1 million households in May 1992 in comparison to 8.9 million households in August 1991) and consequently in advertising revenue. Still, there is not yet a German programmer in the MTV team, and MTV is wary of the danger of 'Germanising' the channel or for that matter favouring any particular country. 'If music from the Continent is going to be treated with respect,' says Diamond, 'it has to be treated just like British and American music, not as "Oh, this is from France!"'[26]

Helmut Fest, regional managing director of EMI in Germany, Austria and Switzerland, has a different sense of respect for music. He stresses that MTV has a great opportunity to expand its own and its viewers' horizons but does not adequately fulfil its responsibility towards Continental and up-and-coming artists such as Herbert Groenemeyer, BAP, Marcus-Meuller Westernhagen or Vasio Rossi. MTV has a limited understanding of the Continental market and repertoire. 'If you see the German charts, you will see the same names occurring over and over again. We need to break new artists and MTV could really help there.'[27] However, MTVE's quarterly survey in July 1992 showed that 76 per cent of MTV's German audience said that MTV already plays enough German music, and 59 per cent are happy with the amount of Anglo-American music. Dial MTV's top ten German requests in 1991 included nine American and one British clip, which complicates the question of what young Germans want or should get on MTV.

Since 1992, MTVE has been transmitted on a further satellite link, Astra 1B, extending the channel's footprint to the southern regions of the Mediterranean countries and to North Africa. MTVE is also discussing the possibility of transmitting special 'Latin' programmes southwards to these marginal territories, broadcasting in different languages and featuring more indigenous music. The aim is to boost ratings and link into previously untapped advertising markets – Spain being among the strongest advertisers in Europe. This would make Brent Hanson's aim of creating a product all young Europeans could share simultaneously quite problematic, and he would have to change his strategy.

The increasingly high-quality look of MTV presents further problems for local bands waiting to break through. While the costs of producing the music for an album today might be £5,000, one can calculate an average of £30,000 for a video of one of the tracks, and another £20,000 to promote the album adequately.[28] European video quality often does not conform to MTV's slick and highly professional visual gloss. Only very few bands have the 'drive' and finance to speak the increasingly sophisticated MTV image language. MTV is high-density TV. In a primetime slot such as *Greatest Hits* or *European Top 20*, millions in production value float past.

Although high budgets and extravagance are often the key to success, they are not indispensable or the only prerequisite. Some videos work because of simple but powerful ideas. Massive Attack's striking video, *Unfinished Sympathy*, directed by Baillie Walsh, consists of just one shot following the lead singer Shara Nelson walking down a street in Los Angeles. The video of Sinead O'Connor's *Nothing Compares 2 You*, accompanying her European 1990 no. 1, is just a static close-up of her stunning performance. Army of Lovers' video maker, Frederic Martinsen, became famous by producing videos for an eighth of the price asked for in Britain. UB 40 have made videos for £500, giving their music a homely, friendly touch.

MTV does feature video material shot on Super 8, Hi 8 or VHS, mainly on the image shows such as *120 Minutes*, *Headbangers Ball*, or *Party Zone*, which are broadcast at weekends. *120 Minutes* shows mostly independent music – low-budget videos and groups whose producers prefer making records rather than videos. Up to half its output is specially produced by the show itself, including features and specials (Laibach, The Pogues, Nirvana), interviews, news and concert footage. Low-budget and self-produced videos by indie bands such as Wedding Present, Sonic Youth and The Jesus and Mary Chain are featured frequently. In this way the show has served as a breaking-ground into heavy rotation for some bands. Examples are Nirvana's smash hit *Smells Like Teen Spirit* (which had its premiere on *120 Minutes* in September 1991), Primal Scream and R.E.M. But to make a really international impact, heavier rotation than that available on *120 Minutes* alone is needed.

Eastern Europe is another important territorial as well as ideological issue for MTVE. For Russian viewers, 'The network of a non-stop stream of hedonistic images has political (arguably revolutionary) consequences beyond George Michael's bum. They are suggestive of an alternative social order that is almost impossibly attractive.'[29] A mere six months before the Berlin wall fell, MTV entered Poland, Hungary, Czechoslovakia and East Germany. In 1990, a one-hour weekly show was launched in Russian and became the country's most popular programme. In February 1991, MTV became the only Western cable channel in St Petersburg, and the Deputy Manager compared the network with Peter the Great, who opened Russia to Western influences. By May 1992, with almost 2 million households, Eastern Europe (including the former Yugoslavia) constituted 5 per cent of the MTV territory, with 530,000 Polish, 399,336 Yugoslav and 346,624 Hungarian households plugged in. While for the moment MTV's 'colonisation' of the East seems to have purely ideological importance, there is also potential for huge audience growth and lucrative markets.

In the political climate of the post-communist world, MTV's Janus-faced nature comes to light. While constructing its appeal around the rebellious image and anti-authoritarian values of Rock'n'Roll, at the same time it typifies and exists to serve the interests of advanced consumer capitalism. The flood of phone calls and letters (increasingly from Croatia and Bosnia) seem to prove that it provides welcome escapism, a lifeline out of daily drudgery. While most young Europeans can feel that their music is occasionally represented on MTVE, the East's ticket to MTVE membership is through consumption. In economies unable to provide for basic needs, the music industry is completely underdeveloped. For now, MTVE can only give young people in the East a marginal voice through concert footage and the youth documentary items planned by Brent Hanson.

The Eastern European situation demonstrates the need to be critical of the kind of Europe MTVE portrays. 'Their experience of rock and roll, after all, has taken place outside its intended cultural context, and lacks the unabashed consumerism of late-stage capitalism which has made us Westerners all so jaded (for good or for ill) when it comes to pop.'[30] Antony Tosiek from Poland writes:

> MTV is highly professional and I pray every evening our performers can learn something from it. The voice is not enough any more. How expressive Whitney Houston is, how cold and at the same time exciting Sinead O'Connor. When I recall Monika Bory's short breath after her half-minute dance while performing I lose my optimism. Do we have to produce 'Polenzes' (Polish cars)? Because it's got four wheels and goes? And because it is ours?[31]

MTVE's presence beyond the rusted Iron Curtain stimulates Western guilt and worry about what 'our' cultural perversions do to 'them'. But it must not be forgotten that MTV is exceeding the role which pop records and jeans had previously played as valuable and illicit contraband. There is a serious danger of patronising those 'victims' of the globalising, dictating forces of the North European music and culture industry.

The fact that black artists are taking an increasing percentage of airtime is a radical change from the early days of MTV in the US, when it was criticised for its white bias. MTV's executives at the time claimed that MTV was a Rock'n'Roll channel, and that in the 80s Rock was in fact a white phenomenon. In 1988, MTV US was forced to accept black input after incurring the wrath of Michael Jackson's management, which had forced Epic records to threaten to withdraw all support from the station if it failed to back its promotional drive for Jackson.[32] However, it was the launch of the US-produced *Yo! MTV Raps* in 1988 which most emphatically signalled the end of MTV's all-whiteness. *Yo!* is now bought in from America and aired daily on MTVE at the peaktime slot of 6 o'clock CET (Central European Time) – despite the fact that it is a non-sponsored programme. *Yo! MTV Raps* typifies the arguments about MTV, and in Europe especially it is the most controversial show on the air.

Rap as a form of black popular music started in the late 1970s in the South Bronx, New York. The urban experience of young lower-class blacks of racial discrimination, unemployment, crime, drugs and poverty provided the ingredients for Hip Hop, the subculture of which Rap is the most prominent feature. The rough edge of Rap as a music form lends itself to documentation of these living conditions, often expressed through angry lyrics, most notoriously by gangster Rapper Ice-T. However, Rap's spectrum is large. 'Edutainers' like Public Enemy, or bands like Big Daddy Kane, Lakim Shabaz and Rakim, associated with the Nation of Islam, use the format to introduce critical and socially conscious lyrics and messages. Native Tongue Posse, a loose collective of rappers who include Queen Latifa, A Tribe called Quest and De La Soul, challenge the aggressive stance and machismo often associated with Rap as a whole.[33]

The frantic pace and streetwise edge of *Yo! MTV Raps* complements the Hip Hop style. *Yo!* is the key to Rap's access to a larger, more diverse audience. It was an instant success in America, gaining the station its largest ever viewing figures. *Yo! MTV Raps* is 'institutionalised counter culture'. In the US, and subsequently in Europe, Rap has become big business. Arch rappers like Ice Cube or Ice-T, who went as far as no. 2 in the US charts, or 'pseudo rapper' Hammer, frequently on MTV's A-List, are shrewd business people. Kris Kross, a pair of 13-year-olds produced by Hermain Dupree, turned their clothes back to front and coined gold when they signed with New York hard-core label Ruffhouse. With *Jump* they have outgrown *Yo!* and have had several consecutive weeks on MTVE's A-playlist. It is the fastest-selling no. 1 single the US has seen in fifteen years.[34]

MTV's undeniable influence in bringing Hip Hop culture into the main-stream and turning it into an accessible consumer item has spread to other areas of entertainment. In 1991, Fab 5 Freddy, New York's arch rapper who hosts the weekend edition of *Yo!*, co-produced the film *New Jack City*, which made $50 million from a relatively minor investment from Warner Bros. John Singleton, director of *Boyz from the Hood*, who was voted most talented newcomer at the MTV US movie awards in July 1992, thinks that one of the reasons the new wave black films have been so successful (and with young white as well as black audiences) is that 'kids have been conditioned by the videos and imagery they've seen on *Yo!*'[35]

Yo! is produced by MTV US and imported into Europe. British Rap, often reflecting the American prototype, suffers from lack of exposure. 'Black people aren't dealing with the music business on any significant level in this country ... and DJ's that say they support British Rap ain't doing no shit about it,' says MC Bee from Caveman.[36] But according to Max and Dave, Hip Hop DJs on London's Kiss 100 FM radio station, the lack of European Rap 'is not *Yo!*'s, it's MTVE's fault.'[37] *Yo!* was in fact invented in Europe in 1987 by Sophie Bramley. Although the European Rap scene was also packed with US acts in those days, the European *Yo!* played bands like London Posse, King Bee and DJ Pogo, who have now lost access to TV and pan-European exposure. The concept was adopted by the American producer Ted Demme in 1988. In 1990, MTVE decided to drop MTVE's *Yo!* in favour of the American version. Since then there has been very little room on *Yo!* for European Rap acts, except for bands like Cookie Crew, who scored successes in the US charts, and Monie Love, who emigrated to Los Angeles for her career. In 1991, Fab 5 Freddy recorded his first European special in Brixton, featuring British rappers MC Mello, Young Disciples and Galliano. A second attempt at exposure followed in spring 1992 in Cannes, introducing French acts MC Solar and Ideal Junior. But these remain exceptions, and European Rap is more likely to be on regular MTVE shows than on *Yo!*, if at all.

If Rap is an Afro-American and marginally British phenomenon, what is its significance for Europe? Transplanted across the Channel, Rap suffers a further sea change. PETAR audience ratings show that German viewing figures have their highest peak during *Yo!*, while in Britain ratings dive to rock bottom.[38] These ratings must be judged sceptically since they can be easily manipulated by a minority of passionate viewers. Besides, the show is on air in Germany's primetime, while (because of the time difference) potential British viewers are still at work.

Nevertheless, there is plenty of resentment against *Yo!* in Europe, for its alleged sexism, aggression and irrelevance to the European cultural experience. The show epitomises the recent shift of MTVE's audience towards male and younger viewers.

Still, *Yo!* is the second most frequently watched European weekly show and the most popular Saturday viewing on the Continent, while in Britain it is not among the top ten shows. To a certain extent this is because MTV is still dependent on satellite reach, which remains very patchy in the United Kingdom, with only 2.3 million households having access. More important factors are the music industry itself and the musical history of the countries involved. Britain is the fastest moving European music market, followed by Holland, and is rapidly outgrowing what's on offer on MTV. In Britain the Rap club scene, the diverse offerings in record shops, on London radio stations such as Kiss FM and on Tim Westwood's Rap show on Capital Radio are more important for forming music consumption trends than MTV. As a high-profile show under commercial pressure, *Yo!* is becoming more and more mainstream and arguably more popular for white than for black audiences. In general, the cultural confidence of the British music scene acts as a barrier against MTV's influence, while Germany is much more taken by it.

Desolate urban landscapes, drugs and crime, black subculture: where is the breeding ground for the love of Rap in the squeaky clean streets and tight social security systems of western Germany, where MTV is mostly watched? Whereas in France and Italy some innovative local Rap collages have emerged, Hip Hop culture in Germany is predominantly one of consumption. According to Richie Rich, Rap musician and Hip Hop DJ on London's Kiss FM, 'They like it when there's a lot of swearing in it. They like the image that goes with it, the feeling of being rebellious kids.' [39]

Is MTV producing a watered down version of Hip Hop culture, a visually packaged display of a mysterious adventure land, an exotic black underground for curious, saturated North European consumers? It seems that the original rebelliousness of Rap lasts as far as wearing your baseball shirt back to front (Kris Kross charted in top positions all over Europe) and being 'seriously Krossed out'. However, Hip Hop DJs Max and Dave argued that 'the Kris Kross record, as commercial as it is, is probably one of the best representations of the way the Hip Hop audience do behave, having a good time without any images of violence.' [40] Or does *Yo!* hold a more seriously political message for Eastern

European viewers, who might not be able to decode the lyrics which reflect their own experience?

Loved by its fans and detested by its adversaries, *Yo!* is a contentious piece of the jigsaw puzzle which is MTV Europe. Whether the interest of some white Europeans in the subcultural voices on *Yo!* is just a momentary fashion, whether it might open minds or actually reinforce racist stereotypes, are questions at the heart of this controversy. A Europe-produced show is planned, modelled on MTV US's *Fade to Black* and featuring a wide range of black music. It remains an irony that, despite the range of black communities within Europe, MTVE imports its principal black music show from the US. But certainly *Yo!* brings race into the spectrum of European mainstream youth culture, further blurring Europe's already dissolving cultural boundaries.

The different responses to *Yo!* also demonstrate that the MTV generation is more unpredictable and more diverse than it seems at first sight. This will not appease those who bewail MTV as an omnipotent, homogenising cultural force, producing bland and uniform Euromusic. But MTV's message is not monolithic. The differing reactions to *Yo!* in Germany and the UK, or to the channel as a whole in Sweden, Poland or Italy, indicate that as MTVE strives to build its European profile it is at the same time reflecting and helping to create a range of diverse and surprising 'imaginary continents' for and with its young audiences. Nevertheless, a question remains about this range. Given the nature of the television market-place in which MTVE operates, how inclusive of the many ethnic, cultural and social identities that make up contemporary Europe can it afford to be?

This chapter would not have been possible without the friendly welcome I received at MTV. I am very grateful to Brent Hanson and Brian Diamond, and everybody else at MTV, for their great help, patience and time. (The chapter was written in the summer of 1992, so does not deal with any changes since then.) Special thanks also to all interviewees, and to Philip Wood for his support and advice.

NOTES

1. R. Harrington, 'MTV, after 10 years, Still Rocks Round the Clock', *International Herald Tribune*, 2 August 1991.
2. S. Faith, *Music for Pleasure* (Cambridge: Polity Press, 1989), p. 208.
3. J. Heileman, 'Rebel Without a Cause', *The Modern Review*, Autumn 1991, p. 5.
4. S. Jhally, *Daily Mail*, 28 February 1992.

5. W. Hobel, 'Eine Kulturschande', *Newmag*, Germany, August 1991.

6. B. Hanson, interview with author, November 1991.

7. B. Steinberg, Director of Advertising Sales, MTV Europe, interview with author, June 1992.

8. B. Diamond, interview with author, November 1991.

9. B. Diamond, interview with author.

10. B. Webster, 'Cocacolanisation and National Cultures', *Overhere*, vol 9 no. 2, 1989.

11. D. Morley *et al.*, 'Spaces of Identity: Communications Technologies and the Reconfiguration of Europe', *Screen*, vol. 30 no. 4, 1989, p. 18.

12. Quoted in C.W.E. Bigsby, 'Europe, America and the Cultural Debate' in Bigsby (ed.), *Supercultural: America Popular Culture and Europe* (Bowling Green, Ohio: Bowling Green University Popular Press, 1975), p. 26.

13. B. Diamond, interview with author.

14. B. Hanson, interview with author.

15. L. Levine, Director of Programme Acquisition, MTV Europe, interview with author, November 1991.

16. *Hollywood Reporter*, October 1990, p. 14.

17. H. Staggers, 'Gallic Sauce', *NME*, 6 January 1990.

18. S. Frith, 'Europop', *Cultural Studies* (UK), 3 February 1989.

19. Quoted in P. McNeill, 'Miming in Prime Time', *The European*, 6–8 December 1991, p. 22.

20. Ibid.

21. Quoted in T. Coleman, 'The MTV European', *Hollywood Reporter*, October 1991, p. 15.

22. P. Flodin, 'Kulturskandal om MTV forsvinner', *Aftonbladet* (Sweden), 17 January 1992.

23. Figures released by MTVE's research department (July 1991).

24. Quoted in S. Price, 'Swede Jesus'. Publisher and date unknown.

25. B. Diamond, quoted in T. Coleman, 'The MTV European', p. 11.

26. B. Diamond, interview with author.

27. H. Fest, 'MTV Europe Ignores Local Acts', *Billboard* (USA), 7 March 1992.

28. Jambo van Renon, Mango Records, interview with author, July 1992. These figures should be taken to indicate the relationship between production and promotion costs.

29. J. Heileman, 'Rebel Without a Cause', p. 6.

30. Ibid., p. 5.

31. In *Pawie Oko* (Poland), July 1991.

32. 'Yo! Fab 5 Freddy Raps', *CT Incorporating African Times* (UK), 28 January 1992, p. 18.

33. H. Querl, 'Lyrical Culture, Rap Music as a Cultural Form of Resistance' (London, May 1992, unpublished).

34. A. Higginsbotham, 'Straight outta Primary School, Kross Dressing for Beginners', *Select* (London), July 1992, p. 31.

35. 'Yo! Fab 5 Freddy Raps', p. 18.

36. Quoted in D. Fousham, 'Rubble without a Pause', in *Hip Hop Connection* (UK), June 1992, p. 15.

37. Interview with author, July 1992.

38. Source: PETAR MTVE 1991.

39. Richie Rich, interview with author, July 1992.

40. Max and Dave, Hop Hop DJs at Kiss FM, interview with author, July 1992.

GLOBO VILLAGE
Television in Brazil

Roberto Mader

Brazilian television is one of the most developed systems in the world. It also provides some of the most outrageous examples of the effects deregulation can have. State-run channels are almost non-existent and have insignificant audiences; private networks control the market and dictate the rules. The main network, Globo Television, is well managed and achieves high standards of broadcasting quality, producing 80 per cent of Brazil's programming and employing nearly 15,000 people. It is the fourth largest commercial television network in the world – following ABC, NBC, CBS in the United States – and only in the last few years has it experienced occasional threats to its dominance of the ratings.

Globo penetrates 99.93 per cent of Brazil's territory (as large as Europe without the former Soviet Union), and is the main communication channel for 150 million people. A quarter of Brazilian adults are illiterate and millions more are semi-literate. The country has 40 million TV sets, six national TV networks (one state-run) and two regional networks. There are 247 TV stations – 227 commercial and twenty educational – of which Globo controls seventy-nine. Globo's audience share never dips below an average of 45 per cent in any state and the nationwide average hovers around 70 per cent.

What circumstances made this private monopoly possible? A realistic portrait of television in Brazil would include three basic characteristics. First, there has never been any notion of public service broadcasting and private networks are free to broadcast whatever they find will attract the largest audience and therefore advertisers. Insignificant amounts are spent on quality programmes such as educational material or investigative journalism. TV Cultura, a state-run channel in São

67

Paulo, is exceptional in terms of its high quality but its ratings are not encouraging. Secondly, licences for broadcasting have been bargaining instruments in the hands of politicians, who also own most of the channels. Approximately 20 per cent of Brazilian members of parliament, and fourteen senators out of seventy-five, own shares in at least one radio or TV station. Regulation of media ownership is vague and not respected. In 1988 the former president, José Sarney, bargained for a wider mandate in exchange for franchise concessions to 1,250 radio and TV stations. The third significant characteristic of television in Brazil is that advertising is the *raison d'etre* of every channel, except the weak state-run channels. Advertising comes before, during and after every programme, without any warning or rational regulation. In addition, news items can be sponsored, which paves the way for many different sorts of censorship.

I will consider here the problems these features have caused and examine some of the solutions attempted so far, such as alternative video production, which has flourished since the early 1980s but which still has very limited distribution, and the radical review of state policy on television, which is gathering support from a growing number of organisations and social groups who see the control of the media by democratic institutions as a major step towards a democratic society.

Dynasty: Family control

The history of television in Brazil is one of powerful families running regional services. The chaos and the lack of concern for public service broadcasting which characterises Brazilian television is rooted in the development of a system of political favours that has benefited powerful businessmen and influential politicians since television started with TV Tupi in São Paulo in September 1950. By 1953 there were also Tupi Rio, Radio Televisão Paulista and TV Record Rio, all concentrated in Rio and São Paulo. Tupi, the first television station to be established in Latin America, was owned by Assis Chateaubriand, an early media baron who controlled a thick slice of the communications market. Later his group would control thirty-six radio stations, thirty-four newspapers and eighteen television channels. Industry in Brazil was still virtually non-existent, so equipment and technical assistance came from General Electric and RCA.

Commercial considerations have been fundamental to Brazilian television from the start, and financial, as well as technological, models derive from the United States. Initially few advertisers were attracted, but agencies working in Brazil saw the potential in a medium reaching the well-off who could then afford a television set, which cost at that time not much less than a car. Advertising campaigns were launched to encourage consumers to buy TV sets, with the argument that they needed to play their role in 'modernising the country'. Trying to popularise the new medium, Chateaubriand himself ordered some TV sets to be installed in city squares for public viewing, and more popular programming such as soap operas and variety programmes was squeezed between programmes aimed at an elitist audience: classical theatre, dance and music and many US-produced documentaries.

The sponsoring model for programming set up at that time indicates the regulatory chaos that has always marked television in Brazil. The whole production process was totally dependent on sponsors who retained the ownership of programmes. If they were not happy it could mean the end of the programme, no matter what the TV station or the audience thought. TV stations only provided the studios and equipment and broadcast the programme. These productions were usually named after the sponsor, like *Cine Max Factor*, *Mappin Movietone*, *Teatro Walita*, *Espetaculos Tonelux* and *Reporter Esso* from TV Tupi, adapted from radio and broadcast on television from 1952 to 1970. *Reporter Esso* was entirely produced outside Tupi, by an advertising company using the services of United Press International (UPI), and it contained hardly any national news. The first advertisement filmed was produced by J. Walter Thompson, working for Ford, which sponsored *Telenoticias Panair*, one of the first televised news bulletins on TV Tupi in 1952.[1] It was not until 1961 that the government limited advertising breaks to three minutes; before then nobody could say how long each commercial break would last. Sponsors also controlled the main artists, who would be moved, along with their programmes, from one station to another if it was thought they could reach a larger audience.

During the 1950s technical limitations and the lack of an administrative structure in the Brazilian broadcasting industry meant that TV was entirely a regional phenomenon. However, in 1955 the newly elected president Juscelino Kubitscheck promised to make Brazil achieve fifty years of growth within five years with his National Industrial Development Plan. Television was seen as a centrepiece for capitalism's expansion in the country, importing foreign ideas and spreading values which would gradually create a more urban society. Starting from Rio and São Paulo, the expansion of this cultural industry stimulated industrial development on a national scale.[2] Kubitscheck was also the first politician to use television as a mass medium in Brazil: the inauguration of his government was broadcast live.

In the 1960s, with expanding industries and markets and the arrival of videotape and cheaper TV sets making advertising on a national scale more attractive, programming at a national level began to be standardised. Programmes, once produced with a different cast in each region, were now centrally produced in Rio or São Paulo and then distributed to the regions, which lost ground in both cultural and labour markets as a result. Videotape, besides facilitating programme production in the economic centres, encouraged commercialisation of programmes and opened the market to foreign productions such as US-made series. North American values started to penetrate Brazilian television, which had relied on the hitherto cheaper alternatives of home-made products.

Videotape was also a significant turning point in the production of Brazilian television's most popular product: *tele-novelas*. These are best described as a mixture of soap opera and mini-series, and before the early 60s they were broadcast live and not more than twice a week. Recorded on videotape, however, they could be broadcast daily, creating the basis for a 'horizontal schedule' where programmes of the same kind (soap operas, live variety shows, US-made series, journalism) are broadcast at a particular time of the day in strands, conditioning the audience to switch on every day at the same time. Since then national integration through television has meant an imposition of a Rio/São Paulo culture on the other regions.

The first daily *tele-novela* opera 2-54-99 was broadcast by TV Excelsior, established in São Paulo in 1959 and owned by Mario Wallace Simonsen, a coffee magnate and airline (Panair) proprietor. Excelsior is considered to have been the forerunner of today's properly administered television networks. Within two years it was also established in Rio and was threatening the region's leader, TV Rio. Its daily soap opera *Redemption* (1966) had 596 episodes and some of Brazil's most popular stars. The real success for the *tele-novelas* came at the end of 1964 with TV Tupi's *The Right to be Born*. This was an old-style Latin American drama, about a poor wet nurse and her relationship with a rich family, and was broadcast for eight months. People may argue about whether soap operas divert attention from the real world, but few can deny that they are, especially under tough censorship, a relatively harmless kind of programme, a welcome light entertainment in hard times. So *The Right to be Born* was the audience's right to dream, sponsored by Colgate-Palmolive. At the end of that dream a crowd of 25,000 gathered at Maracanazinho, a Rio stadium, to celebrate their stars.

Lethal Weapon: military TV

1964 was also the year in which a military coup seized power from the democratic government of João Goulart, which was implementing a series of reforms perceived by the right wing as communist manoeuvres. Under the military regime, Brazil was pushed into fast economic growth and industrialisation that was dependent on imported technology and foreign capital. Television promoted consumer goods on a massive scale.[3] This had sharp social consequences, and provoked a huge conflict of interest between national and foreign capital, reflected in television when indigenous television stations fought against the entry of North American capital.

Time-Life Broadcasting Stations was the first group to penetrate the opening market. It had signed the first co-operation contracts with Globo in 1962, creating a joint venture even though, according to the Brazilian constitution, national communication companies holding a television franchise could not (and still cannot) have foreign partners or intellectual and administrative direction from abroad. Globo, a national newspaper group based in Rio which also runs three local radio stations, was then owned by Roberto Marinho, who was interested in expanding into television. Time-Life needed a way to enter the market, Globo needed money and assistance: there were all the characters for the perfect plot, written and directed by a local media baron, financed by a multinational as the executive producer, with the military an appreciative audience conveniently ignoring the unconstitutional nature of the arrangement.

Between 1962 and 1966 the Time-Life group invested over US$6 million (or US$4 million as admitted by Roberto Marinho) in Globo Television, which started broadcasting in 1965.[4] It was certainly a broad interpretation of a 'technical assistance contract'. Time-Life set up their administration, techniques for programming and commercial activities. The package also included the training of personnel from Globo in the United States and Time-Life providing assistance in Brazil. Joseph Wallach, a Time-Life representative who could hardly speak Portuguese, was sent as technical 'adviser' – he had been director of Time-Life's TV station in California – and soon became Globo's executive director. The foreign investment was camouflaged by Globo selling the station's building to Time-Life and paying 45 per cent of net revenue as rent and 3 per cent of its gross income for assistance and training. The heavy entry of foreign capital, with sums that had never been seen before in other Brazilian stations, shook the television market and helped Globo become the first major Brazilian media group to have a modern management structure.

A strong reaction from the interests of national capital led to a parliamentary investigation. Despite government pressure, the commission appointed concluded that the Globo/Time-Life assistance agreements were illegal.[5] João Calmon from TV Tupi, giving evidence to the Congress, accused Globo of unfair competition not only because of direct Time-Life finance, but also because of indirect investments through supplying US films in a package that Marinho called 'extraordinary business'.[6] Although the report of the investigation in 1966 recommended that Globo should lose the concession because of foreign participation in its administration, the government delayed the process for more than a year, giving Roberto Marinho enough time to clear Globo's situation. Eventually the contracts with Time-Life were cancelled and Marinho repaid Time-Life with money borrowed from a state bank.

Another criticism faced by the military government in its relations with Globo concerned the obscure circumstances in which Globo updated equipment. Two fires (in 1969 and 1971) provided Globo with perfect opportunities to renew equipment with the best of foreign products. Walter Clark, Globo's top executive from 1965 to 1977, admits that not only Globo but other TV stations imported equipment without paying taxes. By this time Globo was already taking the lead in the television market. With the gradual support of multinational advertising agencies, attracted by the US-style administration and Time-Life's lobbying, a virtual monopoly was in place.

Even Tupi, the main challenger at that time, could compete no longer. The old-style station could not find a way forward in this modernised version of capitalism and so its light faded throughout the 70s. The fate of Excelsior TV exemplifies military intervention in the sector. Connected with the previous Goulart government, Simonsen's group were able to run an innovative kind of national station with Brazilian-style soaps and millionaire musicals while their coffee businesses were successful. However, Excelsior's condemnation of the coup meant hard times for their coffee interests and consequently for the station. After a period of agony, the station had its concession cancelled in 1970 for alleged financial insolvency and delays in service contracts.

A very Brazilian coup: state TV policy
The interest of the military in telecommunications had started even before the coup in 1962. Congress approved a Telecommunications

Code based on military ideas propagated by the Superior War School, which was anti-communist and modelled on the American National War College; it was designed to reinforce public power and protect national interests, to develop and integrate a country with continental dimensions. The Code prepared a National Telecommunications Plan aimed at setting up a reliable network of telephone, telex and television which, combined with the expanding electricity network, would link the whole country. A new telecommunications system was considered vital to ensure the circulation of economic information needed by the market. The electronics industry was encouraged, and the government boosted the television market by enabling the sale of television sets on credit. In this way the government established its political and economic control over the expanding media.

The National Council for Telecommunications, strongly controlled by the government, was set up by the Code. The Council was to be responsible for supervising the concessions (franchises) for TV stations awarded by the government for a fixed but renewable period of fifteen years. The government can cancel these concessions at any time, turning them into *de facto* objects of political bargain.

In order to implement their communications policies, the military regime – which lasted from 1964 to 1985 – created an institutional framework. In 1965 the Brazilian Enterprise for Telecommunications (Embratel) established a modern telecommunications system that would benefit the economic sector as a whole but above all anyone ready to start broadcasting at a national level: in other words, Globo. In 1967, by which time Globo was already well established, the Telecommunications Code was changed in order to make clearer the prohibition on foreign groups participating in the ownership or administration of radio and TV concessions. It also limited to ten the number of TV stations that could be owned by any one company, a rule that the networks would later evade by various means, such as owning stations under relatives' names. Embratel was also responsible for setting up a microwave network to link up even the country's most remote regions through live broadcasting; a huge country with a population in 1991 of almost 150 million people needs a sophisticated network to link remote places like the Amazon with the main centres.

The Brazilian Communications Satellite Programme was implemented by Embratel in the 1970s, a decade that saw some developing countries following more independent paths. By the early 80s, both Brazil and India had modern communications systems with their own satellites, but the decisions to develop them were taken by authoritarian governments. The first programme to be broadcast live to the whole of Brazil was Globo's national news bulletin in September 1969. Its first item announced the take-over of a new junta to replace General Costa e Silva. It was the starting point of the most repressive period of the military dictatorship.

Globo benefited from the military's political campaigning and carried the TV advert with General Medici's slogan: 'Brazil, love it or leave it.' Brazil's victory at the 1970 soccer World Cup in Mexico was broadcast live, and this nationalist boost was used by the military to 'unite' the country.

The inauguration of colour television in Brazil in 1972 was another coup for Globo, consolidating its technical, visual and organisational superiority, and for the electronics industry which had almost exhausted the market for black-and-white TV sets. The number of television sets in the country quadrupled in ten years, from 2.2 million in 1964 to 8.9 million in 1974 (43 per cent of households), benefiting above all the multinationals which dominated the sector. In Brazilian shanty towns electronic goods are still frequently regarded as a higher priority than food. By the end of 1974 Brazil was already putting pressure on other Latin American countries to replace their black-and-white systems, and soon Brazil was exporting television programmes to them.

To keep the ratings lead it had achieved in the late 60s (with programmes predominantly aimed at urban centres and at the poverty belts on their outskirts), Globo pioneered programming policy in Brazil, creating an analysis and research department in 1971. It was a crucial tool for planning advertising slots and adapting programmes to audience tastes following elaborate socio-cultural research. According to Homero Sanchez, head of the department for many years:

> Television needs to know its viewers as human beings. Using this data, at a certain point we began to study programming before broadcasting it. I received the subjects for the *tele-novelas* and analysed whether their contents were suitable for the television viewers. They had to satisfy the expectations of one of the classes the audience would include.[7]

The government's concession policy for TV stations was once again criticised when Tupi, having contracted huge debts with the state, finally collapsed and had its concession cancelled in 1980. Five different groups with media interests competed for the concession. Abril, Brazil's largest magazine publishing company, and Jornal do Brasil, a traditional national newspaper group with radio stations and an old interest in TV concessions, were among the bidders. After a process in which the only consultant was the National Information Service, the 'most reliable' candidates were chosen: the family-owned Manchete, a powerful editorial group which started with an initial investment of US$52 million in state-of-the-art equipment to make programmes aimed at an up-market audience; and Silvio Santos, presenter of a very popular variety programme centred on a 'Happiness Box' scheme which distributed fabulous prizes. Santos had already acquired 50 per cent of TV Record in São Paulo and targeted his station at a working-class audience. Needless to say, Abril and Jornal do Brasil had both occasionally been critical of the regime. Once the Bandeirantes network acquired former Tupi-affiliated stations around the country, Brazilian television began to take its present form: five national TV networks – Globo, SBT (Silvio Santos), Bandeirantes, Educativa (educational and state-run) and Manchete. In March 1992 OM, the first network to broadcast from outside the metropolitan centres of Rio and São Paulo, was inaugurated. Its owner, José Carols Martinez from the state of Paraná, is said to be linked with President Collor, whose government had been spending up to US$1.5 million in monthly advertising with the new network. Another group believed to have connections with the present government is IBF, who bought Manchete TV in June 1992 when the network was in debt to the tune of US$125 million.

Globo's ratings lead has never been seriously challenged, although in the last few years it has faced occasional threats from SBT and Manchete in some regions and at particular times of the day. The end of the military regime in 1985 meant that Globo's privileges were scaled down, and the existence of a national satellite communications network allowed developing networks to extend their coverage. Nevertheless, Globo has developed a competent and powerful empire which is unlikely to crack under isolated pressures. Its average share of the audience is still around 45 per cent, while Manchete achieves 10 per cent, Silvio Santos 9 per cent and Bandeirantes 3 per cent. Furthermore, it has already shown its ability to relate well to different governments.

Antonio Carlos Magalhaes, the Minister of Communications in the first civilian government after the military period (he had also been active in the previous regime), was an old friend of Marinho. One of his first acts as Minister was to suspend all state payments to NEC Brazil, cutting the cash flow to this subsidiary of NEC Japan. NEC is one of the Brazilian government's major suppliers of telephone and telecommunications equipment and its majority shareholder was Mario Garnero, accused by the Japanese of enriching himself with company money. In 1986, Roberto Marinho acquired Garnero's shares and the government's payments started to flow again. A parliamentary investigation concluded that the transfer was illegal. The Ministry of Communications was accused of having forced a private company to transfer its shares to a government ally at a price below market value. Marinho was later accused of 'returning the favour' in 1987 when he terminated the affiliation which TV Aratu, in the state of Bahia, had with the Globo network for eighteen years. TV Bahia, linked to Magalhaes, was Globo's new affiliate. In 1990 Magalhaes was elected governor of Bahia.

Globo's power is visible in other continents, not only through the global success of its soap operas but also through other attempts at international expansion. Having created an international division in 1980, Globo set up Globo Europa to try to penetrate the European market before ownership restrictions were introduced. The acquisition in 1985 of Tele Monte Carlo from Italy was the biggest step. However

Roberto Marinho, photo by Antonio Ribeiro, © Abril Imagens

Marinho was not wholly successful in this European enterprise and sold 40 per cent of Tele Monte Carlo shares to the Italian group Ferruzi. Another step taken was a move towards acquisitions or alliances with television stations or satellite broadcasters around Europe. More recently, Globo has launched co-production initiatives with the Cuban Radio and Television Institute and with RAI in Italy.

Entertainment programming

Chacrinha throws vegetables and salt cod at the audience before he interrupts Brazil's leading singer in the middle of a song. Semi-naked go-go girls dance on separate stages. Amateur artists are ridiculed but keen on returning to the programme. Chacrinha, the enormously popular, charismatic and anarchic presenter who died in 1988, was considered the most important mass communications phenomenon in Brazilian television.

Xuxa is another presenter, a blonde ex-model dressed in sensual clothes. She is also a top-selling singer, a film star and one of the world's forty highest paid entertainers. For five hours on five mornings a week her young clones (in even more sensual clothes) dance while she announces the next cartoon, which will probably get 50 per cent of the total adult and 80 per cent of the total child population watching. Xuxa is known as the 'Queen of the little ones'. Xuxa will show in front of the cameras an example of a healthy breakfast, which less than a third of her audience can afford.

It is Sunday and Silvio Santos advertises the 'Happiness Box' scheme, which attracts people to pay for vouchers that can later – if the payments are regular – allow them to acquire goods from 'happiness box' shops. In the next segment the audience can also dream, dream that they could come one day on to the programme and enter the 'gate of hope' to have their wishes come true – the more sensational they are, the higher the ratings. Santos has been presenting this programme for years, but now he does it on his own TV network.

The audience knows the television schedule by heart. From Monday to Friday it follows the same basic order of programme categories, changing only at the weekend, when live variety shows are predominant. *Fantastico, the Show of Life*, with news and entertainment, is Globo's attraction for Sunday evenings. The programme's coverage of medical treatments most of the population cannot afford gives its title a special irony. Brazilian television is fundamentally an entertainment vehicle. One in every ten hours is dedicated to current affairs or news programmes, one to educational programmes and eight to entertainment. Films take up 22 per cent, the largest share of broadcasting time, *tele-novelas* 12 per cent and sports 5 per cent. The information share is as small as 12 per cent and education only 4 per cent. Although Globo produces nearly 80 per cent of the programmes it broadcasts, the figures are lower for other stations and as a whole the country still imports 39 per cent of programmes broadcast. Regional (4 per cent) and local (13 per cent) productions are rare.

The commercial base and the lack of regulation in TV lead to an anarchic struggle for audiences. In the heat of the fight, TV stations increase their doses of sex and violence to keep up their ratings at the expense of information or art. Recently, TV Manchete posed the first real ratings threat to Globo with *Pantanal*, a *tele-novela* which combined eroticism and an ecological portrait of the stunning landscape of western Brazil. When Manchete achieved the top ratings, the other stations, including Globo, by-passed the eroticism and started broadcasting straightforward porn programmes.

Telejournalism
In 1971 General Medici, the third military president, said:

> I feel happy when every evening I turn on the television to watch the news. While there is news of strikes, agitations, crimes and conflicts all over the world, Brazil is peacefully marching towards development. It is as if I had taken a tranquilliser, after a day's work.

Two years previously 100,000 people had been in the streets protesting against the regime. The government, having declared an open war against left-wing guerrilla groups fighting the military's 'revolution', took total dictatorial control. Parliament was shut and pre-censorship of the media was established.

During the military period there were hijacks, kidnaps, institutionalised torture, robberies, and anti-communist death squads bombing newspapers, theatres and universities. But the war between left and right was totally ignored by television. This was the result of both institutional and self-censorship, as Walter Clark admitted:

> We would have been awarded medals for any act of courage but it would have cost the existence of the network. We hired a professional censor to anticipate possible clashes with the regime. We

would prefer to decide what we were broadcasting rather than hearing it from the military's censors.[8]

Globo was heavily censored, as were the other stations. But to say that self-censorship was due solely to pressure from the regime is to forget that the company openly supported the government. It is more of an excuse now in more democratic times. The military have gone but their anti-democratic heritage remains. Television coverage for peaktime news bulletins, especially those involving delicate political issues, still conforms to the interests of TV owners and to their relations with the government. The larger the audience, the heavier the pressures. Globo was the slowest network to follow the course of political openness when contradictions within society began to be more openly debated, at least in the streets. Armando Nogueira, head of Globo's journalism during the military years, complains that 'the job of informing people is more difficult when television stations are afraid of losing their concessions. It is even worse when we return to democracy and people know the official censorship has finished, but we are still not corresponding to expectations.'[9]

The situation is in fact far more complicated than it appears. Globo pays the best salaries and employs some of the best journalists, who are often sharp critics of the government. Beth Costa, president of the Rio de Janeiro journalists' trade union, works for Globo and tells the local joke: 'People say the high payment here is not salary any more. It is a bribe to cope with this journalism.'[10] Costa explains that Globo's journalism is built on half-truths, softening the impact of bad news and not showing the real Brazil. 'The orders come from above.' From personal experience I know it is not an easy task to keep your integrity as a journalist in one of the main Brazilian television networks. Having worked for two of them – Manchete and Bandeirantes – I know that in one way or another you are always serving the interests of sponsors or TV station owners. I experienced several occasions when the audience had to live without information which might have damaged the sponsors' businesses. And whether it is sponsorship by the state or by a private company makes little difference. There is no formal rule. You simply know that some issues are not to be spoken of in particular ways on that network. Some topics are taboo on all networks, agrarian reform for instance: rural workers are simply ignored most of the time because media barons own significant pieces of land. More than once I received instructions from above to be careful with the questions I was going to ask Antonio Carlos Magalhaes, the former Communications Minister. I was told that he simply asks the network to fire 'inconvenient' reporters. For my colleagues from Globo the situation was worse: they would be fired on the network's own initiative.

Some networks follow the prejudices of their owners. At Manchete, after making numerous vox-pops with a wide range of people, I was told, 'You shouldn't bother about interviewing black people. Mr Bloch doesn't like it.' I kept wasting tapes. Still, at Manchete I experienced an unusual situation. An increasing awareness of Globo's bias against trade unions meant that at one point strikers would not allow their crews to cover the rallies but other networks, like Manchete, were welcomed. Manchete did not exactly support the strikes, but it took a slightly less biased approach.

The censorship practised by the Brazilian media in the last few years leaves the country with some gaps in its contemporary history and, sadly, the words of TV journalists are taken as gospel. By 1983 Globo's national TV news bulletin had the largest audience in Brazil, and today, in a country where more than a quarter of the adult population is illiterate, 80 per cent of the population watch the slick *Jornal Nacional* every evening for thirty minutes. The following cases show how Globo has ignored some of the democratic changes which have taken place in Brazil.

— In 1975 the left-wing journalist Vladimir Herzog, head of news at São Paulo Educational TV station, was killed after hours of interrogation and torture in the offices of the military police. The news of his death was reported by the press in the first major act of resistance against censorship. Globo only mentioned the fact later, reading an official communiqué which tried to prove that Herzog had committed suicide.

— The late 70s saw the first post-coup strikes, organised by metal workers from a new trade union movement in São Paulo. Thousands of workers gathered for rallies and their leaders were arrested under national security legislation. Globo showed they were only prepared to cover the strikes on their terms – no sound tracks for shots of rallies, and no interviews with strike leaders, only with the bosses.

— The social democratic Leonel Brizola returned from exile to run for governor of the state of Rio de Janeiro in 1982. Popular in Rio since before the coup, Brizola had always been feared by the military, who had their own candidate, 'coincidentally' supported by Globo. Even before the elections the network was predicting Brizola's defeat. While the official results were not announced – they were slow in coming and constantly postponed – Globo television was releasing partial results and their own projections which showed Brizola would be defeated. The official explanation is that the computers were first registering the votes from less urban areas with more conservative tendencies. Brizola's version is that Globo was preparing public opinion for a major fraud that would take victory away from its most famous enemy. Brizola was elected and is still boycotted by Globo.

— In 1984, Globo ignored for months a broad-based political movement which drew thousands of people to the streets demanding that the president once again be elected by direct popular vote. The first time Globo gave this any notice was when 500,000 people demonstrated in São Paulo. Even so, the event was minimised and muddled with a celebration of São Paulo's anniversary. When a million people took to the streets of Rio, Globo finally broadcast the demonstration live (winning the highest ratings) and for the first time tried to distance itself from the unpopular government.

— The most recent example of Globo's partial journalism came with the elections in November and December 1989. After a month-long campaign – with party political broadcast times proportionately distributed according to parties' representations in Congress – two candidates went forward to the second round. Surprisingly, one of them was Lula (Workers Party), the main trade union leader of the late 1970s strikes. Collor, a conservative state governor with a moralistic anti-corruption campaign, was Lula's opponent. Despite the free broadcasting time, Lula was disadvantaged by the media's boycott of the ordinary election coverage. Collor's family just happens to own the Globo affiliate in the north-eastern state he was governing.

In the second round there were two nationally televised debates. In the eyes of the public, Lula had won the first and he seemed likely to eliminate Collor's lead in the opinion polls. For the second debate, Collor improved his performance and before people had the chance to express their opinion at the ballot box, Globo prepared a special summary of the debate for the main news bulletin. The summary was watched by more people than the unedited version had been and was broadcast two days before the election with no free broadcast time left to allow an answer. Collor was given more time than Lula in the summary and the editing enhanced his good performance since his best moments were intercut with the poorest parts of Lula's performance. Earlier that day a different and fairer version of the summary had been broadcast. Vianey Pinheiro supervised the editing of the first version and protested against the changes made for the later summary, which he called an 'advertising piece'. He was fired. Collor was elected and now has people he trusts commanding Globo's journalism. Ironically, at the time of writing (1992) he is in danger of being impeached for corruption, the 'evil' which he campaigned so vigorously against in the election. [He has since resigned.]

Tele-novelas

Soap operas, or *tele-novelas*, are the most valuable product Globo has to offer advertisers, and careful planning partly explains their success. The network won the absolute lead in the ratings when it started planning the schedules and which advertisements should accompany each programme. Through its competent administration of advertising income, Globo was able to invest in drama and attract leading professionals not only from television but also from theatre and cinema, which simply cannot pay as well.

The first *novelas* were melodramas in traditional Latin American style, but it was not long before they were refined to modern television genre patterns. From 1964 to 1989 Globo produced 155 *novelas*, comprising more than 22,000 episodes. Three different *novelas* are shown in primetime six days a week for an average of six months when, unlike American soaps, they reach a conclusion. The main news bulletin at eight o'clock is sandwiched by two sixty-minute *novelas*. One guarantees the audience for the other. Episodes are written just a few days before being broadcast, which gives the writers the chance to play with current issues, very often weaving political analogies within what is sometimes a loose adaptation of a classic novel. Audience researchers advise on the plot and the development of characters to maximise ratings.

Some television experts credit the success of *novelas* to this openness. The former communist Dias Gomes, one of the main *tele-novela* writers (whose work has occasionally had the astonishing audience share of 100 per cent), believes the genre has developed in a particular way in Brazil.[11] In 1975 his *Rogue Santeiro* (a sharp and critical analogy of Brazilian society) was censored after Globo had invested US$500,000 in the first twenty episodes. It was finally broadcast ten years later. Gomes still thinks the *novelas* were the only form of popular art to develop during the dictatorship, and that they did not suffer as much as theatre or cinema. Nevertheless, *novelas* have been criticised for their folkloric poverty, for the easy solutions they offer to complex problems, and for their capacity to depoliticise information in a country where the education system is weak and illiteracy rife.[12]

Novelas have become more complex over the last two decades, and the latest examples have tended to include a wide range of characters who are not representative of the reality of Brazil since they are still predominantly urban and middle-class. Aesthetic standards, accents and cultural trends come from Rio, more precisely from the southern part of Rio, inhabited by the middle class. In regional *novelas*, artists from the main urban centres struggle to imitate regional accents. Rio's middle-class way of life was first exported to the rest of the country, including remote villages in the Amazon, thanks to satellite and to the standardisation of programming that has slowly inhibited regional cultures. Globo then became interested in foreign markets, and in 1973 *O bem amado*, the first colour soap – based on a regional romance written by Jorge Amado – was its first programme to be sold profitably abroad. Globo's income from international sales rose from under US$300,000 in 1977 to US$14 million in 1985. This success took Rio's accent to Portugal, where it has begun to affect the former coloniser's speech patterns: a sweet historical revenge.

Advertising

Television reaches approximately a hundred million Brazilians, and it is estimated that Brazilian families keep their TV sets switched on for an average of five and a half hours a day. Housewives in Rio and São Paulo spend between 20 and 26 per cent of their time watching television – which is consequently a golden goose for advertisers.[13] Anyone selling Brazilian television to advertisers could claim that in every hour of television there are fifteen minutes of free advertising plus opportunities for product placements in any programme.

Leading advertising agencies have been established in Brazil since the late 1920s, when companies such as Lintas, Standard Propaganda, McCann Erickson and J. Walter Thompson started working with radio stations without any state regulation. This multinational presence also meant the North-Americanisation of advertisements in both style and content. The industrialisation of the 1960s and 70s brought to Brazil the consumption fever of the older industrialised countries. Globo, already looking for slicker advertisements that would bring programmes and commercial breaks under the same aesthetic (and the same consumption ideology), was the ideal vehicle to boost the new economic policy. The government's policies, on the other hand, actually prevent most of the population from being able to buy the products displayed in its electronic shop window, and so TV sells not so much the product as the desire for it. Washington Olivetto, an award-winning copywriter, questions this paradox: 'It's difficult to find the link between our adverts and our country. Advertising in Brazil gives the impression that we have a rich and happy population.'[14]

Television now accounts for nearly 55 per cent of Brazil's advertising spend (in the US it is 22 per cent). Brazil is the seventh largest advertising market in the world, and Globo takes by far the largest share of the money spent on TV advertising in Brazil (70 per cent in 1990), almost two billion dollars. The state does not have a direct financial influence over the networks (except for the weak state-run network), but as a massive advertiser it has unhealthy ways of interfering. Government campaigns are more like political propaganda than public education. In 1990, the federal government, together with ministries and public companies, was the fourth largest advertiser in Brazil.

Its large share of ratings and its potential to reach virtually every TV set in the country make Globo the favourite advertising vehicle for major companies, both national and multinational. Globo's share of the advertising market is even superior to its share of the ratings. The consequence is a trend towards concentration, not only in terms of television market hegemony – smaller TV stations are strangled by the lack of finance and unable to produce programmes with the same technical standards as Globo – but also in more general market terms. Smaller companies cannot afford to advertise through Globo, while more powerful companies have 'economy of scale' agreements with the network, proportionally reducing their advertising costs for a larger area of coverage.

Advertisers have been able to diversify their techniques in order to maximise their television time. Besides sponsorship and the growing variety (in length and format) of television advertisements, product placement has become increasingly intrusive since advertisers became aware that ratings fall during commercial breaks. *Novelas* are their main vehicle, and sometimes a whole scene can be fashioned to open the way for a placement. Advertising agencies arrange separate contracts with the networks and with the artists, some of whom have refused to be used without getting a share of the profits.

Alternatives
Over the last few years, TV Globo has been faced with competition in parts of the television schedules. This threat comes mainly from stations

that are simply Globo clones, offering less glossy versions of the same. Neither market expansion nor the recent opening up of UHF broadcasting have led to significant changes; and since once again the groups in control of the new media are the same as those controlling the main networks, the so-called segmentation of the market (with channels broadcasting only sport, journalism, music or movies) is unlikely to democratise Brazilian television.

Within the main channels in Brazil the one exception in terms of programming comes from TV Cultura. Run by an independent foundation but financed by the state of São Paulo, it carries an emphasis on high-quality educational and cultural programmes but does not have a competitive share of the audience – it hardly ever has more than 1 per cent of the ratings. In Rio, the channel funded by the government has improved journalistic standards over the last few years, after a long period of subordination to politicians. However, low ratings are again the main obstacle to success.

Alternative groups have been trying to penetrate the mainstream market since the early 1980s, when video technology became accessible to a wide range of social groups and organisations. With rare exceptions television networks closed their doors to independent producers, arguing that they did not meet broadcasting standards.

Election times offer political parties rare chances to penetrate the defences of commercial television. In campaigns that last months, with political parties sharing airtime proportional to their representation in Congress, more radical political groups have their opportunity to air their points of view. They can criticise not only the government but also the media monopolies. The social democrat leader Leonel Brizola frequently uses his airtime to attack Globo's monopoly, and the campaign broadcasts by the Workers' Party in the last presidential election were a major boost for Lula's campaign. The 'People's Network', as it is called, produced parodies of politicians, denunciations and serious proposals. It parodied Globo's style at the same technical standard (many of Globo's employees also worked on a voluntary basis for Lula's campaign).

Young film and video-makers, individuals and alternative organisations have been responsible for a huge amount of material not usually seen on the Brazilian small screen. The areas covered have been varied: educational, ecological, scientific, training, domestic, social, touristic. Video has also become popular among artists and video-art groups have spread. Political organisations such as trade unions, women's groups, tenants' associations and ethnic minorities have benefited from the new medium, even though distribution has always been a major problem. Local and First World non-governmental organisations contribute funding to productions of this kind.

This grass roots video movement created an alternative to traditional ways of covering current affairs and brought to some screens faces hardly seen before. TV Viva in Recife is an outstanding example of alternative production in Brazil, having for many years produced a wide variety of videos screened in different town squares in the centre or the outskirts of this northeastern area. In simple, sharp language they rediscover the 'grass roots'. All they need to attract enthusiastic audiences is their van with a large screen and a few actors who also perform in their videos. The live performance and interviews with the audience will later be part of the follow-up work, in a continuous process of debate. Their style and language have gradually been incorporated by other groups and even mainstream programmes like *Casseta e Planeta* from Globo. In Santarem, in Amazonia, the 'Circo Saude-Alegria' have used a video-boat to circulate educational video-letters about health issues, at the same time recording the visits. TV Maxambomba from Centro de Criação de Imagem Popular (CECIP) in Nova Iguacú (Rio de Janeiro) works with what is now known as 'video-process' in a similar way. In the north, the Projeto Video Nas Aldeias (video in the tribes project) is co-ordinated by the Centro de Trabalho Indigenista, who work with Indian tribes, advising on politics, law and economics in the hope that Indians will find their own images and eventually recover their cultural identity through video production. The technology is handed over to the tribes, who now record traditional events and ceremonies, music, dance, legends and celebrations, and their contact with urban white society.

Other political movements have developed through the use of video. In Recife, the women's group Sos Corpo produces programmes for TV Viva on issues like birth control, sexuality and abortion. In São Paulo the Coletivo Feminista Sexualidade e Saude produces feminist videos. The black movements of Rio, Salvador and São Luis use videos in their campaigns, as does the movement of street kids in Fortaleza. In the industrialised state of São Paulo, powerful trade unions acquired professional TV equipment which enabled them to portray their movement – strikes, rallies, conferences – from a different perspective. Apart from the usual alternative circuit (taking the videos to the factories), TV Dos Trabalhadores (Workers' TV) can produce cheaper material for alternative organisations or parties which cannot afford airtime on the main TV stations – their work was crucial for the Workers' Party campaign in the last presidential elections. Some unions now advertise rallies on TV. Other examples of trade union videos are TV Sinitel in Rio Grande do Sul, Minas and Rio, and TV Do Trio in Campinas.

As a result of this video boom, several associations were set up in Latin America to co-ordinate the exchange of material and experience between grass roots producers around the continent. In Brazil in 1987, the ABVP (an association for grass roots videos) pioneered the difficult task of cataloguing and distributing the work of thousands of organisations. They also run courses and encourage production. But how will they ever extend beyond the alternative circuit?

Brazil's 1989 constitution consolidated the privilege of the few and powerful media groups which had a strong lobby in the Constituent Assembly. Revision of the broadcasting franchises was made extremely difficult. However, on franchise matters power has now been transferred from the executive to the Congress, and there are opportunities for legislation to make significant changes. Different segments of Brazilian society, as well as alternative video-makers and television professionals, have sought to affect changes in the broadcasting scenario. Access to video production facilities with restricted distribution is no longer enough. There is a broad demand for the democratisation of all communications in Brazil. Lasting reform of the Brazilian media will necessarily mean a profound revision of state policies on the concession of television franchises and on programming regulations. If media ownership and programme content remain subject to market forces, many social groups will stay marginalised and misrepresented.

Today, the concentration of capital and technology around television is accepted as inevitable. The challenge is to create democratic mechanisms to provide the necessary social control over the media. Only a wide range of properly represented social groups can guarantee real power of choice for the audience, and allow room for diversity and conflict. The creation of a Social Communication Council to represent these groups and advise the Congress on franchise matters is therefore at the top of their agenda. Most groups favour maintaining the commercial system, but in order to avoid monopolies and oligopolies they would like to see statutory limitations on the production capacity of TV networks, and the encouragement of competition based on quality rather than economic or political power. Decisions would also have to be made as to which frequencies would be allowed to carry advertisements, which would be guaranteed for non-state public service stations and which non-commercial stations could be controlled by communities, cultural and ethnic groups, trade unions, educational groups or political parties. A tax would have to be introduced whereby commercial TV stations would finance the non-commercial ones. A guaranteed minimum of broadcast hours would have to be agreed for local and regional programmes, and independent productions encouraged.

These objectives may take a long time to achieve and may not arrive in the expected form, given the power of the organisations involved. However, encouraging steps have been taken towards a more democratic environment in Brazilian communications. If changes cannot come from within the broadcasting organisations, they will certainly occur through the steady growth of alternative production.

In 1986, I worked on a documentary series called *Movimento*, which portrayed grass roots communities around Brazil. They had their problems, but they also showed the audience their creative solutions, based on hard work and organisation. The series was optimistic and stimulating, even though it dealt with some of the poorest areas of the country. After a few months, the sponsors (in this case the federal government) withdrew funding for the series. Perhaps those smiling faces were too disturbing for them, or didn't suit their political propaganda. But I still dream about the day we will fill our small screens with those subversive smiles.

NOTES

1. G. Richeri and C. Lasagni, 'Precocious Broadcasting', *Intermedia*, vol. 15 no. 3, 1987, p. 23.
2. S. Caparelli, *Televisão e Capitalismo no Brasil* (Porto Alegre: L&PM, 1982), p. 21.
3. S. Mattos, *Um Perfil da TV Brasileira: 40 Anos de Historia 1950–1990* (Bahia: A Tarde, 1990), p. 4.
4. D. Herz, *A Historia Secreta da Rede Globo* (Porto Alegre: Tche Editora, 1987), p. 193.
5. C. Lacerda, *CPI Time-Life* (Brasilia: Diario de Congreso Nacional, 1967), p. 72.
6. E. Adler, *The Power of Ideology: Technical Autonomy in Argentina and Brazil* (1987), p. 37.
7. H. Sanchez, *Revista Playboy* (São Paulo: Editora Abril Cultural, 1985).
8. W. Clark, *O Campeao de Audiencia* (São Paulo: editora nova cultural, 1991), p. 253.
9. A. Nogueira, from an interview for the programme *Beyond Citizen Kane* (Large Door Productions for Channel Four, 1991).
10. B. Costa, interview for *Beyond Citizen Kane*.
11. D. Gomes, interview for *Beyond Citizen Kane*.

12. M. R. Kehl, interview for *Beyond Citizen Kane*.
13. *Rede Imaginaria: Televisão e Democraçia* (São Paolo: Editora Schwarcz, 1991), p. 257.
14. W. Olivetto, interview for *Beyond Citizen Kane*.
15. Bill Hinchberger, 'Brazil's Media Monopoly', *Multinational Monitor* (Washington: Essential Information, 1991), pp. 13–16.

THE PEOPLE SHALL BROADCAST
The Struggle for a Post-apartheid
National Television Culture in South Africa

Willie Currie and Michael Markovitz

Introduction

South Africa's political landscape is changing. We write as members of The Film and Allied Workers Organisation (FAWO), which was formed in August 1988 as an organisation of oppositional film and video producers who felt the need to challenge the dominance of apartheid in the film and broadcasting sector. As part of the broad anti-apartheid forces inside the country, FAWO has focused on the question of how to rid the film and broadcasting environment of the effects of apartheid and of how to promote a progressive film and television culture as part of a non-racial democratic society in South Africa.

The focus of national attention is now (in the summer of 1992) on the Convention for a Democratic South Africa (CODESA), where nineteen political parties are trying to negotiate South Africa's future. The struggle is over the shape of a constitution for the new South Africa, heralded in February 1990 when President F. W. de Klerk released Nelson Mandela and unbanned the liberation movements. De Klerk wants a constitution that will protect 'minority' interests and block any radical changes that may threaten the privileges accumulated by the white minority during the apartheid era. Mandela wants a constitution that will allow for majority rule in a unitary state that will enable the new government to redress the effects of apartheid on the black majority. In De Klerk's scenario, economic power would remain in the hands of the private sector and the state's role would be minimised. In Mandela's scenario, the state would intervene to ensure a redistribution of economic power within a mixed economy. This has precipitated a precarious battle for position which is impacting on all sectors of South

Africa, including the systems of communication, of which television is a part.

The main protagonists in this battle are the following:

The National Party (NP) is the party of apartheid which came into power in 1948 as a coalition of Afrikaner interests. Its main platform was the policy and practice of the institutionalised racism known as apartheid. Over the years it changed its focus to the constituency of whites as a whole and under President F. W. de Klerk is now attempting to broaden its constituency to attract conservative coloureds, Indians and Africans.

The African National Congress (ANC) is the leading national liberation movement in South Africa with a history going back to 1912. Its platform is the formation of a non-racial democracy in one South Africa, and its central policy document is the Freedom Charter adopted in 1955, which declares that South Africa belongs to all who live in it, black and white.

The Inkatha Freedom Party (IFP) was formed out of the Inkatha cultural movement which Chief Mangosutho Buthelezi set up as the political power base for Zulu ethnic nationalism in the 1970s. When the ANC was unbanned in 1990, Inkatha became a political party and attempted to broaden its base to include other South Africans, but it remains essentially Zulu in character.

The United Democratic Front (UDF) was a front of anti-apartheid grass roots organisations formed in 1983 to challenge President P. W. Botha's unilateral attempts to restructure the South African constitution to include coloureds and Indians but to exclude Africans. These constitutional changes introduced the tricameral Parliament which South Africa still has and which the current negotiations are designed to replace. With the return of the ANC from exile, the UDF decided to disband.

The Congress of South Africa Trade Unions (COSATU) is the major trade union federation in South Africa. Formed in 1985, COSATU, together with the UDF, played a leading role in the internal resistance to apartheid.

Television in South Africa
Since its inception in 1976, television has been monopolised by the National Party government to promote its policies of apartheid. Initially only the South African Broadcasting Corporation (SABC) was licensed to broadcast television. This monopoly was challenged in 1983 by BOP

TV, which tried to broadcast from the homeland of Bophuthatswana into South Africa. SABC tricked BOP TV into using its signal distribution network and then put shields on the transmitter to limit BOP TV's transmission to Soweto. In 1986 M-Net was established as an encoded pay-TV service owned by a consortium made up of the big four newspaper groups. SABC has two TV channels (TV1 and Contemporary Community Values TV, previously TV2/3/4), which reach an audience of 8 million viewers. M-Net has 600,000 subscribers with an audience of 1.5 million viewers, while BOP TV has an audience of 120,000 viewers.

SABC TV embodies the principles of apartheid in its structures of control and management, and its programmes were, and mainly still are, imbued with the apartheid imagination. The State President appoints the SABC Board, which over the years has included important members of the Afrikaner Broederbond hierarchy. The SABC management has been dominated by Afrikaner appointments, vetted by the security establishment, particularly in the News departments. The apartheid division of South Africa was entrenched in the structures of the TV channels themselves. TV1 addressed whites in English and Afrikaans. TV2 addressed blacks in Zulu. TV3 addressed blacks in Sotho.

Racial separation was the order of the day on most SABC TV programmes until the late 1980s. Blacks in TV1 drama series played subordinate servant roles, while there were few whites in black drama series on TV2/3. Racial integration on commercials was forbidden until the mid-80s. TV 2/3 dramas reinforced the apartheid notion that blacks belonged in their rural homelands with narratives that showed black people coming to the city and, after realising that urban society was corrupt, returning to their homelands. A white person watching TV1 would imagine that he or she lived in an almost white world, while a black person watching TV2/3 would feel that he or she lived in a primarily black world, a citizen of one of the homelands. SABC TV defined a South African as a white South African. Blacks were Vendas, Transkeians, Bophuthatswanans, Ciskeians, Zulus, Ndebeles and Tsongas, but not South Africans. TV2, TV3 and TV4 were combined in January 1992 to form Contemporary Community Values TV (CCV TV). This channel has cut down on African-language programmes and is attempting to be a crossover station for blacks and whites, driven mainly by American series.

In the 80s, as the cultural boycott took effect, more American TV programmes started appearing on SABC TV. This predominance of US soaps, mini-series, comedies, crime series and films reached incredibly high proportions during the State of Emergency. The reasons for this are partly economic, relating to the cheaper cost of buying imported programming (R300 per minute as opposed to at least R3,000 per minute costs for home-produced material). But the ideological effect during the Emergency was to offer a stressed and battered society a channel for relief and relaxation that could shield people from the nasty repressive reality in the townships and countryside.

The promotion of market forces was the other pre-eminent TV discourse in the 80s, coinciding with the sense of the ruling Afrikaner Nationalist Party having arrived as middle-class entrepreneurs, professionals, financiers and businessmen. This middle-class ruling bloc then followed the international trends towards the privatisation of state enterprises, the deregulation of the economy and the promotion of a free market. In television the free market trend is represented best by M-Net, which limits its programming almost entirely to films and sport and shows very little of South African origin. Even education programmes on TV 2/3 extolled the virtues of free market capitalism and despised all socialist systems.

The notion that African governments had failed was another powerful ideological discourse on both white and black channels. For whites, this reinforced the notion of white South Africa as the last bulwark of Western civilisation on a continent ravaged by the political and economic mismanagement of black African governments that were reducing Africa to barbarism. At its peak this discourse was represented on TV News by the image of the 'African' Aids virus ravaging the continent. For black audiences, it suggested that blacks in South Africa did not have it as bad as their brothers and sisters elsewhere in Africa, and warned that the consequence of liberation in South Africa would be violence, chaos, collapse and starvation, as had happened in the rest of Africa. A documentary series, *Africa in Focus* by Al J. Venter, carried out most of this ideological work in the 80s, ably helped by TV News and by drama series like *Shaka Zulu*.

Strategies of resistance in the 70s and 80s
The introduction of television in South Africa coincided with the Soweto uprising in 1976, which also made South Africa a focal point for international news and foreign news crews. The Nationalist government had delayed the introduction of television because of its fears that it would allow a high degree of foreign information and foreign culture

into the country, which would destabilise the core values of apartheid. Ironically, during the uprising the South African government still had not grasped how powerfully television would reveal its coercive force: the police were delighted to perform in front of the cameras, beating up demonstrators and showing off their power.

The SABC was nevertheless aware of how to structure the news in favour of apartheid. In the late 70s and early 80s, the developing mass organisations began to see how the SABC was manipulating the news and to develop counter-strategies. Trade unions were the first to realise the power of television and in 1979 COSATU commissioned a film on the launching congress of the federation. In the 80s, with the implementation of the tricameral parliament and the resistance of the mass-based UDF, the government began to appreciate the power of the medium and started controlling TV coverage in the country. However, the restrictions were unevenly applied: at times police would confiscate film and harass TV crews, at other times they would give TV crews free rein to cover what they wanted. In the political struggle against the implementation of the tricameral parliament, the UDF and other mass-based organisations boycotted the SABC because they had no confidence in its reporting news events fairly and impartially.

The first major steps to restrict TV coverage were introduced after the uprising in Sebokeng in 1984 and mass organisations in this period started to use video to express their own views and to communicate with their constituencies. Afrascope was set up to service mass organisations, but it was not long before the government confiscated its equipment and forced its members to skip the country. From 1985, COSATU was using video widely to communicate with its members. By then, images of resistance to apartheid were in the top three news stories on international television virtually every day. The 1985 State of Emergency led to the first systematic clampdown on the media in an attempt to restrict international coverage. But it was only the declaration of the State of Emergency in June 1986 that led to images of South Africa being wiped off international TV screens in a total clampdown on all mass-based organisations and the imposition of emergency media regulations which prohibited TV crews from covering 'unrest'.

It was in response to this that small video production units like Video News Services (VNS) and Dynamic Images (DI) came into action. Before the emergency period, VNS had already been in discussion with the ANC, who were worried about the effect that the media restrictions would have on the coverage of the apartheid issue internationally and were prepared to support counter-strategies which would enable images to continue to flow out of South Africa. During the period of restrictions small video units, along with foreign TV crews, continued to distribute material internationally against great odds and draconian prohibitions: a video culture started to emerge. Video recorders were now more accessible in homes, organisations and townships. A number of small video production units like VNS, DI and others grew up in centres around the country, and video as a tool for information and communication became widespread. The work raised the issue of government-controlled state media versus people's media: the video units tried to show images of people's lives in struggle, as opposed to the pictures of tribal conflict and nascent black middle-class life presented by the SABC. VNS, for example, produced 'video pamphlets'. These were 15-minute pieces which dealt with events like the 1987 railway strike and the miners' strike from a workers' perspective.

In order to survive, these small production units hid in the shadow of the foreign media networks. They were also protected to a certain extent by COSATU, which managed to maintain its structures publicly through most of the Emergency, unlike the UDF which was driven underground. Local video crews faced a high level of harassment. There was a constant danger of being picked up, detained and beaten up. Video material was often confiscated and there were many alarms, which led units like VNS to move their entire video libraries out of their offices at short notice. VNS circulated their videos through COSATU networks to reach audiences ranging from 500,000 to a million people. Workers would watch the videos at home, in factories, all over the place. Besides the union networks, videos also circulated in youth, student, church, civic and political organisations. These distribution networks operated informally. VNS would make copies of videos which would then be copied by people in organisations and circulated. There was no consideration of copyright.

Local production of videos was also supplemented by tapes sent into the country by individuals or groups like the International Defence and Aid Fund. Virtually every TV documentary aired on British or US television found its way into these networks, and those which carried the images and voices of the ANC and the liberation movements were highly valued despite the risk of detention that possession of these videotapes carried. It was an informal network which achieved wide distribution. Abroad, South African exiles also produced anti-apartheid videos, which were circulated to TV stations internationally, were used by anti-apartheid solidarity movements and found their way into video distribution inside South Africa.

State restructuring strategies in the 90s
The period of transition from authoritarian rule which began in 1990 has produced a slight liberalisation in the SABC. The people of South Africa have been able to see demonised leaders of previously banned organisations on their TV screens. We have even seen former 'terrorist' Carl Niehaus being asked what it feels like to be speaking on the same SABC which, a few years ago, he was allegedly planning to blow up. However, the news personnel are still roughly the same as those who vilified the liberation movements, and the structures of control relating to news and current affairs broadcasting remain in the hands of white Afrikaans-speaking men.

Even so, SABC News in the 90s is not as crude as it was in the 80s. There is some live debate and there are attempts at balancing viewpoints across the political spectrum. When it counts, however, the SABC News team comes out on the 'right' side, for example in the coverage of the signing of the Peace Accord in September 1991. The Peace Accord was a multilateral event involving a wide range of organisations, including the National Party, the ANC, Inkatha and COSATU, all committing themselves to peace. However, the SABC gave only one political leader the opportunity to express his views on the current affairs programme *Agenda* – F. W. de Klerk. This enabled De Klerk to be represented as the Peacemaker, and minimised the contribution of the other organisations to the Peace Accord. Early in 1991, *Agenda* claimed a victory in getting spokespeople from the liberation movements and Inkatha on the same show, to discuss violence. But the fact that they did not also invite police or government representatives on to the show reinforced the racist discourse of blacks being unstable tribalists incapable of governing a country by themselves and the ANC, despite its claims to be the major liberation movement, being unable to control its own people.

SABC TV News bias raises questions about the continued representation of people and events in South Africa in terms of an apartheid logic that simply has to puff up the white president as the single-handed initiator of the transition to democracy. The apartheid state is unwilling to relinquish control of its premier propaganda machine unless it is forced to, and it is clear that a key strategy of the National Party government is to keep the SABC under its wing as long as possible while it transforms it from within. To effect this transformation, the government has set in motion a restructuring of the SABC and the broadcast sector which aims to prevent any future government having such a centralised national propaganda machine at its disposal. To do this, the government plans to break up the monopoly structure of the SABC through a programme of commercialisation and creeping privatisation on the one hand, and the deregulation of the broadcasting sector as a whole on the other.

The government set about restructuring the SABC into commercial business units (which can be seen as a prelude to its privatisation) in 1991, and had already appointed a Task Group on Broadcasting in South and Southern Africa, under the chairmanship of Professor Christo Viljoen, to make recommendations about the deregulation of the broadcasting sector. The Viljoen Task Group consisted almost entirely of white Afrikaans men, many of whom have a vested interest in the broadcasting establishment. A token black man was added after public complaints. The Task Group completed its report in August 1991, recommending that the broadcast sector should be deregulated by the establishment of an Independent Broadcasting Authority (IBA) which would take over the government's regulatory powers. The mission of the IBA would be 'to ensure that broadcasting in South Africa serves the public in such a way that the ideals of a democratic, non-racial, non-sexist and prosperous society are pursued and advanced.'[1] A somewhat surprising statement from so conservative a group.

If we put the commercialising of the SABC together with the deregulation of broadcasting by the government, this strategy seems to indicate the transfer of control over broadcasting from the political to the economic sphere and the fragmentation of the national public broadcaster in the process. This roughly corresponds to the De Klerk strategy in the CODESA negotiations – to fragment the centralised power of the current state into semi-autonomous regions which could exercise a veto over any future government.

One aspect of the SABC's commercialisation was to reposition it so that it could compete effectively with M-Net for the advertising rand. The SABC gets 75 per cent of its income from advertising and only 25 per cent from licence fees, which are largely boycotted by the black population. The SABC's Chief Executive Officer, Wynand Harmse, refers to the SABC as the largest commercial broadcaster in Africa and clearly has no notion of it as a public service broadcaster. M-Net, however, has its eyes on the TV markets of Africa and has begun to extend its operation. To quote M-Net Managing Director, Ton Vosloo: 'M-Net has the technical potential to bring the global village to Africa. It has established a viable and profitable service in darkest Africa.'[2] M-Net aims to open services in African capitals aimed at elite communities, international hotels and hotel resorts. On 17 December 1991, M-Net announced that it had bought a 50 per cent shareholding in the privately owned Kenya TV Network. It planned to rebroadcast M-Net programming with an 'African flavour' into Kenya through a decoder network. M-Net also has a temporary licence to broadcast in Namibia and Lesotho. Judging by M-Net's current lack of commitment to indigenous programming, it seems likely that its dream of a new Cape to Cairo route over the airwaves will make it a conduit for Western programmes and the wonderful world of the international elites.

The SABC has agreed in principle to employ a satellite for direct-to-home broadcasting. They aim to introduce it by 1994, and it will enable the SABC to cover areas in South Africa falling outside the present terrestrial transmitters. However, it will also open South African audiences to global broadcast networks on a much greater scale; and the future democratic government of South Africa may find its sovereignty undermined by direct satellite broadcasting from around the world. The management of the SABC, however, interpret the development as the ultimate 'depoliticisation' of broadcasting. They argue that all attempts by governments to control and regulate broadcasting will come to nothing because broadcasters can simply cross the border and transmit their programmes directly to people's homes by satellite. This position fits in well with the global pattern of the dominance of market forces (rather than domestic regulations) as the governing mechanism for cultural and information activity.

FAWO began to organise in response to the appointment of the Viljoen Task Group and the proposed restructuring. On 25 August 1990, under the banner 'The People Shall Broadcast', thousands of people from trade union federations, media unions and cultural and political organisations marched on the thirty-storey SABC headquarters in Johannesburg. It was the first ever public protest against the SABC in the corporation's long, shameful, sycophantic history. The main demand of the protesters, who danced and sang while nervous management peered down from the 'tower of power', was that the restructuring of broadcasting had to take place democratically.

FAWO had always argued that the control of broadcasting was a constitutional issue and could not be resolved without the participation of the ANC, COSATU and other groupings in the democratic movement.

Campaign for Open Media demonstration, The Star, *September 1991*

In August 1991, over fifty anti-apartheid South African organisations and individuals met in Doorn in The Netherlands for the 'Jabulani Freedom of the Airwaves' conference and drew up 'Recommendations towards the Future of Broadcasting'. The conference broadened the base of resistance to apartheid broadcasting and began preparing a vision of the future. By the end of 1991 both the ANC and COSATU had accepted the important tenets of FAWO broadcast policy and were committed to preventing any unilateral government restructuring of the broadcast sector. SABC chief executive Wynand Harmse began a sleazy, covert process of trying to make deals with the democratic movement. As one ANC leader commented privately: 'Has the SABC not yet realised that I don't eat lunch?'

By February 1992, FAWO had organised an independent broadcasting and film industry bloc. A group of media lawyers were commissioned to draft legislative proposals and by the beginning of March a number of memoranda were submitted by the bloc to CODESA. The submissions outlined the necessary legislative amendments that would enable an interim government to establish a non-partisan Media Commission, which would in turn appoint a new, representative SABC board, an Independent Communications Authority (ICA) and a Broadcasting Ombudsman. A crucial proviso to the bloc submission was that there could be no agreement on an ICA until a new SABC board was appointed. This 'linkage argument' maintained that agreement on the restructuring of the SABC was more important than the immediate establishment of an ICA. The ICA would take some time to establish and South Africa could not move into free and fair elections when the medium with the largest audience was partial to one interest group.

In early May 1992, CODESA agreed on an 'Independent Body to Regulate the Telecommunications Sector', but failed to achieve consensus on the SABC. While the agreement is yet to be ratified, waiting has potentially dangerous consequences: the SABC and the government sycophants who run the Corporation may go into an election with a free hand to malign the democratic movement and promote De Klerk. If CODESA fails to address this imbalance, 'free and fair elections' in South Africa are unlikely.

Despite CODESA's failure to agree on the SABC, the consensus on an ICA was a positive development after decades of state repression and control of the broadcast media. Nowhere else in Africa has the control of broadcasting been independent of political parties or supervised by independent structures broadly representative of society. However, since there is no precedent in South Africa of a truly independent regulatory authority, media organisations will have to be vigilant in monitoring the ICA when it is established in order to ensure that there is no slide into the world of corruption and kickbacks that South Africans have come to know so well. The appointment of ICA members should not be done secretly in some CODESA committee room or in an office in the Union Buildings but should be done publicly by a respected group. It was a small victory that CODESA accepted FAWO's proposal that no ICA member should be an office-bearer of any political organisation, or have a vested interest in the film and broadcasting industries or any other conflicting interest. Nonetheless, the dividing line between legitimate lobbying and undue influencing is very thin. South Africans are tired of the future of the country being decided secretly in committee by people who say they support the public's right to know. Therefore, any future ICA must hold all its hearings in public and the minutes of Authority meetings must be made available to the public.

The private sector, excluded from the CODESA negotiations on broadcasting, has a healthy but sometimes over-zealous suspicion of a politically determined structure for broadcasting. The word 'regulation' and the idea of an 'independent regulatory authority' for broadcasting arouse great passion amongst commercial broadcasters. After years of state monopolies, protectionist policies and a myriad of boards, it is not surprising that South African business people throw their hands up in horror when confronted with the concept of regulated industry, but regulation provides the only means of ensuring freedom in a sector prone to unfair competition, overconcentration of power and political manipulation. Unfortunately, although regulatory issues will be crucial in determining the South African broadcasting landscape, the CODESA agreement did not deal with them. The agreement contained only principles, not detailed legislative proposals. The ICA will be a damp squib if it fails to address the imbalances, inequalities and unfair competition already existing in the broadcast sector.

It is vital that the ICA adopts licensing criteria appropriate to this end, and that they act effectively to curb media monopolisation and cross-ownership and promote affirmative action in the interests of historically disadvantaged sectors of South African society. FAWO insisted in its legislative proposals that agreement must be reached on important regulatory provisions before the ICA is established since there is no guarantee that the Authority will have the will to address these issues once that happens. 'Democracy of the Airwaves' will become an empty slogan if the new broadcasting dispensation does not provide for a diversity of voices from a broad range of communities. FAWO will take the struggle against apartheid broadcasting back on to the streets if constitutional negotiations fail.

The battle for local, independent television production

If South Africa is to develop a viable indigenous film and television industry, it is essential that there are minimum local content regulations in a future broadcast dispensation. But with SABC TV, M-Net and BOP TV enthusiastically embracing 'market forces', the struggling independent film and video industry has a battle on its hands to stem the tide of cheap American programming. Will television broadcasters sustain a healthy commitment to the local industry or is there a need for state subsidies?

FAWO has argued that although local production is far more expensive than imported programming, the existing broadcasters do have the revenue to increase their commitment to the local industry significantly. However, SABC TV has cut back 60 per cent on local productions, and M-Net and BOP TV both broadcast less than 5 per cent local content. These broadcasters have continued to underdevelop the independent film and video industry in South Africa in the quest for superprofits. The Viljoen Task Group made no criticism of M-Net's blatant refusal to comply with local content percentages negotiated in 1986 (a domestic content of 30 per cent after 500,000 subscribers have been reached). The renegotiated licence conditions required M-Net to spend only R12m on local production. Although M-Net claimed it would spend R30m on local production during 1991, the company has clearly not been making any real attempt to support the local industry. After producing a R15m Afrikaans drama series during 1991, M-Net cynically fulfilled the conditions of its licence agreement through the funding of just one tele-serial, *Egoli*. M-Net has consistently refused, 'on the basis of confidentiality', to release the percentage of local content in their overall schedule. They also refused to release figures on the percentage of total expenditure spent on local drama. The only conclusion one can draw is that these percentages were embarrassingly small. Our own calculations show that both figures were less than 5 per cent. Local content on SABC, M-Net and BOP TV falls well short of what would be admissible in France, the UK, Spain, Finland and a number of other countries.

The need to develop and protect the local film and television industry is urgent. BOP TV and M-Net's almost exclusive promotion of American programmes, SABC cutbacks and the establishment of SABC private companies are already contributing to the collapse of the industry. The Viljoen Task Group's recommendation that broadcasters should contract at least 30 per cent of their local content commitment to independent production houses and facilities is welcome, even though it flies in the face of massive cutbacks by the SABC. Unfortunately, the Task Group does not explain how it defines an independent production house. Broederbond patronage has taken its toll on the local industry, with only a few companies benefiting from SABC and M-Net commissions. Both the SABC and M-Net decline to release details of what percentage of outside production goes to which companies. As a public broadcaster the SABC must have a much larger commitment to local content and their productions must be commissioned fairly, in a way that stimulates the industry as a whole – not just four or five companies traditionally run by Broederbonders.

During the early 1990s FAWO will have to fight not only for a significant increase in non-ideological state support for local cinema production, but for statutory support for the local TV and video industry. At present we do not have a developed indigenous film and television culture, and in order to build a national picture the predominance of American programming must be severely curtailed through clearly defined and sustainable regulatory provisions.

Building a national picture

With the changes after 1990, progressive video units and film-makers have turned their attention to getting their programmes aired on SABC television. The success of their attempts has tended to depend on whether they have the backing of mass-based organisations. An example of this is the VNS programme *Hlanganani: A Short History of COSATU*. COSATU had commissioned VNS to make a film on the history of the federation for its Fourth Congress. COSATU and VNS decided to see if they could get the SABC to broadcast it and entered into negotiations with Madala Mphahlele, the recently appointed controller of CCV TV and the first black person to occupy a senior management position at SABC. Mphahlele agreed to broadcast the programme subject to reducing its length to 26 minutes and imposing two cuts – one of a scene showing a white COSATU member. The programme blends interviews with key unionists, businessmen, politicians and workers, with a montage of impressions of workers on the streets, in factories, at rallies, in townships. It was screened the day before the COSATU Congress and succeeded in getting a crossover audience of black viewers and white management. The SABC, however, could not resist showing, immediately after *Hlanganani*, a 3-minute American insert which attacked socialism in Cuba. Its anti-communist reflexes are still knee-jerk.

The screening of *Hlanganani* was a first for progressive film-makers seeking access to the closed world of the SABC and for the representation of the black working class on their own terms. It also showed up the difficulty for progressive film-makers in getting access to the airwaves without the backing of the powerful COSATU or other mass-based organisations. After commercialising into business units, the SABC reduced its outside commissions from independent TV producers who did not have the backing of a powerful institution like a trade union federation or funding from elsewhere. Individual film-makers have simply been ignored by the SABC.

There are clearly no guarantees that the struggle for a national television culture will be won. The current management of television broadcasting is in the hands of free-marketeers whose main concern is the advertising rand they can get from primetime TV by scheduling cheap global product. Quentin Green, the chief executive of SABC's Television Division, is an accountant whose mission is to privatise the SABC and compete successfully with M-Net. The SABC cannot conceive of how they could function as a national broadcaster for all South Africans and not simply for the white minority, and they still operate a structural division between whites and blacks. TV1 still addresses whites, has white news presenters and alternates between English and Afrikaans. The multicultural CCV TV still addresses a primarily black audience. This perpetuates the racial division of South African society and makes the SABC's professed commitment to national reconciliation an exercise in rhetoric. Outside the TV fortresses, the dramatic changes South African society is experiencing go largely unrecorded and unrepresented. Meanwhile in the black population there are few with the means (skills or resources) to represent these changes. The potential for television to play a role in making sense of the changes is not there. Free market ideologies and the bankrupt imagination of apartheid clog the airwaves and do their best to prevent the emergence of a new national picture.

The full implications of a new national identity and consciousness for all South Africans need exploring in relation to the heterogeneity and diversity of the population as a whole. The black population needs massive affirmative action programmes, but at present there are very few training schemes in place. FAWO runs a small Community Video School with the support of Channel Four Television in Britain. The state runs a film school at the Pretoria Technikon which until recently was for whites only. There is a film course at the Afrika Cultural Centre in Johannesburg. There are also a number of private training initiatives, which are expensive. The future democratic government will have to be persuaded to support the development of film, video and television schools as a means of redressing the effects of apartheid on the televisual landscape, especially because the game plan of the existing broadcasters is to maintain their domination of the airwaves as conduits for global product.

If the globalisation of South African television is allowed to continue, our TV stations will continue to be video distributors at the mercy of global television markets. The reconstruction of South African society after apartheid will be impeded because television will be unable to fulfil the role of representing the full complexity of South African life, building national reconciliation and a new national picture, contributing to the education and development of the country, and unleashing the imagination of all South Africans. The choice is stark. Will we have an American TV culture, or a post-apartheid national television culture?

NOTES

1. *Report of the Task Group on Broadcasting in South and Southern Africa*, Chairman: Professor Christo Viljoen (Pretoria: The Government Printer, August 1991), p. 62.
2. Quoted by Nigel Bruce, 'Broadcast', *Leadership* (Johannesburg), vol. 10, October–November 1991, p. 8.

SINGING THE ELECTRIC
Aboriginal Television in Australia

Philip Batty

In 1984, a family of Pintupi people were escorted into the remote Aboriginal community of Kiwirrkura, located on the edge of the Gibson Desert, Western Australia. They had never seen white people or the artefacts of white culture before. Their thoughts on seeing cars, houses, windmills, aeroplanes and fences, for the first time, are difficult to imagine, although one of them said that he felt as though he was being ensnared in a cobweb when one of his relatives (a man who had met Europeans years before) covered his naked body with a shirt and a pair of trousers. A few months after their entrance into the world of the non-Aboriginal, they sat and watched a live news report from Washington, on a battery-operated television set, linked to a local satellite receiver.

Global television is a fact of life for almost all of us. We can follow the latest regional war or witness the collapse of nations as they happen, from the comfort of our sitting rooms or, in the case of the Pintupi, under the shade of a mulga tree. During the Gulf War, George Bush was reputed to have said that he watched television in order to get the most up-to-date reports of the war. Apparently, Cable Network News (CNN) could get information to the President of the United States quicker than his official intelligence machine: for a few minutes, George Bush may have known as much about what was happening in the Gulf War as the Pintupi in Western Australia.

What effect, if any, has the spread of global television had on minority groups and their cultures? Do the children of these marginalised groups learn to despise their own cultural inheritance after prolonged exposure to the dazzling cosmos of network television? Do they gradually abandon their own traditional languages for the dominant language heard via the television set? Does global television act as a kind of subtle drug of acculturation, seducing then destroying indigenous peoples? Or has the emergence of global television given all peoples throughout the world the opportunity to become citizens of a common global village, with equal access to all manner of information and 'global knowledge'? Has television, in fact, opened a window to the world for all minority people and released them from their cultural ghettos?

There was a time when I could have provided easy answers to all these questions. There was no doubt in my mind that imported or 'alien' television programming, especially delivered direct from satellite, would have devastating effects on local Aboriginal cultures and languages. But after many years of work in the field of rural and indigenous broadcasting development, I'm not so sure.

I don't think it is entirely true or particularly helpful to characterise the emergence of what might be described as 'Aboriginal television' simply as the result of Aboriginal people taking an oppositional stance to the introduction of European-style television into their communities. This would be too simplistic a description of the many and varied 'styles' of Aboriginal television in Australia today. Some groups have indeed taken a highly oppositional approach to the imposition of global television on their lives. Others have used the technologies associated with television to support and even strengthen traditional cultural activities. Some Aboriginal people have simply intervened in existing television services to ensure that Aboriginal issues are appropriately presented, while others are only interested in owning, as private shareholders, a piece of the commercial television pie, like any other commercial participants in a private business.

It would be a comfort perhaps to romantics who tend to regard Aboriginal culture as a static entity, immune from change, located forever in some timeless never-never land, to believe that Aboriginals have rejected the 'evils' of global television and banned the intrusion of such spiritually impure rubbish from their communities. Most people, including Aboriginal people, aren't like that. Aboriginal kids love Kung Fu movies, and Michael Jackson clips even if they can't understand the lyrics. The local football team in every Aboriginal community in the Northern Territory is glued to the TV screen when the grand final is telecast live from the city, and everyone is intrigued by news stories featuring indigenous peoples from other countries. This is not to say, however, that Aboriginal people living in remote communities have little interest in locally made television programmes. On the contrary, anything featuring local news, local cultural events, community concerts or even coverage of local council meetings is as eagerly watched as programmes made in Hollywood.

The available evidence seems to indicate that when television of a 'global' nature becomes available in a community populated by indigenous people or minorities, it rapidly assumes a substantial physical presence, in one form or another, in the day-to-day life of that community. It would appear that the activity of television viewing is as seductive for indigenous peoples as it is for those in the developed world. The problem here of course is that global television, by its very nature, requires an endless stream of programming to satisfy its viewers, and in the main it is the developed world that has the technical and economic clout to produce the vast amounts of material required to feed this global monster. Inevitably, however, the viewers in the developed world will almost always watch forms of television produced within their own cultural milieu, while viewers located at the outer limits of the global networks, the Pintupi for instance, will see a world that bears almost no relation to their own.

I want here to examine the various forms of Aboriginal television which have evolved in Australia over the last decade (1980–90). I am also interested in looking at how Aboriginal people have attempted to create or 'invent' their own television through a process of 'negotiation' with the settler nation, and how this kind of inter-cultural bargaining has in itself influenced, in quite profound ways, the emergence and nature of these varied television services. I have limited myself to discussion of Aboriginal-controlled television services, and omitted detailed reference to the production and distribution of Aboriginal television programming through the Australian Broadcasting Corporation or the Special Broadcasting Service (both national, European-controlled TV stations).

Contemporary Aboriginal culture

Casual observers often make the mistake of seeing the Aboriginal community or 'nation' as an unchanging social order, free of any internal differences or conflicts. Nothing could be further from the truth. The 'Aboriginal nation' as such is an extremely complex entity, containing many internal variations. Millions of individuals regard themselves as European, for example, but will also recognise that other Europeans speak different languages, hold divergent political opinions, or live in varying social circumstances. The same applies to the Aboriginal 'nation' within Australia. Indeed, the Aboriginal population probably represents the most diverse single community of people in the country. Over a hundred Aboriginal languages are still spoken, of which twenty or so survive in a healthy, robust state. Some Aboriginal people, such as the Pintupi, first came into contact with non-Aboriginals as recently as 1984, while others, living in Sydney for instance, have a contact history stretching back over eight generations. In the political arena too there are Aboriginal factions both on the extreme right and the far left. Aboriginal fundamentalist Christians live side by side with groups that maintain traditional religious beliefs, and as in any social grouping there are also relatively wide social and economic differences.

While there are deep cultural commonalities connecting the 250,000 people who identify themselves as Aboriginal, it must be understood that when we talk about contemporary Aboriginal culture and therefore Aboriginal TV, we are not talking about just one thing. Discussion about any Aboriginal initiative invariably pulls in a whole raft of issues, from the meaning of 'Aboriginality' (pan-Aboriginalist vs. federationist or localised ideologies) through to the hidden agendas behind the concept of 'Aboriginal self-determination' (the generic term applied to official federal government policy on Aboriginals). The inclination to extend the examination of a particular issue about Aboriginals into a broad discussion about everything Aboriginal is due, I think, to the deep uncertainties and confusion about what it is to be Aboriginal (from both an Aboriginal and non-Aboriginal perspective). It seems that Aboriginal people suffer from a constant identity crisis, so that 'contemporary Aboriginal culture' is always being reinvented. The unfortunate consequences of this can be seen in places like Alice Springs, where Aboriginal unemployment, alcoholism and violence remain a regular feature of local life. Obviously all peoples, whether they be Australian Aboriginals or white middle-class Americans, live in social and cultural environments that are (and always have been) 'emergent' or in constant states of alteration, but Aboriginal culture is far more 'emergent' than most. Of course, when 98 per cent of the people living on your land are deemed to be foreigners, the pressure to change, adapt, adjust and 'emerge' is enormous, if not fundamental to your basic survival.

The Ernabella model
Ernabella is a remote Aboriginal community located in the semi-arid regions of northern South Australia. This little community is home to approximately 550 Pitjantjatjarra people, who continue to maintain a

relatively traditional lifestyle. Pitjantjatjarra is still spoken as a first language, and ritual ceremonial activity continues to play a central role. Like the Pintupi, the Pitjantjatjarra have settled into a sedentary way of life in comparatively recent times.

Over the last ten to twenty years, the Pitjantjatjarra have fought many battles asserting their rights as an independent indigenous people. Through the Pitjantjatjarra Land Rights Act, for example, they have won secure tenure and control over their traditional lands, which encompass an area half the size of England. They run their own health service, a network of community stores, and extensive community development schemes. It is little wonder, then, that the Pitjantjatjarra at Ernabella were prepared for the arrival of satellite-delivered television, and aware of the impact this event might have on their local languages and culture. At a Pitjantjatjarra Council meeting held near Ernabella in 1983, a prominent member of the community, Anmanari Nyaningu, said, 'Unimpeded satellite transmission in our communities will be like having hundreds of whitefellas visit without permits every day.'[1]

Past experiences with 'whitefella' media seem to have alerted the Pitjantjatjarra to what they might expect from the satellite. Videocassettes, for example, had slowly found their way into their communities. Many people were concerned about the alien social values portrayed in such video programmes and the effects this had on young Pitjantjatjarra viewers. Once the satellite became operational, similar programmes would be available on a twenty-four hour basis and have an even greater corrosive effect. There were already problems with the younger generation with regard to respect for traditional authority structures and laws governing social behaviour, and it was felt that the satellite would hasten the process of social disintegration. They knew also that archival material on film and video, of secret-sacred ceremonies, had often been shown publicly by white film-makers. The introduction of satellite television would increase the likelihood of this happening. For these and many other reasons, the Pitjantjatjarra at Ernabella decided to establish a media committee to monitor developments with the satellite, and initiated what became known as the Ernabella Video Project.

The Video Project began in 1983, with the simple aim of producing local video programmes that would reflect the interests and activities of the Ernabella community. The programmes were to be presented only in Pitjantjatjarra. When these locally made programmes were released on videocassette and distributed throughout Ernabella, there was an enormous response. Everyone, it seemed, wanted their particular event or story recorded so that it could be seen and enjoyed by the whole community. Soon other Pitjantjatjarra communities were asking that the video crew from Ernabella come and make similar programmes in their respective local areas. Over a period of a few months, the Video Project began to assume a powerful momentum of its own, becoming the *de facto* television channel of the Pitjantjatjarra people.

Initially, events of a communal nature were recorded, such as sporting activities, music concerts, council meetings, bush trips and community work projects. But gradually the video crew began to record material of a more cultural nature. Women asked that video programmes be made about local bush foods and medicinal plants so that their children could learn about them and the tapes could be stored for later reference. Eventually, the Ernabella Video Project developed into an organisation: Ernabella Video and Television. And EVTV, as it came to be known, gradually assumed a pivotal role in the cultural life of the Pitjantjatjarra.

Those familiar with traditional Australian Aboriginal beliefs will be aware of the concept of the 'dreaming line' or, as Bruce Chatwin would have it, the 'song line'. These terms refer to journeys taken by mythic ancestors during the 'dreamtime' over particular tracks of land. These paths or tracks are delineated by actual physical features such as an outcrop of rocks, a creek, a mountain, a water-hole or a cave. All such features were created by the mythic ancestors as they travelled through the land. Associated with each journey there is a song 'cycle', made up of hundreds of verses, as well as dances and ritual performances. By learning the song for a particular ancestral journey, one will also learn about the 'dreaming story' associated with that journey and how each particular physical feature came into existence, and also how the ancestors themselves emerged from the earth. There are hundreds or perhaps thousands of dreaming lines criss-crossing Pitjantjatjarra country. Acquiring a knowledge of these lines is fundamental to Pitjantjatjarra religious understanding and takes a lifetime of patient learning. Unfortunately, since they abandoned a nomadic life the Pitjantjatjarra do not travel over their country as much as they used to do and it is therefore difficult to pass on to the younger generation a full appreciation of the dreaming lines. Through the judicious use of video equipment, however, these dreaming lines and their physical manifestations, along with the associated songs and dances, can be recorded on tape and stored back at the community. Such recordings can then be used in instructing young men and women in the ways of the ancestors.

111

The recording of significant dreaming lines became one of the major preoccupations of Ernabella Video and Television, and the central reason that EVTV came to assume such importance in the eyes of the Pitjantjatjarra. According to Neil Turner, media co-ordinator with EVTV:

Most significant [productions] have been the cross-country expeditions organised with up to thirty custodians of *Tjukurrpa* (dreaming) from several communities, for several days at a time to tell and re-enact Dreaming Stories and perform the song and dance for each successive site on video.... We have completed the shooting of the entire *Kungkarangkalpa* (seven sisters' dreaming) line as it traverses the Pitjantjatjarra lands ... over a hundred kilometres of spinafex and dune country.... The custodians have found video a particularly apt tool for recording the unique and integral combination of story, song, dance and visual arts and landscape through which the *Tjukurrpa* is expressed . . . as it can be entirely directed, produced, and distributed by themselves, without the expertise of literate white anthropologists.[2]

EVTV filming traditional dance at a sacred site in the Central Australian desert,
© *CAAMA*

Such was the local interest in the use of video to record the dreaming lines that EVTV produced, over a relatively short time, close to a thousand hours of footage which was roughly edited and subsequently multi-copied onto cassette and distributed throughout the Pitjantjatjarra lands. This process had the effect of engendering a kind of local renaissance in traditional dance, performance and singing. The various video programmes depicting the actual land where the dreaming lines were located gave renewed strength to traditional beliefs and values within the communities. This in turn led to EVTV hosting a number of traditional dance festivals at Ernabella, and the organisation of performances throughout Australia.

Apart from the recording of traditional activities, EVTV had always planned to establish a local television broadcasting station, on an experimental basis, at Ernabella. The major obstacle was funding. EVTV had been advised that even a small, low-powered TV transmitter would cost $20,000 or more. While there were government funding bodies that could supply such financial assistance, all were reluctant to support what would in effect be an unlicensed television station and therefore an illegal project. Undaunted, EVTV sought the assistance of a local amateur electronics enthusiast who could install a basic TV transmitter, made from second-hand parts, for $1,000. In order to raise the required cash, the community store agreed to place a surcharge of 10 cents on all soft drinks sales. The money was available in a matter of months. In April 1985, the world's cheapest TV station went on air from the studios of Ernabella Video and Television, to the delight of the local community.

The station was managed on a relatively strict basis by the local media committee, made up almost entirely of older, traditional Aboriginal people. It was switched off during the weekends, so that television viewing did not interfere with the social activities of the community, and during funerals and council meetings. Initial broadcasting hours were between 6 p.m. and 10 p.m. four nights per week. Programming consisted of a mix of locally made material, programmes made by other Aboriginal media organisations, and material relating to Aboriginal issues recorded off regular TV services such as the ABC. The local school began to run a weekly educational programme and there were some 'live' performances from the Ernabella Choir and other local musical groups. The station even ran an 'Aid for Africa' appeal and raised $1,600 from local viewers.

A year or so after local television transmission at Ernabella began, the national satellite AUSSAT was launched and began beaming the national television service, the ABC, into every remote corner of the nation. At this point EVTV decided to purchase a satellite receiving dish (from the sale of videos) so that it could take material off satellite and rebroadcast such programmes on a selective basis as part of their nightly programme mix. The media committee felt that EVTV had gained substantial experience in managing a television service through the operation of their local TV station, and had shown members of the local community how television was controllable, and how it need not be an overpowering force. The committee now felt that it could patch together a local television service drawing on a variety of sources, including a substantial selection of their own locally produced material.

Today, Ernabella continues to operate a locally controlled television service, broadcasting a selection of programming composed of satellite feeds (from both commercial and public sources) and locally made programmes. It also continues to produce a seemingly endless stream of video programmes based on traditional activities, which are sold on a regular basis throughout the Pitjantjatjarra lands and beyond. Despite perennial funding problems and limited production resources, Ernabella Video and Television have managed to use television technologies in productive and genuinely beneficial ways, and indeed have been able to incorporate such technologies into their local culture in ways appropriate to themselves. Beyond this, I think it can be shown that the Pitjantjatjarra at Ernabella found ways of using television technology for their own cultural purposes which were very different from Western mass media practices. For example, secret-sacred ceremonies of both women and men continue to be recorded on video for private purposes and not for broadcast. One of the interesting aspects of the approach taken by the people at Ernabella was that they did not reject television outright; in fact they embraced it wholeheartedly. They had managed to establish their own local television service, funded through their own local resources, and became familiar with the basic processes of production long before the arrival of television via satellite.

There are important lessons to be learned here. Firstly, if the community had taken a completely oppositional approach to the introduction of television into their community (in other words, had banned it) and had not established their own local TV station and local production techniques on their own terms, then it is almost certain that they would not, as a community, have been able to deal with the introduction of direct satellite television in an experienced and informed way. When satellite television became available in most other remote Aboriginal communities where there was no previous experience with television, there was neither local ability to control the influx of external television nor the technical understanding needed to produce local programming. So when we talk about 'resistance' to global television, it seems that this can only be accomplished, in any effective way, by gaining an active if basic knowledge of television technology, and by applying that knowledge in locally relevant and significant ways.

Secondly, the people at Ernabella established local TV and production facilities using relatively low-tech, cheap and easy to use equipment. In other words, they were able to develop a kind of local 'television culture' using technologies that could be rapidly learnt and applied to local conditions. There have been so many development projects initiated in Aboriginal communities that have failed because of the complex technologies employed. In such projects, outside 'experts' and technicians are required to operate equipment and manage the associated administrative structures that invariably hamper involvement by the local people. In this case, however, the TV project was largely initiated and controlled, in both a technical and an administrative sense, by the local people.

Thirdly, most of the initial funding for these developments was generated by the Ernabella community itself and not provided through the often constraining avenue of government funding. Indeed, they would not have been able to establish a local TV station at all if it had been funded through government money; without a television licence, no government would have provided assistance to set up what amounted to an illegal TV channel. Finally, the Pitjantjatjarra, unlike the majority of Aboriginal people, live in an environment where they are in the majority: they have relatively secure tenure of their land, a strong connection to their traditional cultural base, and adequate support services in place. While they continue to suffer from a wide range of health, housing and educational problems, the Pitjantjatjarra are nevertheless in a politically strong position compared with other Aboriginal people. This ability to call at least some of the shots certainly had an influence on the successful development of locally controlled television services at Ernabella. As we shall see, in other rural or urban settings where Aboriginal people are in the minority, and so have to conform to the vagaries of government policy to a much greater extent, the effort to establish Aboriginal television services has not been so successful.

The Broadcasting in Aboriginal Communities Scheme (BRACS)

The BRACS service grew out of a federal government report entitled *Out of the Silent Land*, commissioned by the Department of Aboriginal Affairs in 1985 to assess and make recommendations on Aboriginal broadcasting.[3] The authors of the report modelled their concept of the BRACS system on the experiments at Ernabella and the activities of the Walpiri Media Association at Yuendamu, which have been well documented by Eric Michaels.[4]

In technical terms, a BRACS station is capable of picking up commercial and national signals (radio and television) off the domestic satellite, AUSSAT, and rebroadcasting them in a selective manner (or not at all) into the local community via low-powered transmitters. The BRACS system can also be used for the production of limited, low-budget local radio and television programmes. At the time of writing there were twenty-eight BRACS facilities operating throughout the Northern Territory.

While the intentions of the federal government (to provide local communities with a measure of control over incoming television and radio services) are to be commended, the effectiveness of the BRACS system at the community level has not been an unqualified success – and some would say it has been a fiasco. It appears that with a few notable exceptions these facilities are used mainly as a means simply to rebroadcast outside television programming within the communities, rather than as a device to broadcast a mix of local and incoming material, as originally intended. The government facilitators of the BRACS system did not appear to have any realistic notion of the time-consuming effort required to produce television programming (even using low-budget, domestic-standard equipment), or of the basic administrative infrastructure required to manage a BRACS system, which is in effect a small-scale television station. In most cases, the BRACS facilities were installed in communities without proper consultation. In some instances, the actual physical control of the BRACS facilities (possession of the key to the equipment shed, for instance), ended up with the white local teacher or the policeman's wife!

The various elements that made the experiment in locally controlled TV at Ernabella work were, in nearly all respects, missing in those communities where BRACS facilities were installed. The notion of a locally controlled TV station did not emerge from these communities as a particular issue of concern to the local people themselves; there was no training, or development of a community consciousness about television, prior to BRACS being installed; there was not the basic administrative structure required to operate a community TV station, or the skills needed to produce programming. Typically, it was an initiative based on a policy developed according to the experience of one or two Aboriginal communities in Central Australia (Ernabella and Yuendamu). This policy was then applied across the board to many other locations, far from central Australia, all with very different local concerns and experiences. Regardless of these current difficulties with the BRACS facilities, I think it can be said that the successful development of Aboriginal television services in remote Aboriginal communities, even through BRACS, is a far more likely proposition than in rural or urban situations where Aboriginal people are invariably in a minority, and therefore must compete and negotiate to a much greater degree with the dominant non-Aboriginal population for access or control over available television and radio services.

Negotiating an Aboriginal television licence

When the Central Australian Aboriginal Media Association (CAAMA) set out in 1985 to intervene in the introduction of satellite television services in the Northern Territory, it had not envisaged owning and operating a commercial television service. CAAMA only wanted to gain access to the new satellite system in order to provide culturally appropriate TV programming to the substantial Aboriginal population within its region. But after a long and heavily contested negotiation process, CAAMA in fact became the major shareholder in Imparja Television, a private company created to hold and operate the central Remote Commercial Television Service (RCTS) television licence, and suddenly became responsible for providing a commercial TV service across a third of the Australian landmass, an area the size of Western Europe. The following is a brief description of events that led up to these extraordinary developments.

A group of Aboriginal and white people, including myself, had set up CAAMA in 1980, initially to produce and broadcast radio programmes in Aboriginal languages using the facilities of the local commercial radio station in Alice Springs. In 1981, we became aware of plans by the federal government to introduce direct broadcast satellite (DBS) television services to the remote regions of Australia. There were to be four discrete satellite footprints, technically capable of distributing a range of telecommunication services, including television and radio, to anywhere in Australia. One of these satellite footprints (the central zone) would cover all of the Northern Territory and South Australia. CAAMA was immediately concerned about the potential effects of foreign television on the many hundreds of traditional Aboriginal communities located throughout the proposed central footprint area, most of which had no radio, television or telephone services, let alone direct satellite facilities.

CAAMA felt strongly that the Aboriginal people living within the central footprint area should have a fundamental involvement in the new satellite services, for a number of reasons. In a submission to the then federal Department of Communications, CAAMA demonstrated that the Aboriginal population within the central footprint was substantial. At the time, it was almost 40 per cent of the total proposed audience – on the basis of demographics alone, wide Aboriginal involvement was indicated. The main arguments for Aboriginal participation centred on concerns about the potential effects of unimpeded television on traditional Aboriginal life. For example, CAAMA pointed out that 90 per cent of the Aboriginal languages spoken throughout Australia had been rendered extinct in the relatively brief period (200 years) of European colonisation, and all the remaining 10 per cent were located in the areas where the new satellite services were to be introduced. Ceremonial life, social structures and traditional values were also felt to be under threat. Apart from the potentially negative effects of the satellite, CAAMA also believed that it could be used to advantage, particularly in the field of Aboriginal education.

When CAAMA presented its 1981 submission to the federal government, plans for the actual technical configuration of the satellite had not been finalised, so it argued that the satellite should be engineered in a way that would allow non-profit organisations some access to the new technology and should not be entirely dominated by commercial television operators. Sadly, such arguments were never considered by the authorities.

At this point, the Australian government was under the spell of economic rationalism and believed that free enterprise could solve any conceivable problem. They decided that the satellite transponders set aside for non-government television broadcasting, in the four footprint zones, should be licensed to commercial television companies only, and that if anyone else wanted to use these transponders they would have to work out a deal with the successful commercial licencee. Indeed, these four transponders would operate what would become known as the Remote Commercial Television Services (RCTS). This meant that commercial interests would have a large measure of control over all non-government television, educational services, data distribution systems, community telecommunications and medical communications services. In late 1984, the Minister for Communications invited interested companies to apply for the licences to operate such services.

The government's decision to hand over control of the RCTS to commercial interests presented CAAMA with a real dilemma. Should it wait until a private company was given the licence, then ask for some airtime and hope for a favourable response? Or should CAAMA take the plunge and apply for the licence itself? Some argued that CAAMA's integrity and purpose as an independent Aboriginal media organisation would be distorted beyond recognition if it engaged in the operation of a commercial TV station; that it would necessarily have to become to some degree commercial in outlook, and would most likely be forced into making compromises that could undermine the very reasons for intervening in the television licensing process. Others felt that if CAAMA did not at least attempt to acquire the RCTS licence, it would never get another chance of gaining some control over the satellite. As the closing date for the submission of applications grew nearer, CAAMA finally decided to apply.

In a sense, debate about whether CAAMA should have gone for the licence or not was somewhat academic. First, it had no money, even though $6m would be needed just to buy the equipment to run the new service. Secondly, it had no expertise, even though direct satellite television is an extremely complex piece of technology and had never been tried in Australia before. To make things worse, all financial projections seemed to indicate that no matter who operated the central RCTS, it would never be able to support itself on a commercial basis. Nevertheless, with the assistance of hired consultants, CAAMA very quickly put together an impressive licence application (in two volumes). It also created a commercial company, known as Imparja Television Pty. Ltd., as the vehicle for the licence application. While various funding bodies were approached for funds, they were slow to make any real commitment. The only strength that CAAMA had was in its programming proposals. Here it outlined a comprehensive and innovative plan to broadcast a wide range of television programming that would reflect the diversity of the audience within the central RCTS service area. Although commercial programming was included as part of the total programming mix, CAAMA proposed a high level of weekly Aboriginal programming, presented in the Aboriginal languages of the region, by and for Aboriginal people.

The only other applicant for the licence was Television Capricornia, a company owned by an existing commercial television station, NTD8, located in Darwin, capital of the Northern Territory. NTD8's application was in most respects a reverse of CAAMA's. They seemed to have the financial backing and the experience to implement the new service but did not plan to develop any new or appropriate programming; instead they proposed to use their existing commercial programming, making a few minor changes to the local news. Their application did not include any plans for Aboriginal programming.

The Australian Broadcasting Tribunal (ABT) convened a hearing in Alice Springs, Northern Territory, in August 1985 to consider the licence applications. The hearing lasted for almost two weeks. CAAMA, realising that this might be the only opportunity it would get to air its views about Aboriginal involvement in the proposed new satellite, whether it won the licence or not, presented twenty-four witnesses, most of them traditional Aboriginal people from remote communities in central Australia. Much of CAAMA's evidence centred round the need for appropriate television programming for the new service, and the impact that ill-conceived programming might have on traditional Aboriginal cultures located in the remote communities within the proposed new television service area.

No one was more surprised than CAAMA when, towards the end of 1985, the ABT released its report on the hearing and concluded that, 'neither applicant qualifies for the licence. The Tribunal [has] serious reservations about the financial capability of the Imparja [CAAMA] application and doubts as to whether the service proposed by Television Capricornia [NTD8] would be adequate having regard to all the circumstances and characteristics of the area to be served.'[5] The Tribunal called for a further hearing to be held in March 1986, again in Alice Springs. There was now a real prospect of CAAMA becoming the owner and operator of a commercial satellite television service. Again, there was lengthy debate within CAAMA about whether the organisation really wanted to have anything to do with running a commercial business, which would inevitably involve providing a service to the more commercially attractive non-Aboriginal audience. But the momentum created by the Tribunal's decision proved to be an irresistible force, and CAAMA decided to prepare for the second hearing in earnest.

In effect, the Tribunal sent both applicants out on a treasure hunt: CAAMA had to find $6m and NTD8 some Aboriginal programming proposals, all in six months. Fortunately for CAAMA, the federal government had just created the Australian Bi-Centennial Authority (ABA), an organisation charged with the task of co-ordinating the celebration of 200 years of white colonisation. The ABA was given a substantial budget to fund the celebrations, and of course quite a lot of money was set aside for Aboriginal groups. Financing an Aboriginal television station appeared to be just the right antidote for two centuries of white guilt. A lengthy submission, asking for $2.5 million, was presented to the ABA, and a further $1.8 million was approved by the Aboriginal Development Commission, a body set up to provide government funding to Aboriginal enterprises. An extra $2.0 million was sought from the federal Education Department to underwrite educational programme production. It seemed that CAAMA could go back to the Tribunal with the required cash, even though only one lot of funding had been approved. Meanwhile NTD8 had managed to acquire the services of a group called United Australian Television to provide the Aboriginal programming required by the Tribunal.

The Tribunal hearings were duly reconvened in March 1986 and lasted for four days. When the hearings opened CAAMA had still not received confirmation of the ABA's funding, but it was received during the hearings in a telex from the Minister of Aboriginal Affairs. The Education Department funding did not, however, materialise. In the end CAAMA had managed to scrape together $4.3m; this was nearly $2m short of the target, but a strong case was put forward for the likelihood of further sponsorship becoming available if it was granted the licence. NTD8, on the other hand, had not put up a very convincing case for better programming. It appeared that its consultants, United Australian Television, instead of developing a comprehensive plan for Aboriginal programming, had spent the intervening months running a campaign to discredit CAAMA's application. It had not succeeded. In August 1986, a year after the Tribunal began its hearing into the central RCTS, it concluded that the licence should be awarded to CAAMA.

The Tribunal indicated that although both applicants had satisfied the criteria to be awarded the licence,

> The Imparja (CAAMA) program proposals offer an innovative development in Australian commercial television and [are] clearly based on the applicant's perception of the needs of the RCTS area.... The program proposal of Capricornia (NTD8) changed considerably during the course of the enquiry and its adequacy for the Aboriginal population of the service area is debatable.... The Tribunal concludes

that the Imparja programming proposals will provide a more adequate and comprehensive service than those of Capricornia ... [and]
that Imparja is the most suitable, and therefore appropriate, for the
grant of the licence.[6]

Clearly CAAMA had won the final round in the licence battle through
its proposals to service the Aboriginal audience. This represented an
extraordinary achievement for CAAMA and Aboriginal people in general. It had won the right, through its commercial offspring Imparja
Television, to deliver both radio and television programming to every
remote Aboriginal community in the Northern Territory and South
Australia, as well as to the relatively large outback towns of Alice
Springs, Catherine, Tennant Creek and Coober Pedy. Indeed, CAAMA's
new broadcast service area was home to more than 60 per cent of all
Aboriginal groups still living in a semi-traditional way.

Self-determination or self-destruction?
In 1991, six years after CAAMA's original intervention into the television licensing process, a visiting student from Nigeria came to Alice
Springs to inspect Imparja. He had been told that this was the only
Aboriginal-owned television station in Australia and was therefore keen
to see how an indigenous group ran such a service and how it differed
from mainstream stations. He was amazed to learn that the federal government had given the local Aboriginal people more than $18m to set
up and run Imparja over three years, but perplexed that the station only
employed four Aboriginal people out of a total staff of thirty-two and
that Imparja's programming was 98 per cent white! While Imparja is
today cloaked in the rhetoric of 'Aboriginal self-determination' and is
supported by many millions of 'Aboriginal dollars' provided by the government, the major beneficiaries do not appear to be Aboriginal. Over
80 per cent of the audience is non-Aboriginal, practically all the local
and national businesses that take advantage of the highly subsidised
commercial rates offered by Imparja are non-Aboriginal, and all senior
operational management are still white.

Although CAAMA never had any intention of televising 'wall-to-wall
corroborees' on Imparja, as some earlier critics believed, it did intend to
produce and broadcast a moderate level of weekly programming for its
Aboriginal audience in a variety of local languages. Such programmes
were not to be placed in 'programming ghettos' but scheduled in normal
rating periods along with the more regular commercial fare. But these

plans (which so impressed the Tribunal) have not come to fruition. During the whole of 1991 only six and a half hours of programming in Aboriginal languages were transmitted. Ironically, one of the other RCTS operators (GWN in Western Australia), which is owned by commercial interests, manages to broadcast on a community service basis far more Aboriginal programming than Imparja. Equally ironically, Imparja is now no different from its rival for the licence, NTD8. The management of both stations is white, the primary aim is to be commercially successful, they even buy their programming from the same source.

Freda Glynn, an Aboriginal woman of considerable experience in the field of Aboriginal development, was the co-founder and Director of CAAMA (from 1980 to 1991) and the chairperson of Imparja for the first three years of its existence. She resigned from both organisations in late 1991, as I did, largely as a result of internal disagreements over the way Imparja was being managed and the general direction in which the station was heading. Ms Glynn is now disillusioned:

> Our original aim was to get some control over the satellite so that we could use it to suit our own purposes.... I remember saying that television was like the second invasion of our country, that it would be just as destructive as alcohol.... We wanted to see a lot of black faces, people speaking our local languages.... We were especially interested in using it for educational purposes.... Maybe this can still happen... but look at Imparja now, it's no different to any other commercial TV station.... In a way, it has become what we tried to stop.[7]

I believe that Imparja represents an example of how government policy towards Aboriginal people, while apparently designed to encourage them to manage their own affairs, has actually worked both to defuse any genuine notions of 'self-determination' and, more distressingly, to deny Aboriginal claims to a separate cultural identity.

On the one hand, the Federal government has a generally stated commitment to the right of Aboriginal people to self-determination, and through the ABT's decision in favour of CAAMA's application recognised the specific need for Aboriginal control over the introduction of satellite television in the area. On the other hand, its rejection of CAAMA's initial arguments for non-profit access to the satellite, combined with its decision to award licences only to commercial TV companies, effectively forced CAAMA/Imparja into the global television

Simon Tjiyanu of EVTV setting up a shot, © *CAAMA*

market-place. The realities of this market-place mean that it costs Imparja about twenty times less to buy top-rating international TV shows than it does to commission their own Aboriginal programming, and the (white) advertisers whose money supports the station are obviously keen to reach the more affluent (again, mainly white) audiences who watch the top-rating shows. In these circumstances it is not difficult to see why CAAMA has been unable to create its own form of television. Instead, Aboriginal people were simply given the right to 'own' a small piece of the established global television pie.

Unfortunately, it must also be pointed out that there were some people within Imparja who were more than willing to allow it to become just another commercial television station in line with government expectations. Indeed, the current management of Imparja has stated that Imparja cannot, in any real sense, be classified as an 'Aboriginal television service'; rather, it is first and foremost a commercial business, with obligations under its licence to serve all viewers. The fact that it is owned exclusively by Aboriginal interests is of no consequence: 'All sorts of people own commercial television stations'.[8]

It might be worth noting that another operation established by CAAMA, the radio broadcasting network 8KIN, has proved to be a success. 8KIN goes on air via satellite over the same area as Imparja and has a devoted following in the footprint's Aboriginal communities. Sixty per cent of its spoken material is in local Aboriginal languages and the station's staff are all Aboriginal. There is no space here to analyse why 8KIN has succeeded and Imparja failed. I mention 8KIN simply to draw attention to the fact that, given the right circumstances, indigenous groups can utilise the relatively sophisticated technology of satellites to their advantage.

Aboriginal people must be in a position to use such new technologies in ways relevant and acceptable to themselves. The Pitjantjatjarra people at Ernabella demonstrated that it is indeed possible for indigenous groups to negotiate successfully, in both a technical and a cultural sense, the introduction of television into their lives. On the other hand, CAAMA's attempt to conduct similar 'negotiations' (on a much larger scale of course) to establish Imparja ultimately failed, largely because their right to develop such a service in ways appropriate to themselves was not properly acknowledged.

It is only in relatively recent times that the industrialised West has come to haunt almost every corner of the globe. Very few people today remain unaware of or free from the influence of the all-pervasive juggernaut of Western culture. It is encouraging, then, that some groups at least have been able to meet this global force head-on, and to produce as a result new and powerful forms of television which are uniquely their own.

NOTES

1. Neil Turner, 'Pitchat and Beyond', *Artlink* (Adelaide), vol. 10 no. 1–2, 1990, p. 44.
2. Ibid., p. 45.
3. Department of Aboriginal Affairs, *Out of the Silent Land* (Canberra: A.G.P.S., 1986).
4. Eric Michaels, *The Aboriginal Invention of Television* (Canberra: A.I.A.T.S.I.S., 1986).
5. Australian Broadcasting Tribunal, *Remote Commercial Television Services Fourth Report Central Region* (Canberra: A.G.P.S., 1986), p. 172.
6. Ibid., p. 181.
7. Personal communication.
8. Ibid.

HONOURING THE TREATY
Indigenous Television in Aotearoa

*Derek Tini Fox**

The debate on indigenous television in Aotearoa (New Zealand) has to begin by considering the position of Maori people in New Zealand society, and how that is reflected in the media; more particularly, by considering how Maori people are represented in the two public broadcasting systems of radio and television in the country now known as New Zealand, since as citizens Maori people are their direct shareholders. By some current estimates Maori make up 25–30 per cent of the total population. However, Maori argue for their stake in the broadcasting system not on the basis of this percentage but by virtue of their being full and equal partners under the Treaty of Waitangi. The Treaty, signed in 1840 between the British Crown and the chiefs of Aotearoa, guaranteed to the Maori people *tino rangatiratanga*, or absolute authority over all their resources; and a large number of Maori communities are currently reclaiming, under the Treaty, land which has been stolen from them over the last 150 years. Like the land, the public broadcasting system is a vital present-day resource, and as such Maori are legally entitled to an equal share of it.

However, the number of Maori or Maori-related programmes on television is less than 1 per cent of the total broadcast time, and the total extent of Maori language heard on New Zealand national radio – which is owned and funded by the state – is under an hour a week. This represents a slight improvement on the situation a quarter of a century ago, when I began working as a journalist and broadcaster.

I grew up in very remote rural areas barely penetrated by any form of mass media. My first language was Maori, and everybody around me

---

* Based on interviews with the New Zealand journalist Mark Derby

spoke Maori most of the time. We had no electricity, so when the sun went down we went to bed and when it rose again we got up. I remember my grandfather coming home from work on the farm at around five o'clock, and my grandmother saying, 'I would like crayfish for tea.' He would climb back on his horse, ride into the surf and bend down and flick a couple of *paua* (abalone) off a rock. Still on his horse, he would mash up the *paua*, put them in a little flax basket and hang it in a rock pool. The crayfish would come out and cling onto it and he would pull the basket out and be home twenty minutes later with dinner.

The nearest town, Gisborne, produced a daily paper but my family never bought it and in any case it would not have arrived until a day or so after it was published. No radio stations reached our area, and it was quite a long time before we got any public services at all.

In these areas Maori people predominated, so to be Maori then was to be what the term 'Maori' actually means, which is simply 'mankind'. All this changed in 1965 when I went away to St Stephens (a Maori boarding school near Auckland) to finish my schooling. After that I went to university and then to work in broadcasting. So for the first five years of my life I spent up to 90 per cent of my time speaking in Maori, but for the next thirty years I spoke Maori only about 5 per cent of the time. My Maori language didn't come back into its own until I helped establish the Maori broadcasting unit within Radio New Zealand, and later the Maori television news programme *Te Karere* for Television New Zealand.

When I first started work in the mid-60s in the then combined public radio and television system, Maori people were rarely seen on television, and then usually as fugitives from the law, described as being 'of part-Maori descent'. The only other occasion Maori might appear on television was when performing traditional song and dance, either to welcome the Queen of England when she arrived on her infrequent visits, or on Waitangi Day, the annual celebration of the signing of the Treaty of Waitangi. There were no television programmes made especially for the Maori population. The Maori language was almost never heard on the airwaves, and the whole spectrum of social and political issues important to Maori people were largely ignored both by radio and TV.

Today, nearly thirty years later, the situation is little changed. There are still no people in the senior management of Radio New Zealand or Television New Zealand who speak or understand Maori. The standard procedure is still to pay little attention to Maori activities except as they impinge on the Pakeha (white) establishment. So crime and land claims get publicity, as do achievers in sport and show business, although the Maori element in the success stories is liable to be played down. Losers may be Maori, but winners are New Zealanders.

The country's first Maori broadcaster was Wiremu Parker, who began regular Maori-language broadcasts on radio during the Second World War. A short space of time was made available on Sunday evenings for Parker to read out the names of the Maori war dead. This short weekly programme was continued after the war and still survives today on national radio. For many years Parker worked as the lone Maori broadcaster, with no support from anybody else in radio. When I began working in the national broadcasting newsroom in the mid-60s, Bill Parker was still there, a lonely figure who came in on Sunday evenings and looked through the box where copies of stories which had any remotely Maori content had been placed. He would sift through the stories, but often ended up simply broadcasting material that he had gathered himself over the course of the week.

In the early 1970s a television documentary series on Maori people was produced, called *Tangata Whenua*. It had a Maori director, Barry Barclay, and for those times it was quite radical in its content. It featured a *tangi* (mourning ceremony) at a *marae* (meeting house – the physical and spiritual focus of every Maori community); this and many similar scenes, which were regular and important parts of life for most Maori, had never properly been seen on television before. The main point about the *Tangata Whenua* series is that it was not made by Television New Zealand but by an independent company. There was simply no will and no vision within the broadcasting system to deal innovatively with Maori programming.

In the mid-70s the first real development in so-called Maori television was a series called *Koha*, which was a studio-based magazine programme on Maori issues. It was about fifteen minutes long, in English, and it went out on Sunday afternoons. Its brief was first to satisfy the general audience and then to address the Maori audience. As the original presenter of *Koha*, I soon found that the way the programme was regarded by the broadcasting authorities was indicative of the grudging, minimalist attitude that bureaucrats in general have towards Maori issues. At the same time as I fronted *Koha*, I worked as a producer for a mainstream current affairs programme called *Eyewitness*, which went out twice a week at peak-time. *Eyewitness* had a big budget which enabled us to travel widely, to commission material inside and outside the country, and to appeal to a large general audience. *Koha* had none of these advantages. It was really a soft, cute window on Maori society through which Pakeha people could peer. It had an 'ethnic' set with some tasteful pieces of artwork, and its producer was not a journalist but had a background in theatre. A typical episode might include an interview with a traditional weaver, or with a Maori author. I spent a couple of seasons with it as the presenter and then went back to the mainstream to produce current affairs programmes, although *Koha* continued for several years. The low-cost approach to Maori programming set at that time is maintained in broadcasting to this day.

The next development in Maori-related television didn't occur until the early 80s. It happened almost by accident, at the time of Maori Language Week, which as far as television was concerned did not usually mean anything. The continuity announcers might start the evening by saying '*kia ora*', the Maori greeting, but there was no other Maori language heard over the air. It always seemed peculiarly appropriate to me that Maori Language Week took place between Conservation Week and Hiroshima Day. But in 1982 the editor of news and current affairs for television asked me if I could spend the following week, Maori Language Week, presenting a two-minute news programme in Maori. His view was that I should simply present a two-minute translation of whatever else had been gathered that day. But I made up my mind that I would provide, as opposed to two minutes of news in Maori, two minutes of Maori news. I made this choice because there are significantly different perspectives on what the two peoples see as important. In an English-language news programme a Maori might be captioned as the chairperson of the New Zealand Maori Council. In the Maori programme that person is as likely to be captioned with his tribal affiliation. When giving a background on somebody, Maori people will always refer to them as being *Ngati Awa* or *Ngati Porou* or whatever their tribe is, or mention that they come from a certain *rohe* (tribal district), even if they don't live there any more. These things are important, because Maori people need to know someone's tribal affiliation in order to properly consider what they are saying in public.

So, instead of just translating and reading the news, I decided to chase stories and present a bulletin, and for a week I begged and borrowed camera crews. In that very brief time-slot I managed to cover a number of important Maori events around the country, like the opening of a new *marae* or the registration of Maori language students. This meant the bulletin often exceeded its allotted two minutes. I kept claiming extra time, and the programme ended up being about seven minutes long. It was presented from a continuity studio which had only one camera. I followed a Pakeha newsreader who gave a headline bulletin in English, and significantly, while I was waiting my turn in front of the camera, I had to sit on the floor at his feet. When he finished there was a very short tape-recorded weather report, giving me ten seconds to take his place and gain some sort of composure before reading the news.

Simply because it was entirely in the Maori language, that little week-long news bulletin caused quite a stir, and the Maori people who managed to see it asked publicly why it could not continue on a regular basis. Television New Zealand was not keen on this and, as often happens in these situations, it was not the system but an outside individual who happened to effect change. In this case it was the then Minister of Broadcasting, Ian Shearer, who told me privately that he would take up the cudgels on behalf of a regular Maori news broadcast. By the beginning of 1983 I was fronting a new programme I called *Te Karere*, which means 'the messenger'.

Te Karere differed from *Koha* in that it was entirely in Maori. It was only four minutes long, and this time there was no possibility of going over the allotted time. It went out just before 6 in the evening, Monday to Friday, and had to be over by exactly 6 o'clock. It had a staff of just two – myself and a Maori-speaking journalist named Whai Ngata. We continued to struggle with the back-of-the-bus treatment accorded to all Maori programmes. *Te Karere* was the first network programme to air each night, and should, in theory, have had priority for camera crews and other production resources. Yet the main English-language news programme, which went on air half an hour later, would always try to pull rank. My colleague and I developed devious strategies to overcome these limitations.

The day before a shoot, we would book the first available ENG (video) crew. This meant writing the name of the story to be shot on a booking sheet, but quite often we had not decided on a story by that time, so we would write down a word like *hoiho*. *Hoiho* simply means 'horse', but such was the ignorance of the Maori language within television that none of the other staff knew this. Then, after presenting that day's programme, I would plan with Whai Ngata our stories for the following day. Next morning the crew would shoot a story which had nothing to do with horses at all.

Often we would go to an event and deliberately interview a Pakeha who could speak Maori. There are very few such people in New

130

Zealand, but we would find members of a religious order, or elderly individuals, who had learned to speak our language and we would interview them in Maori. The point was to show our Pakeha viewers that this person was not going to die because he or she was speaking Maori, and nor would our viewers die from listening to it.

The key story in the programme's first year swayed the whole nation. It was to do with the Motunui synthetic fuels plant, a multi-million dollar project by the petrochemical industry on the west coast of the North Island. It was decided that the plant's waste products would be disposed of through an outfall directly into the sea. A group of Te Ati Awa people living at Motunui opposed this idea because they gathered shellfish (and have done for over a thousand years) from a small reef onto which the petrochemical waste was to be discharged. These local people exhausted every possible avenue of objection open to them without success, until their only remaining course of action was to take a claim for traditional fishing rights to the Waitangi Tribunal, the judicial body recently established to advise on traditional Maori claims under the terms of the Treaty. The Tribunal does not have the power to intervene directly but only to recommend to government, and in the case of the Motunui claim it recommended that the waste outfall should not proceed. However, the Prime Minister of the day, Robert Muldoon, rejected the Tribunal's decision and little notice was taken of the issue except that *Te Karere* ran the story. Over a period of a week we reported that the people of Te Ati Awa, led by a worker named Aila Taylor, objected to the waste disposal plan. We ran pictures of the reef where these people gathered their shellfish. We showed the Tribunal meeting giving its decision, and the Prime Minister rejecting it.

Throughout this time *Te Karere* did not have a budget to travel to Taranaki. Instead we commissioned a local Pakeha cameraman, who couldn't speak Maori, to take pictures of the reef at low water while the people were gathering seafood. We arranged for this stringer to ask questions in English of Aila Taylor, who would answer in Maori since he was fluent in both languages. Then this material was flown to Auckland where the English questions were dubbed into Maori for broadcast.

At the same time, the British Queen was about to visit New Zealand. One by one Te Ati Awa and other Maori tribes joined in a revolt against welcoming her while her New Zealand government continued to treat Maori people in this way. Eventually the government gave in and the recommendations of the Waitangi Tribunal were carried out. I don't believe that would have happened as rapidly as it did without those nightly four minutes of Maori news.

As the only regular vehicle for the Maori language on television, *Te Karere* faced a barrage of requests for subtitles. These came from people who held to a principle that New Zealand was basically an English-speaking country, and so everything on television should be under-standable to them. We were called separatists and racists for broadcasting in a language which Pakeha people couldn't understand. This argument was simple to parry because the subtitling technology available at that time was not adequate to the task the public were demanding of it. Sometimes we were still editing a news item less than two hours before it went on air, and there was no time for subtitling. But the demand for subtitles, and for written translations of our nightly broadcasts, continued both inside and outside television. I pointed out the irony to my superiors: resources could not be found to make *Te Karere* a bigger and better programme but they might be willing to com-mit more resources to subtitling. And why demand English subtitles on *Te Karere* but never consider providing Maori subtitles on the main net-work news?

The programme's success contributed to this debate because we were showing images not seen anywhere else on television. We occasionally shot material in the Pacific Islands, and these images were novel and tremendously powerful. The conventional media were not interested in covering events like the South Pacific Festival of Arts in Tahiti, but we went up there and showed the various Pacific peoples performing and making art works, and you could almost feel the sultriness of the occa-sion in the pictures. Pakeha people at home could see something excit-ing going on but they didn't understand the words and were highly frustrated. I would try to steer the debate in a different direction and say, 'If these events are so important, why aren't they being covered in the half hour of English-language news?' Today *Te Karere* continues to be screened, five nights a week, but it is still just ten minutes long. It shuts down altogether at Christmas, and when its time-slot conflicts with coverage of World Cup cricket it is cancelled or transmitted in the lunch break.

As a daily dose of fluent, accurate Maori, *Te Karere* has always made a priceless contribution simply towards preserving the Maori language. In the last twenty years our language has been brought to the very brink of extinction, more than anything else by the influence of monolingual broadcasting. Today only a small minority of Maori, mainly the elderly,

132

can speak their native tongue with fluency, and most cannot understand it at all. I am one of the lucky ones since I grew up with my grandparents speaking Maori as my first language, and even after thirty-five years working in a foreign and occasionally hostile environment I am still comfortable in that language. So it is difficult for me to realise how it might be lost. Yet all the available statistics show that, year by year, the number of fluent Maori speakers is declining. There may already be insufficient teachers or fluent Maori speakers to ensure the survival of the language in a healthy state. It is likely to survive in academic circles and in small pockets of the country, but not as a living, changing national language with the same status as English.

So broadcasting has an enormous responsibility in the recovery of a language it has helped to push towards extinction. In Aotearoa it is clearly failing to meet this responsibility. Maori have argued in court, with some success, that the Maori language is one of the *taonga*, or ancestral treasures, which in 1840 the Waitangi Treaty guaranteed to the Maori people in perpetuity. For Maori people the Treaty is like owning half of a treasure map. We are clinging to our half even though it is practically worthless on its own, and hope that the Treaty is going to be honoured so that we will find the other piece and everyone can end up with the treasure. In broadcasting terms the Treaty of Waitangi did not really come into prominence until 1988 when the government moved to corporatise its broadcasting services. The existing legislation required the public broadcasting system to reflect, in very general terms, the culture of the country and should therefore have required it to include a higher Maori content. However, the legislation specifically forbade the use of the judicial process to rectify the situation, and the broadcasting authorities paid scant attention to the lack of Maori coverage. It was not until the last Labour government created the state-owned enterprise Radio New Zealand Ltd and Television New Zealand Ltd, and prepared to hand back all its broadcasting assets to these new enterprises, that we were provided with an opportunity to press the claim for more Maori on air.

A clause in the new State-Owned Enterprises Act required the government to pay heed to the Treaty. I was part of a group of people, the NZ Maori Council and *Nga Kaiwhakapumau i te Reo* (guardians of the language), who took out an injunction restraining the Crown from handing over its broadcasting assets until provision was made to ensure adequate time and resources for Maori broadcasting. We went to the Waitangi Tribunal and championed the case for the Maori language being a *taonga*, a treasure, and therefore, under the terms of the Treaty, something the Crown had a duty to protect and guarantee. The Tribunal found in our favour, but the case is still proceeding because the government has so far refused to accept its decision. It has been before the courts for three years now and has been fought all the way to the highest court in the land, the Court of Appeal. The Maori claimants are currently considering taking the case to the Privy Council in London which, strange though it sounds, is the final legal remedy under New Zealand domestic law. As claimants, we do not actually want to go to the Privy Council because this would be extremely costly and the legal battle has already cost hundreds of thousands of dollars which we cannot afford. We would rather go to the United Nations and have the world community scrutinise the deficiency of the New Zealand government in this area, but before matters like that can be taken to the UN all domestic remedies must be exhausted, and the one remaining 'domestic' remedy is the Privy Council.

While this legal tussle has been going on, disaffection with the mainstream media has recently been translated into a rapid and spectacular development in Maori tribal radio. In the past three years about twenty small regional stations have started broadcasting. The appeal of radio may be in part because Maori society is an aural society and places high value on people being able to speak out and win or lose the day on the merit of their words alone. Radio is also an economical medium because it requires only a microphone and a transmitter to reach a large number of people. However, the critical shortage of skilled Maori radio journalists and broadcast technicians makes these tribal stations a terribly under-used asset.

The rapid growth of tribal radio has fuelled an idea that there should also be tribal television stations. Already several groups are proposing to establish their own stations, and at least one has made a trial broadcast this year (1992). Tribally-based Maori TV is favoured in particular by tribes who are relatively strong and confident, and who want to retain control of all the resources within their *rohe*, or tribal boundary. Elements of the Tainui people, for instance (based along the Waikato River in central North Island), want to establish several small tribal stations.

I do not altogether support the idea that tribal television can develop in a similar way to radio, because the economic natures of these media are so different. I have no difficulty with Tainui people making Tainui programmes, but I think they are selling themselves short. A radio station can be set up for NZ$100,000, but television stations cost many millions of dollars and that sort of funding is unlikely ever to be delivered to tribal groups. The promise of tribal TV seems to be another minimalist ploy, fuelled by bureaucrats who are really looking for low-cost, low-grade, unexciting programming. Children are not likely to watch such a station, nor is it likely to capture a wider audience.

I believe that instead there has to be a national Maori television station, which would cost around NZ$300 million to set up. This could satisfy tribal aspirations by buying programmes from tribal production centres for screening on the national network. Tribal regions could also break out of the network at certain times to cover localised issues and events in their local dialects. That way Tainui people could, if they choose, produce their own programmes either as an independent production company or as a regional station using the British commercial network model. In either case their programmes would be reaching the widest possible audience, so that all Maori people, in fact all New Zealanders, would at least have the chance to see them. Programming for this network should give priority to language programmes for children, including animated cartoons in Maori. We should also look at making bilingual comedy, and major documentary series on our traditional and contemporary arts. All our history can be found in the carvings, the weaving and the painting of the great Maori meeting houses of Aotearoa, yet they have never been seen in any detail on television.

The current reality is that television does not take the broadcasting needs of Maori people into account. We have a few 'official' Maori inside the mainstream system and they produce some very limited programmes. There is now a Maori department within Television New Zealand, but the programmes it makes, by no means all of them presented in the Maori language, are mainly restricted to a 'ghetto' slot of two hours on Sunday mornings. They tend to rely on studio-based talk which is cheap, or they are archival programmes, consisting of lengthy interviews with old people. Programmes like this are usually little more than a quaint window on Maori society. What is missing are debates on the real issues of today. One quarter of all adult Maori are not registered on any electoral roll and 45 per cent of the Maori workforce is out of work. There are still no Maori current affairs programmes, nor programmes designed to strengthen the language which is rapidly being lost.

This is why my two partners and I set up Mana Maori Media Ltd in 1989 as a professional news-making organisation. We could see no sign of the mainstream media developing the capacity or the will to provide professional coverage of Maori news. Most of us now working for *Mana News* have worked at different times within the mainstream radio and television system, but we were quite unable to make the sorts of programme we wanted. Eventually the only option we could see was to step outside the system and to have editorial control of what we produced. Although Mana Maori Media has made and contributed to a number of television programmes, our main function so far has been to supply regular news, current affairs, sports and other programmes to the network of twenty tribal radio stations around the country. So far Mana Maori Media's broadcasts have been restricted to 22 minutes, five nights a week on national radio, and to a total of less than 90 minutes on the tribal radio network. But we have an audience, and our airtime is likely to expand significantly. We are now moving into print with a national news magazine and into television as well.

Mana Maori Media concentrates on stories of significance and interest to the Maori communities, seeking the Maori element in events throughout New Zealand society and focusing attention, when merited, on Maori achievers and achievements. In our news broadcasts we tend to select stories that are of particular interest to the people listening to the tribal stations, but we also cover major national news stories from a distinctively Maori perspective. Pakeha journalists are generally not aware that in their work they are drawing on their own cultural perspective, since they assume it is universal; we have shown that there are at least two differing perspectives in this country. This process is already empowering Maori organisations because they now have a much greater understanding of what is going on around the country. And we are helping to break down the ignorance and the resistance of some of the Pakeha power brokers.

One of our early aims was to move out of the ghetto and to affect the mainstream, so our first task was to argue with Radio New Zealand that we should also provide programmes for them. The *Mana News* programme which we now present on radio each night is preceded by a half-hour current affairs programme produced by Radio New Zealand called *Checkpoint*. The *Checkpoint* people themselves have noted how the two programmes can often deal with exactly the same news item but end up with two entirely different stories. An example of this is how the current energy crisis in New Zealand has been covered. The hydro lakes from which we draw the majority of our electricity are all at a critically low level. The story is currently being worked hard in all media, with countdowns on how many days' water is left in the lakes before electricity blackouts become necessary. On one night *Mana News* led with that story but referred to the spiritual values of those hydro lakes to the Ngai Tahu people, who have lived on the shores of the lakes for a thousand or more years and can see them being destroyed to supply electricity to homes and factories in Auckland. So our coverage of the power crisis was very different from the *Checkpoint* story half an hour earlier.

Mana News also looks at international events from a Maori perspective. We do not restrict ourselves to the coastline of Aotearoa. We had Maori correspondents at the Earth Summit in Rio in 1992, who quickly identified similarities between their perspective on certain issues and the perspectives of other indigenous groups. In this way we provided a point of view excluded from New Zealand for the last 150 years.

Relationships between Pakeha and Maori have suffered greatly because the Maori dimension has been missing from our media for so long. The redneck element in New Zealand attempts to create division by saying that Maori people are seeking privileges under the Treaty of Waitangi which are racially based. In fact these claims are not based on race, but on prior occupancy. It was recognised many times in the last century by the British Parliament that the Crown had to treat the Maori people equally since the Maori held *tino rangatiratanga*. This principle, which the colonial authorities ignored and transgressed as soon as they had the power to do so, is again being implemented in a number of areas. For instance, there are currently several hundred land claims from tribes in all parts of the country. However, lack of proper information through the media about the historical roots of claims under the Treaty is feeding a wave of anti-Maori sentiment.

Television in particular is a long way from catching up with the realities of Maori life and how it impacts on the wider New Zealand society, which is why I see the need for a national, adequately resourced Maori TV station as a matter of urgency. Even before this happens, I hope to see established a Maori Media Authority which can ensure wide input and set appropriate priorities, because the funding is certain to be difficult to find. We are starting to build a national Maori media system, which should have a substantial impact on New Zealanders over the next few years. They will be receiving information they have not been hearing elsewhere in the media, and we will have a growing capacity to tell the full New Zealand story to an international public.

PALESTINIAN DIARIES
Grass Roots TV Production in the Occupied Territories

Daoud Kuttab

Although Palestinians in the occupied territories have no television stations of their own, they probably watch more television during the
evenings than most people in other countries. The political situation in
the West Bank and Gaza and the frequent night curfews mean that
people are fearful of going outdoors, so the incidence of television viewing is very high. Israel has had a government-controlled station for the
past forty years and a second channel has been established recently.
There is a move to install cable TV throughout most of the major cities,
although it will not be available to Palestinians.

Palestinians mainly watch Jordanian or Israeli TV, but homes in
northern Palestine can also receive Syrian and Lebanese TV while those
in the south receive TV broadcast from Egypt. Most programmes available to Palestinians originally made in Arabic are Egyptian films or soap
operas. These are commercially produced, cheap imitations of American
TV shows like *Dallas* and *Dynasty* and deal mainly with the lives of rich
Egyptians who live in beautiful villas with servants, phones and luxuri-
ous trappings – things which neither Palestinians nor other Arabs in the
area have experienced. The second TV channels in Jordan, Syria,
Lebanon and Israel are usually used to carry foreign programmes, old
Hollywood movies, TV sitcoms, Western music and major international
sporting events.

Few alternative programmes dealing with the problems people actually experience ever make it to these TV screens. Jordanian and Syrian
television stations recently broadcast a number of plays by Dureed
Laham, a popular Syrian comedian whose work is critical of existing
Arab regimes. TV documentaries about the Israeli occupation made by

foreign crews are often shown on patriotic anniversaries. Some progress has been made in children's programming, although most of the animation is Western and then translated or Arabised. TV news in Arabic on both Israeli and neighbouring Arab stations is closely controlled government propaganda, even though some signs of democratisation have appeared on Jordanian TV.

For the past forty years the state of Israel has basked in generally favourable international press and TV coverage which until recently has largely excluded mention of Palestinians even though Israel has been occupying Palestinian territory since 1967. However, in December 1987 Palestinians in the occupied West Bank and the Gaza Strip rose up in protest against the continued Israeli military occupation of their land. The *intifada*, as it is called in Arabic, is a largely non-violent protest movement with self-reliance as one of its basic tenets. Palestinians boycotted Israeli products and encouraged the purchase of their own products and services. Nightly television coverage of the Palestinian protests had long-lasting effects on viewers around the world.

Footage usually showed Palestinians equipped only with stones challenging Israeli soldiers carrying machine-guns and other arms. Television provided Palestinians with a valuable opportunity to show the world how they are not terrorists but are terrorised. The tenacity and size of these demonstrations demolished the Israeli-propagated myth of Palestinians enjoying the 'benefits' of Israeli occupation and having no desire for change in the status quo. TV coverage of the *intifada* changed many people's impressions of Israel and of Palestinians: the brutality of the army and its lack of restraint shifted the world opinion of Israel as a democratic, peace-loving country surrounded by powerful enemies, to one of a powerful military state uninterested in peaceful negotiations.

The ugly Palestinian terrorist of the 1970s was now being replaced with the heroic Palestinian youth challenging the Israeli Goliath with a stone, but TV viewers were rarely introduced to Palestinians who were neither masked stone-throwers nor professional politicians. People in the latter category, especially Hana Ashrawi, did leave important impressions, but ordinary Palestinians were still not getting their voices heard. Television coverage of the *intifada* was neither informed nor comprehensive. By and large television producers and reporters who knew little about the situation would spend a few days in the area, at best a week or so, and then leave with a story as though they were experts on the Middle East. Most disturbing for Palestinians was the predictable requirement of television producers for dramatic and violent pictures around which their stories could be framed.

Although Western TV producers were often well-meaning, their attitudes troubled many Palestinians and especially those involved in journalism. What heaped insult upon injury was that all the camera crews filming for these producers were Israelis, most of whom had to serve in the Israeli army. So it was possible for an Israeli to shoot Palestinian youth with a Beta camera one week and then in an army uniform shoot at them with M-16 guns the next. In fact Israeli camera crews operated for the most part very professionally, but there were a few incidents of improper conduct. A CNN crew provoked anger and mistrust when at the beginning of the *intifada* it agreed to hand over to the Israeli army a copy of a video showing Palestinians stoning the home of a collaborator who had just shot and killed a 4-year-old Palestinian girl. Palestinians then started to think of how to deal with a situation in which they needed to get pictures of the *intifada* out in ways which would not compromise their community.

The occupied territories were dangerous for journalists (especially after the Israeli intelligence service used press decoys), and TV crews and reporters began to insist on having a Palestinian fixer to accompany them to the more troublesome areas. As the conditions for journalists working freely in the occupied territories became more difficult, the role of Palestinians who actually lived there became more vital for the networks dependent on them for their daily coverage. This development had two very important consequences: it introduced many Palestinians to the workings of television, and it made them realise that the job was not so difficult that they could not do it themselves.

Naturally, after a while, ambitious Palestinians were no longer satisfied working as guides and fixers and a number of them started thinking of how to make television economically possible in a politically vital struggle. One of the first problems they faced was the lack of training and equipment, and then there was censorship as the *intifada* continued to provide TV pictures tarnishing Israel's image and the authorities started to look for new ways of stopping 'negative' coverage. Several means were used to curtail press coverage in general and TV coverage in particular. The most frequent method was simply to prohibit journalists from entering certain areas and even cities in which confrontations were taking place. According to the Israeli authorities, if the cameras hadn't caught it then it simply hadn't happened. This prohibition was less successful with print than with TV journalists and photographers whose cameras and recording equipment made them more visible to the soldiers carrying out the restriction orders.

Making Palestinian Diaries

With these restrictions in the occupied territories and no indigenous television production, a formula had to be devised which would provide video footage from behind the barricades that was different, that would not simply add to the libraries full of tapes made in the same superficial ways. To produce such a testimony, it was clear that one could not be bound by a short time-frame. It was also crucial that the daily lives of Palestinians living in the West Bank and the Gaza Strip should be reflected as they themselves saw them. Ways had to be found of equipping Palestinians with the tools to express themselves. Big video cameras were out. They would not only be too visible to the Israelis, they would also make the local community so conscious of being recorded that their spontaneity and informality would be inhibited.

With help from Ilan Ziv of Icarus/Tamouz Media in New York, our company, Al Quds Television Productions (ATP), designed a project which would both act as an educational tool and provide a unique film which would break new ground in presenting what was happening in our lives. We had met Ilan months earlier, when he was preparing a film called *People Power* and wanted to film in the West Bank to show what might happen when the PLO planned to announce the establishment of the state of Palestine on 15 November 1988. Ilan had needed a sound man and some contacts, and we had sent him to the town of Beit Sahour near Bethlehem a day before so that he managed to bypass the tight news blackout we had expected the Israelis to enforce. Ilan had succeeded in capturing the enthusiasm of the Palestinians he had worked with.

Before actually launching the film project we had to select people who had at least some basic understanding of and interest in video. To this end, ATP arranged an intensive three-week video training course. We were quite selective in choosing students. We wanted them to represent a diversity of backgrounds in terms of their training, gender and place of residence. This last consideration was especially important because we wanted to show different areas of the occupied territories, the further away from Jerusalem the better. It is these more distant locations which rarely get attention from the international media and which therefore suffer most cases of violations of human rights. Since the Israeli army often closes these areas to the press, and especially to tele-

141

vision, the presence of a Palestinian camera-person is a major advantage.

Eighteen Palestinians attended the course, given by a professional cameraman who worked with the French network TF1. During three weeks it became evident which of the students had both creative and technical potential. The project had originally been budgeted to keep three Palestinians filming on good salaries for six months, but we had four students keen on the project who showed special abilities and potential. By reducing the individual salaries we were able to take four film-makers on board.

As for equipment, there was quite a bit of discussion and toying around with different models. We finally agreed that Super-VHS cameras would be the most suitable and obtained four JVC compact cassette cameras – three were bought and one was borrowed from IKON Holland, who had agreed to participate in the project. At first we had to have the compact cassettes shipped out from the US because the cost (including the shipping) was less than half the purchase price of the tapes in Israel, but later we were able to find a wholesaler who sold the cassettes to us at a very competitive price. We encountered a few problems with this equipment, notably poor sound quality. To overcome this, we purchased directional microphones which we could attach to the camera and which produced a much better sound track.

Before filming began, we spent a few days giving the students intensive training on the cameras with the help of Peter Chappell, a veteran British film-maker. Where the earlier course had concentrated on filming techniques, Peter Chappell spent most of his time talking about the philosophy of film-making and showing a number of films, which were then discussed. Each film-maker was also asked to shoot a sequence with their new camera; then everyone would watch what they had shot and discuss it. Later, visits were made to each film-maker's community and we had a general discussion about what they should look out for. Again, they were asked to film on site, and we discussed the results. During the six months they were filming all four Palestinians would meet in Jerusalem to present their tapes and, along with staff from ATP, discuss both the quality and the content of what had been recorded. Suggestions were made as to which stories could be followed up, and good material was praised.

A number of challenges and unexpected problems occurred during the filming. Suheir Ismael was our only woman film-maker. She lives in the West Bank farming village of Khader and was planning to marry a

Suheir Ismael filming her aunt in Rafal, photo by Issam Dieh

young man from a refugee camp. We expected her diary to begin with their engagement and end with the wedding six months later. Her engagement was filmed, but soon afterwards her fiancé was arrested and placed under administrative detention for a year. Since family visits were not allowed we could do very little with this aspect of the story except mention it, so the main characters in this film had to be changed. Suheir's father, a member of the PLO, had been killed in the Lebanon in 1976, and her only brother died during the first year of the *intifada*. So her diary concentrates on her mother, on fighting family tragedy and social convention by depending on herself for economic survival and on her aunt, a resilient woman who had spent her life working in the family vines.

We also had to make changes in Nablus. We had intended that the diary should be centred on a local *kenaffa* sweet shop in the old city, since it is a location where a lot goes on and we thought this would be a good way of reflecting the daily clashes. However, there were problems. Many of the Palestinian youths were afraid of being identified on film; but Nazeh Darwase, our film-maker, was their neighbour, and by spending a lot of time with them he won their special trust, which meant he could record what no one else had been allowed or able to do.

143

Another problem Nazeh faced was the curfews, which meant he was stuck at home for long periods. This turned out, however, to be important for the film. Using the scene from his window as a recurring shot, we were able to capture a sense of what the curfew is really like: soldiers running from house to house; times when there are only cats on the streets; Palestinian activists running away from soldiers, hanging flags or scribbling graffiti; finally, people bored with being cooped up in their homes for days without reprieve.

As time went on we discovered that some of the best, but flawed, footage could never be shot again. The background sound of a radio during a unique and moving interview could never be removed. Problems with the lighting or filming of a special scene often meant that we had to choose whether to concede on quality or content during the edit.

Editing took place in New York during the summer of 1991. Our budget allowed us to take two of the film-makers and the executive producer to New York for a month, but as it turned out one of our film-makers (Abdel Salam Shehadeh, from Rafah in the Gaza Strip) was able to stay until the rough cut was finished, which took about four months of intensive editing. The biggest problem of course was deciding how to reduce the work of four film-makers over six months to 55 minutes. In the end we had to make a tough decision and cut out the entire contribution from the film-maker in Jerusalem. There just wasn't enough of a diary there to warrant having to cut material from the other film-makers' work, and we felt that while many people around the world might know about Jerusalem, they would have little or no idea of what was happening in other parts of the occupied territories.

Palestinian Diaries has been shown on Swedish TV (twice), on Holland's IKON TV and on Britain's Channel Four (in May 1992). It was the premier film at the Palestinian Film Week held in Arab East Jerusalem in June 1992. It has also been shown in Nazareth and a number of West Bank cities, and video copies have been on sale since the Film Week. The Israeli Cinémathèque based in West Jerusalem will show it as part of a special two-day exhibition of Palestinian films, and it will be offered to neighbouring Jordanian, Syrian and Lebanese TV. It is highly unlikely that Israeli TV will be interested.

Responses to *Palestinian Diaries* have been largely favourable. Western audiences have used terms like 'intimate', 'refreshing', 'unique' when referring to the programme. Some Palestinian audiences have objected to scenes which do not show Palestinians as they would like them to be seen. To a great extent this is due to the intensity of the conflict and to the feeling that any medium, especially film, must be used to present what they consider to be the 'bright side' of the Palestinian cause.

Some Palestinian film-makers living abroad have been critical of the technical quality of the *Diaries*. But these have been minority responses, and most Arab audiences have appreciated the programme and considered it to be a truthful representation of Palestinian life under occupation. In particular, Palestinians living in the occupied territories have commented that for the first time they have seen the pain of their everyday lives on the screen – thanks to S-VHS cameras and community-based production techniques.

TELEVISION FOR DEVELOPMENT IN UGANDA

Su Braden

Somewhere 30,000 feet over Africa, watching an in-flight television news service on the cabin screens, I began to feel that my mission was not much less pious than the ones earlier evangelists had made to the 'dark continent'. No accident perhaps that cut-price trips to Africa are still called 'missionary flights' by the bucket shop agencies. Being sent to Uganda to help local TV-makers produce programmes about the protection of the environment in their own country, where 90 per cent of the population are still communicating, and communicated to, by word of mouth alone, seemed on the face of it relatively close to old-fashioned idealism. The journey, or perhaps the task, began to appear like a post-modernist version of the Livingstone fervour: the urge to bring cultural change to television itself. How would my arrival be viewed by the Ugandan television makers I was being sent to work with? And still the missionaries come ...

Another moment. In the taxi from the overnight hotel in central Nairobi, along the highway to the airport, talking with the driver about the growth of the city over the last ten years. He said proudly, 'Kenya is a developing country.' I flashed back to my mental imagery of Africa as taught me on the big screen: *Born Free*, *Out of Africa* and countless documentaries of exotic people and beasts and open spaces – the very world that had followed the news on the in-flight video, a publicity programme for tourism in Africa, I had seen just five hours earlier. The highway looked much like the *banlieue* of Bordeaux or the outskirts of Southampton. The prefab factory buildings, the petrol station advertising boardings, were all developing well, in the inevitable heritage of post-colonialism care of the IMF. One message for the worldwide filmgoing public, another for the natives?

146

The route to my employment on this project was punctuated by acronyms. I would be working on a two-month production consultancy with Uganda Television (UTV), employed by Television Trust for the Environment (TVE). They and their partners in the project, the World Conservation Union (IUCN), had planned a series of short TV documentaries on Uganda's wetlands as part of the National Wetlands Conservation and Management Programme, in which it is currently engaged with the Ministry of Energy, Minerals and Environment Protection.

IUCN had produced a business-like and confident brief with all the expected headings: aims and objectives, 'to sensitise UTV viewers, some of whom are in a position to directly influence the utilisation of wetlands [in] the ways in which they can be used wisely.' The brief added: 'In addition to being broadcast on national television, videos of the programmes will be used in training seminars, as part of the National Wetlands Programme's awareness-raising activities over the next three years.' These were the aims of an highly motivated organisation, dedicated to the education of governments and populations in the protection of their environment. They were clear about their strategy: a two-pronged educational attack on those in authority through the broadcast system in a country where television sets are principally owned by the wealthy; and on the educators, rural extension workers in forestry, agriculture and the environment, through seminars and workshops. The message would be taken by the broadcast programmes to the top people, and through the non-broadcast tapes to be shown at seminars the story would be relayed by the rural extension workers to the farmers and agriculturalists. The communication process, in line with the BBC Reithian heritage, was seen as essentially 'top down', imparting scientific fact in a digestible form.

IUCN, ahead of many other organisations concerned to intervene with pedagogical, social or economic messages in the developing world, were taking the initiative by using television as a means of reaching a broader spectrum of society. The messages were intended to bring about mass mobilisation for the protection and sustainable use of Uganda's swamps – the wetlands.

It was in the light of this aspect of IUCN's approach that I was interested by the second part of the consultancy brief, where TVE's contribution to the project and the training role of the consultant were described:

The programmes will be produced by Ugandan Television.... TVE will provide a production consultant and video equipment to ensure that the programmes are produced to an international standard.... By ensuring that the programmes are produced primarily by local film-makers, this project will produce programmes that will more closely meet the needs of an East African audience. In the longer term it will help to build up the ability of the film-makers in Uganda to produce their own programmes on environment and development issues.

This part of the brief interested me because it promised to throw up some crucial contradictions. I had a feeling that the discourses of the Reithian tradition were destined to collide with the discourses of contemporary development practice, especially as it seemed that TVE wanted, through the training process, to address Africans' representation of development issues in their own terms.

Paulo Freire's work in adult literacy (*Pedagogy of the Oppressed*, 1972; *Letters from Guinea Bissau*, 1978) seemed particularly relevant to the question of whose story is represented in any form of communication. He uses important key words such as 'cultural invasion' and, in contrast, the 'empowerment' of the 'oppressed' through what he calls a 'dialogical' process of pedagogy: the use of a two-way debate between teacher and pupil, or in current development theory 'participation'. In short, Freire pointed out that even books designed to teach the illiterate to read contained more about colonialist literacy and culture than about village cultivators. Freire's solution was to encourage those who wished to learn to read to choose the words they use in everyday life to read from – in effect, to write their own primers.

It was Freire who was behind this sense of contradiction I felt at the prospect of sending out top-down, Western-inspired messages about 'their' environment to people who probably have as much experience of it, albeit less accessibly documented, than any of the scientists sitting in Western or for that matter African universities. The question in my mind was how to enable local people to document or recognise what they had probably already observed in such a way that they could recount their own observations and so become conscious of their own knowledge, as well as imparting it to the authorities. I had no doubt that the scientists had a contribution to make, but wondered whether telling the story of the need to conserve Uganda's wetlands as though it were the scientist's story would encourage local farmers to see the protection and sustainable use of their swamps as their own narrative.

While I recognised that the authorities would need to be convinced that single cash cropping on drained wetlands was not the solution to Uganda's dire economic problems but was more likely to lead to aridity and drought, I suspected that on the ground the most important people to involve were those who, scattered throughout Uganda, lived and worked around the 10 per cent of the landmass known as 'swamps'. These wetlands provide a constant and clean water supply, a habitat for birds, fish and other small animals, and a sustainable source of materials used for thatching, basket- and mat-making, as well as a potential for the development of domestic fuel from papyrus stalks. There is evidence that the swamps are responsible for the maintenance of the water table and that, once drained, the water disappears and the land becomes arid.

Thatching in the wet lands,
photo by Su Braden

There was, of course, another narrative with which I should be concerned; that of the Ugandan TV producers, and the story of institutional television production in Uganda. For the time being I only had my consultant's notes to go on.

Behind the Reithian approach, with its cosy assumptions of consensus and national identity, there is the spectre of the media as simply promoting propaganda. For example, television has been effective in interesting ways in Zaire, the largest country in Africa comprising many different ethnicities, under the ruthless dictatorship of President Mobutu. Mobutu broadcasts regularly to his citizens, acclaiming himself as their 'guide', and television and its reception has long been a government priority alongside the promotion of Zairian nationalism. Despite strong opposition to Mobutu's dictatorship, especially in the remoter areas such as Kivu province in the south, it is significant that the population, from whatever region or ethnic background, no longer identify themselves as they did some twenty years ago by region or ethnicity, but as they are identified on television, as Zairians.

The development agenda, at least in its more intelligent versions, questions nationalisms and addresses populations for whom active participation in national as opposed to local identities is not possible. There are literally thousands of agencies, both government and non-governmental, which use the word 'development' either in their titles (the Foreign Office department of the British government that deals with overseas aid is called the Overseas Development Administration), or in their constitutional aims, as Oxfam and Save the Children do. Such agencies would probably agree that development in their context broadly concerns the processes by which the poor or the powerless can be enabled to help themselves. The desirability for these populations to find a voice, to develop sustainable means of survival rather than become the passive recipients of money and expertise handed out from richer parts of the world, forms the common currency of the term 'development' but leaves open a range of questions in relation to implementation. The degree of operational consultation with the 'poor' must, one supposes, vary with the specific abilities, strategies and priorities of each agency.

From the point of view of many development agencies, though, conventional television is of course anti-developmental. It is top-down and non-consultative. Where is the dialogical, participatory process, the joint appraisal of needs, problems and solutions, the long-term sustainability? How is such a project assessed? How can the cost of TV

150

programme production be evaluated alongside the use of longer-term participatory processes? At the same time television is recognised by some agencies and individuals involved in development communications to be an extraordinary instrument for social mobilisation and unity, which can multiply efforts in the development field and contribute to the establishment of an appropriate system for social information. Furthermore, there is an undeniable popular fascination for this medium. The 350,000 TV sets owned in the small region of Uganda able to receive broadcast signals speak of the high priority given to the reception of television by a people living in conditions of almost universal poverty.

In these circumstances, as Alonso Aznar, Communications Adviser for UNESCO in East Africa, has asked: 'Can it be justified to keep television on the fringe of development strategies?' However, the internal institutional histories of the dominant media have led to a natural resistance on the part of those working for development. How can the poor be helped to help themselves if their voices risk becoming simply represented, some might say distorted, or worse, muffled? How can the traditional institutional forms of TV production be brought into some common relationship with the processes of development? How is it possible for the voices of the poor to enter into a dialogical relationship with the means of representation?

My brief was to 'enhance' methods of TV production through the Uganda Wetlands production training, with all the assumptions inherent in that statement. As it happened, some of my mid-flight concerns about the project seemed to be confirmed when I arrived in Uganda. It emerged that the project itself had still not been satisfactorily negotiated with UTV. I was told that this was the result of changes and reductions in ministries and ministerial appointments which had taken place in the Ugandan government earlier in the summer. The new personnel in the Ministry of the Environment had simply not communicated with the changed personnel in the Ministry of Information.

I decided that this was a problem for Ministry folk and the IUCN representative and that in the meantime I would go to meet the people in Uganda Television with whom I hoped to be working and to whom I had previously spoken on the telephone from London about equipment for the project. I knew already that I was to be a disappointment to them on that score. TVE had failed to raise all the funds we needed for the programmes. With a tight budget for three fifteen-minute programmes, I had not been able to hire an edit suite to bring with me.

151

We'd have to make do with UTV's existing equipment and with the hours normally allocated to UTV producers for editing. I was not too sad – if we were to 'enhance' production it might be more useful to attempt to do so within the existing conditions.

The Ministry of Information and Uganda Television sits on one of the ring of hills which raise the more salubrious areas of the city of Kampala above one of the famous Ugandan wetlands. The Nakasero television mast can be seen from most parts of the town. The station itself is housed in a rambling 1930s hospital building. Its long corridors and barely converted consulting rooms, sluice chambers, wards and operating theatres appeared as an impenetrable maze on that first Monday morning. I eventually found Patrick Mawanda, who was to be cameraman and editor on the wetlands programmes. His workshop was formally a pharmacy store. From here, the main sound and vision lines which led to the transmission mast looped across a small compound and the babble of soundtracks and voices from the station's two principal edit suites could be heard all day and most of the night.

Patrick explained the effect of the misunderstanding between ministries about the status of the project. What had been conceived originally as a series of programmes to be made by Ugandan producers for Uganda Television, with the assistance of a TVE consultant (me) and a small amount of additional technical equipment, was now assumed by the new officials at the Ministry of Information to be a TVE film being made on the cheap at UTV's expense. They were naturally anxious to recoup as much as possible of what was thought to be a considerable European film budget. I was thankful for this clear explanation, while being aware that for the time being Patrick probably reserved judgment about whether UTV's assumption that TVE was trying to rip them off was correct. The Ministry of Information is divided into six directorates, of which Uganda Television is one, Engineering another, and Educational Television (ETV) a third. Each directorate reports to the Minister for Information through the usual civil service bureaucracy. TVE had made the original proposal for the Wetlands programmes through the Directorate of Educational Television. So although some of the damage caused by this misunderstanding was resolved at the following day's meeting, the concept of the co-operative nature of the project was never to be fully understood by people outside the ETV Directorate.

Patrick gave me another piece of bad news. Contrary to what had been understood in London, ETV had no ENG (portable broadcast) cameras and UTV had only four for the entire station. We would find it difficult to get hold of a camera to take off for a three-week shoot. Happily, Patrick resourcefully arranged the loan of a Sony 3000 camera and recorder through his church. By the following day things were looking up. We had production equipment and we had learnt that John Kyamaywa would direct the programmes with Patrick operating camera, and John Bwire, with whom they had both worked previously, seconded from UTV as sound engineer. I was disappointed that the only woman promised as part of the team was not available, but felt confident that the three men represented a good spread of the regional and ethnic backgrounds to be found in Uganda.

We had lost two days of the week set aside for pre-shoot workshops. We now arranged a general workshop, to be attended by as many of the young producers from the ETV directorate as possible, together with IUCN researchers from Makere University, to address the specific problem of the intended audience for the Wetlands videos. It emerged from this that the ETV team felt, much as I had, that there was some contradiction between the scientific top-down agenda proposed by IUCN and the other important aim of the project – reaching local people and influencing the debate about the development of a policy for the sustainable use of wetlands throughout the country.

The fact that local producers were emphasising the need for the programmes to involve local debate, confirming my own earlier doubts, reflects a specific characteristic of the politics of modern-day Uganda. Since the early 1970s, the political history of Uganda has been scarred by civil war, famine and poverty. The present government of Yoweri Museveni, the revolutionary leader who led his rebel army to victory against the Obote regime in 1986, is trying against all odds to redress the social and economic decline. Chronic poverty is the result of both the many years of turmoil and crushing international debt. The Resistance Council Movement represents the strength of the Museveni government (as well as perhaps a potential danger to it) since every Ugandan of whatever former allegiance, from parish level through a system of sub-districts, districts and counties right up to the government itself, has automatic membership.

The ideology behind the Resistance Council Movement is one of participation and collective monitoring and evaluation. The theory is that policies are not developed by the government but are offered to the people as proposals to be debated, reviewed and revised through a nationwide process at all levels of elected Resistance Councils. 'The local people are not stupid – they understand their environment,' said President Museveni in an interview for the Ugandan Wetlands programmes in December 1991.

At the workshop, research students from Makere University working with IUCN told us about the debate currently taking place through the Resistance Council structure about the development of a wetlands policy. They insisted that the people of Uganda should see any policy formed around the wetlands and their use as their own, and suggested that we might film some of these discussions. John Kyamaywa supported this proposal and emphasised the importance of rural people seeing others 'like themselves' debating these issues.

A short recce to eastern Uganda with IUCN's technical adviser appeared to confirm the discrepancies between the scientists' and the communicators' views. The ETV team were anxious that the scientific messages should be put over in a form that would be accessible to Ugandans in rural contexts, and that the programmes should be distributed in non-broadcast form in order to reach local people, who would recognise their own experience in the films. In this way the programmes could enter the debate on the government's proposed policy for the wetlands and might enable a two-way communication between those in power and those currently living in and around the swamps.

By the end of the first weekend, John Kyamaywa and the team had agreed outline shooting scripts for three programmes. We were ready to leave for a week's recording in the east, providing the Ministry of Environment paid the crew their *per diems* for the period before we left. The ETV team, as Ministry of Information civil servants, receive salaries of approximately 7,000 shillings (£4.37p) per month, which feeds a family for not more than two days (a stalk of matoke bananas cost 2,000 shillings in Kampala). As a result it is necessary for everyone to maintain a whole variety of often precarious income-generating activities in addition to their full-time jobs. The *per diems* paid to the crew for the period they were to spend away from home were in fact to be left with their families to ensure that they could survive during that time. In the event, the money was forthcoming and we were able to set off for Mount Elgon on the Kenyan border.

Training on the job proved useful and, I think, user-friendly, as well as a personally informative part of the consultancy. None of the crew had received any substantial formal training in television production. The oldest member, Patrick Mawanda, a polytechnic-trained electrical engineer, had until four years previously worked as an electrician in

Kilembe mines, before becoming a technician in Educational Television (ETV). He had developed camera skills mainly as a result of work with his church. John Kyamaywa had taken part in two short courses during three months in Britain, financed by the British Council, where he had observed the work of Coventry Cable and the BBC's *Gardening World* team, and six weeks in the Netherlands on the Netherlands government TV training course. Owing to the shortages of equipment, transport and production funding at ETV, he had developed little experience of pro- gramme production of the kind in which we were engaged, but like the others spoke several local languages and had a good rapport with local people. John Bwire had recently returned from a six-months sound engineering course in Cairo. He was delighted to use the microphones TVE provided, and only sad that they were not going to be able to keep the boom mike, which was on hire.

We set up a system of review/previews after the day's shooting. We viewed the day's rushes, discussed production problems, and whether we were getting what we needed to tell the story. These talks continued during journeys in the Landrover. Previewing the following day's shoot meant that we were able to improve on teamwork and at the same time take account of the processes of debate we were engendering with local people.

In Kabale, in western Uganda, at the end of a long day we were inter- rupted while taking some shots of a small marsh which had been pre- served by local people in an area where rising temperatures and the lack of morning dew are testament to the dangers of draining swamps. Some members of the RC1 (parish-level Resistance Council) wanted to know what we were up to. We explained that we'd been talking with people here and all over Uganda about the need to preserve swamps. 'What are you going to do with your films?' they asked. 'Well, videocassettes will be brought back to the people, and of course it will be broadcast on Uganda Television,' my colleagues replied. 'That's good. We would like to have them here. We don't have television but someone has a video recorder. We could show your films to the people who are worried about what's happening to our climate.' They pressed us for information about the possibility of restoring swamp to the drained areas and about the benefits and dangers of growing cash crops on swamplands. It was clear from this conversation that far from being ill-informed, these local farmers were already well into the debate. Later, we talked about the mobile projection units parked unused in the UTV compound because no film stock is available for production. It would be necessary to get the distribution of tapes such as ours out to the rural people with some-one informed about the issues to answer questions.

My first impression of the editing 'facility' at UTV was of a tropical prison cell. Two edit suites were placed on adjoining tables, around which producers, editors and numerous observers crowded – people and machines melting in the humid heat, with soundtracks and conver-sations competing in the echoing concrete chamber. By now I was aware that editing time is generally at a premium in UTV, and that problems of access to this centrally managed facility for the Wetlands programmes would be exacerbated by the misunderstandings which had arisen earlier about the status of the productions. Throughout the following four weeks our schedule was erratic, depending on the avail-ability and good will (which grew as time went on) of the technical con-troller and obstructed by the frequent breakdowns of the machines. These breakdowns are inevitable and can be traced to overuse of the machines, the poor conditions of their installation, absence of air-condi-tioning in humid and dusty conditions, and the poverty of the station. The lack of cleaning fluid, for example, meant that the engineers them-selves had to buy petrol to use for cleaning the heads – an alarming dis-covery, made late one night as the picture began to dissolve.

Generally we were allocated time on three afternoons a week and at night. In these conditions our well-established relationships and our ability, in UTV terminology, to 'short wave' especially when 'transnight-ing' (working through the night) proved vital. The editing team was composed of Patrick Mawanda as editor, John Kyamaywa as director, and myself. As neither John nor Patrick were relieved of their daytime responsibilities, they often worked an exhausting twenty-hour day. Night working also meant some risky driving through the town, where gunshots and hi-jack robberies are still a nightly occurrence.

Although the initial misunderstanding about the status of our pro-duction pursued us, it was also apparent that any producer in UTV who is able to insist on an even barely adequate period in which to edit a programme must do so in similar conditions to those under which we worked. We were frequently in the company of a team editing a drama on the neighbouring suite, working similar hours. With a total of thirty-six producers in ETV and UTV, the facilities allow the average producer no more than five hours editing time to produce a half-hour pro-gramme. Without the benefit of Time Code (number coding on the tape allowing shots to be logged and edited accurately), with such limited access to the edit suite, and with the fragility of our tapes under the prevailing technical conditions, it seemed unlikely almost from the beginning that we would have the opportunity of off-lining (making a rough edit) as such. Thus we worked from detailed edit scripts to produce the final edited version in one attempt.

Although the final programmes are by no means finely polished, they do perhaps represent a new departure for Uganda Television in their style, which incorporates an informal countrywide debate into the documentaries. They also represent what is possible within the everyday context of Uganda Television, and this is the training the team said they found useful. Picture framing, close miking, sequencing, pre-production planning and edit scripting had all improved through the process of the production. What I had learnt about life in Uganda TV came from first-hand experience. As a result, the 'if only' factor which inevitably excuses flaws and mistakes, as well as the passive acceptance of poor quality which cannot under the circumstances be improved, were beginning to be deconstructed on both sides. If we cannot get it right under these conditions, how can we change them? Well, not by taking productions abroad, I was sure.

'I suppose you're getting the graphics done in Europe?' I was asked by a UTV producer towards the end of the editing process. 'No, they're being done in your workshop – we're having them painted on papyrus mats.' 'Well, I suppose that's cheaper for you,' he said. 'No, we liked the idea, but if it's cheaper for anyone, it's cheaper for you, they're UTV's programmes.' 'Oh.' Or, at the immigration desk at Entebbe airport on my way out. 'So you've been making films here have you – I suppose you're taking them back with you?' 'No, they were for UTV, they're staying here.' But also, 'It looks like an expat who's leaving,' said the once hostile programme controller with a smile, as I walked across the compound of the old hospital on my last afternoon at Nakasero. I was clutching the hired boom microphone and fishpole, the only one ever seen at UTV, which I was reluctantly taking back with me to London.

I felt that experiencing the everyday conditions and problems faced by the team with whom I worked validated for them the debates we had about what it might be possible to improve. It was important to understand the economic stress under which Ugandans live, as well as something of the social trauma they have experienced during twenty years of civil war. Both the economic present and the traumatic legacy have produced everyday insecurities which can easily be mistaken for inefficiency or lack of knowledge, rather than the real need to keep too many small money-making endeavours going while doing a regular job. In terms of my initial brief, it seemed entirely valid to attempt to improve production but equally important to do so within the context in which the ETV team as well as a number of other producers who had joined in our discussions, would continue to work. An idea had been developed to set up a new kind of media unit in Kampala. I was an ex-pat leaving. But we'd used those long journeys across country not only to talk about our different life-styles and programme-making, but also to wonder how it might be possible to re-examine some of the strategies for participation and representation if television were to be seen as a real tool for development in Uganda. I was going back to the UK with a brief from the Ugandan producers to talk to TVE about backing the strategy we had developed.

Meanwhile the Ugandan team, the two Johns and Patrick with another producer colleague, Robby Wodamol, were writing up their proposal for the formation of an independent production unit to meet Uganda's specific needs for television as a tool for countrywide debate. The unit was named 'Television for Development'. Their proposal would be presented to the Ugandan Ministry of Information and to all the development agencies working in Kampala, at a meeting that I was to persuade TVE to chair three months later. This time I felt there was no contradiction in my role. Ugandan producers had invited us to mediate a delicate transition in their own development, when they would need to present a proposal for independence from their own ministry, without risking losing their jobs if the proposal were rejected.

Back in the UK, my consultancy report highlighted the lack of co-ordination in the funding of equipment and/or project training offered to UTV by major donor agencies such as the World Bank, the FAO and even IUCN. I pointed out that in the past equipment had been bought without accessories or spares and apparently without accounting for installation costs. I also explained that in a country as resource-hungry as Uganda a proportion of any development money will be absorbed in ministry overheads. I argued that this material wastage is reflected in the wastage of human resources as young producers, often straight from university or college, learn to accept their underemployment and lack of training. I pointed out that development agencies were more and more looking to the production of video-tapes to express development issues, and would often spend considerable sums parachuting in foreign production teams or buying equipment without any attempt to co-ordinate resources or to develop a workable production base with Ugandans.

ETV crew on location near Mount Elgon, photo by Geoffrey Howard

In their proposal to be presented to the Kampala meeting, the Ugandan team wrote the following:

> To bring about change in the habit, the thinking and the work culture of the seventeen million people who have lived in anguish and uncertainty for over two decades, will take a lot of innovations, patience and money. Virtually every sector needs urgent attention through rehabilitation or development. The level of illiteracy has heightened to about 35% of the population. Poverty and corruption are deeply entrenched. For many people Uganda does not seem to hold any future at all.
>
> In the past five years, however, the government with its international partners has formulated policies and programmes which are aimed at lifting the country out of the quagmire. Nevertheless, for any of those programmes to run smoothly and bear fruits within the stipulated time frame, there is a strong need for an effective project support communication facility such as radio, television and video.
>
> Way back in the sixties, the government had planned rural press, radio and television services which were to address local issues in the various regions in the local languages the people would understand

159

best. It was envisaged that this scheme would generate the necessary forum and enthusiasm and thereby create mass participation in social and economic development programmes. This plan like others was overtaken by a series of political upheavals. The present status is appalling. Newspapers circulate mainly in urban centres. Radio signals reach every part of the country generally but without a serious focus on any particular issue to any particular group.

Television Broadcasting likewise is only for the urban populations who can afford and have electricity. It has also been found to be ineffective as far as tackling social issues is concerned as it is not always targeted to a particular society with a particular problem. It is important to let the people be involved in the communication process such that they address themselves to those problems. This makes them more sensitive to those issues and therefore feel proud to have contributed to their solutions. There is therefore a serious need for non-broadcast video as it brings people closer in the communities and to their leaders.

Three months later twenty-four of the twenty-eight agencies invited to view a demonstration video-tape by Ugandan producers and discuss the proposal for Television for Development (already with a place among the acronyms, now known as TFD) attended the meeting in Kampala.

TVE acted as brokers for the idea, introducing the Ugandans. Robby Wodamol explained the difficulties under which producers work at UTV and how the proposal had been developed. Patrick and John spoke about their experience filming local communities for the Wetlands programmes. The team invited the audience to comment, knowing that now they had to have government approval if they were to have a chance of proceeding. The Hon. Pinto, MP and Chairman of the Ugandan Community Based Association for Child Welfare, spoke first:

There are 4 million youth below the age of 18 and we are not able to reach them. There are 99 radios for every 1,000 people. At present there is no way of reaching the majority of people except by word of mouth. The need for this service is overwhelming. This can become a good tool for development. Those present should agree to become partners.... Only 10% of the population live in Kampala, there is a need for the other 90% of the population to be reached by the media. We need this service to carry messages of development.

160

The Ugandan team had feared two things in making their proposal: that the Western donor agencies would see them simply as another bunch of Africans with their begging bowls; and that the proposal would be seen as a threat to Ugandan Television by the Ministry of Information. The first fear was allayed by the warm response they received for their proposal from TVE and then from the meeting in Kampala. In fearing the Ministry of Information response I think they had ignored the tradition of criticism and debate imbuing the experience Ugandans have gained in recent years through the system of Resistance Councils. Nathan Epenu, Acting Head of Uganda Television, spoke next. He said that the problem of bureaucracy within the Ministry was detrimental to programme-making. For this reason he saw the proposal for Television for Development as essential and as complementary to the work of the Ministry.

TFD was conceived by Ugandan producers, engineers and writers within the context of the Resistance Council government; open debate amidst poverty and debt. In Uganda it may yet be possible to see the modern media used to transmit critical debate rather than as a tool to represent the hegemonic homogenisation of a culture. Out of a mixture of hope and despair it may even be recognised as a model for media development elsewhere in Africa.

On the flight home, and again in that liminal mental state in which place is fragmented and the distance between one culture and another, one political moment and the next, is collapsed in the race through the air, I found Africa and its ethnic, political and economic problems colliding with those of Europe. I was suddenly alone with my experience of the last months. Of course, it had not been the same for my Ugandan colleagues, but had it been as useful and as deepening an experience for them as it had for me? I was not to know for several months. Meanwhile TVE made a small seed grant, and in Kampala they wrote numerous project proposals and fund-raising letters. Then on smart new headed paper they wrote that the TFD office was established in a shared building in central Kampala. They were in dialogue about commissions with several of the non-governmental organisations (NGOs) who attended the founding meeting. The work of TFD had begun.

The Wetlands film project has another postscript in the form of a letter I received from Isaac, a rice farmer whose family we had filmed in eastern Uganda. He was farming on one of the major schemes where the swamp has been partially drained, and he had discussed the problems of yields and the deterioration of the soil. He wrote to say he had had yet

161

another disastrous crop and that his family were suffering because the loss of income meant he could not buy medicine. His elder brother and sister had died.

It is the kind of letter many film producers steel themselves to receive from the subject of a film when the production is over. What can one do? Usually the next production on a new subject is already under way. Then I remembered. TFD have a different aim: the development of the people they film. Isaac's experience is the continuum, the subject and object of this new media unit. Let's show Isaac and the other farmers on the scheme that tape we made with a farmer not fifty kilometres away, who shows how he uses the swamp edge to rotate his crops so that his yields survive both the dry and the wet months.

OLD DOGS AND NEW TRICKS
Access Television in the UK

Jon Dovey

> We have a sense, we know we exist because there we are on
> the screen, and if you do not appear, you or your people do not
> appear on the screen, or only appear in certain roles, it dimin-
> ishes you, you are diminished by that.[1]

Television creates cultural capital; if we are misrepresented or under-
represented our stake in the culture is devalued. So the representation
of identity on TV becomes a site of struggle. A twenty-year tradition
of access TV in the UK has aimed to give a voice to those who are
under-represented or misrepresented by the mainstream, and thereby to
harness TV to a process of widening democratic participation. This
chapter explores the relationship that current developments in access
programming have with this tradition.

We begin with an apparent contradiction. In the wake of the 1990
Broadcasting Act and in the run-up to the BBC Charter renewal in 1996,
the ideals of public service broadcasting continue to be threatened. All
television output is increasingly subject to commercial pressures;
ratings share, delivering good audience profile to advertisers, and sec-
ondary exploitation rights continue to be the order of the day. After a
decade of direct interference by government, news values are increasingly constricted; the capitulations of BBC management, and the threat
to ITV current affairs programming posed by the new scheduling
arrangements since the 1990 Act, together presage a difficult future for
challenging news and current affairs. And yet, despite this unpromising
context, access to TV is thriving. It seems that 'ordinary people', non-

professional broadcasters, have never been more present on our screens. From *Blind Date* to *Beadle's About*, members of the public are the new stars of light entertainment. In *You've Been Framed* and *Video Diaries* the wobblyscope visions of amateur directors find their way into our living rooms thanks to the camcorder revolution. On Channel Four, in programmes like *Right to Reply* and *Opinions*, members of the audience become producers, offering their views on all kinds of subjects, including TV itself; and while *Made in the USA* features the more bizarre manifestations of the public access experiments on US cable, *Free For All* turns the subjects of current affairs into its authors. This is a new world.

Once upon a time, before access was born, the TV audience was the whole nation – addressed by the Queen at Christmas, by the Cup Final or the Eurovision Song Contest. We were united by our television experiences. TV was delivered to the working class mediated by Oxbridge tones which clearly reproduced the prevailing power relations of the time. By the end of the 1960s the need for some kind of access project to open up and democratise the broadcasting process was clear. But who are the unheard, the unseen, today in the 1990s? Who is misrepresented in the diversity of identities constructed by contemporary TV? Who could conceivably be *under*-represented in this plurality and plethora of broadcast narratives? How can we assess the meaning of the word 'access' in this context, or, more specifically, the value of those programmes that lay claim to it?

Within the range of programming described above, the output of the BBC Community Programme Unit which includes *Video Diaries*, and the Channel Four magazine show *Free For All* made by Filmit, most clearly situate themselves within a tradition of access TV. Jeremy Gibson, the current head of the Community Programme Unit, says: 'The maxim that we exist by hasn't really changed. We exist to represent the under-represented, the misrepresented or the non-represented.'[2] Compare this statement with Mike Fentiman's similar account of the Unit, which he led twenty years ago: 'We devised rules that said we should give airtime to the unheard, the rarely heard, the socially inarticulate and so on.'[3] John Samson, series editor of *Free For All*, describes the programme as 'viewer-led' rather than access, but articulates a similar position:

> It [TV] is a mass form of communication. We as viewers ... are fed a diet of material that is often mediated in very specific ways; it's clearly important in a democratic and plural society that they should

be balanced by alternative perspectives, and if those alternative perspectives are not there then we are the poorer for it.... There are often perspectives that we as individuals have on things going on around us that reveal or challenge wrong doings or attitudes that actually need to be challenged, and if one doesn't have a programme like this then we are reliant on journalists to do that on our behalf; and my own view is that culturally we therefore abdicate responsibility for that challenge to the so-called professionals.[4]

There are some fundamental principles that identify access programming; they centre around control and power over the programme-making process. Crucially, access programming is made under the editorial control of the accessee or author, who has the final say; not the producer, director, executive producer, series editor, commissioning editor or any of the other numerous supremos in the media hierarchy whom programme-makers usually have to satisfy. For this power to be in any way meaningful, the authors should have control over the whole process of representation. In practice this is rarely possible, and their power is primarily exercised through their presence in the edit suite during the editing of their programme. A closer examination of the working methods and programming of the Community Programme Unit and *Free For All* might help us understand both how these principles are applied in practice and what the slippery term 'access' means in the 90s.

The Community Programme Unit was established within the BBC in 1972 by a small group of radical programme-makers attached to BBC2's *Late Night Line-Up*; they had been inspired by access work emerging from the US and Canada and began experimenting in the same vein. *Open Door*, the Unit's first programme, invited groups to put forward programme ideas and selection was by a democratic editorial meeting of the whole Unit, including secretaries. Producers then went out and made a documentary under the supervision of the group who had suggested the idea. Successful ideas for programmes were almost always those submitted by groups involved in social action campaigns or cultural development – constructed by the Unit as the representatives of 'the unheard, the rarely heard, and the socially inarticulate'. This focus on working with groups reflected the dynamics of progressive politics at the time, which concentrated on work with grass-roots community action organisations.

Open Door was screened nationally on BBC2 in mid-evening and ran for ten years. The combination of the politically unsympathetic context of the BBC within which the Unit exercised its choices and their focus on social action groups led to uneven and sometimes unintentionally bizarre programming, the diversity of which seemed designed to refute any charges of political bias. The fifth series, for instance, included The George Arthur Road Action Group arguing for house demolition, 'Boy Scouts – the Myth and Reality', the Shotokan Karate Centre explaining martial arts, and the self-help organisation Ginger Bread talking about their problems and aims.

The peculiarities of the first wave of the Community Programme Unit's work have dogged access television ever since. However, the early experiments should not be taken to stand for access TV as a whole, since that would fail to take account of the way in which access, and in particular the Community Programme Unit, has continued to develop. By the end of the 1970s, the Unit had survived the initial battles within the BBC and was an established part of the Corporation. Some of this confidence and security is reflected in its expansion into the area of youth programming in the late 70s, first with the young people's information magazine *Grapevine* and later in 1979 with the ground-breaking *Something Else*. A series of magazine-format shows, each set in a regional city and devised and produced by young people from the area, they featured good music from top contemporary bands, drama sketches, documentary features and studio discussion. The mix was lively, upbeat and populist, quite different from the 'wholemeal TV' image that had attached itself to the access idea. This strand of Community Programme Unit output can be seen as the beginning of the 'Youth TV' style that has dominated whole blocks of scheduling from the mid-80s on, for instance in the *Def II* slot on BBC2 or in programmes like *Whatever You Want* and *The Word* on Channel Four.

This process of development was also reflected in the transformation of *Open Door* into the more substantial *Open Space* in 1983. Still operating on the open access model but with increasing resources and formal sophistication, accompanied by more intervention by the professionals at the Unit, *Open Space* started to look much more like any other high-quality BBC documentary feature, with similar scheduling opportunities. In 1991, *Open Space* transmitted twenty documentaries made under the editorial control of an author or access group, and the programmes occupied a 7.30 p.m. Monday evening network slot on BBC2.

With *Open Space*, the CPU still gives editorial control and the opportunity to participate in the editing process to its accessees, and this is what continues to distinguish it from the mass of other programme producers who may be chasing the same issues. However, it now tends to represent individual 'authors' with a 'story' rather than focus on marginalised groups. Jeremy Gibson has said that he has developed a 'freedom of speech' editorial policy rather than a practice based on any shared set of political principles. So the Unit researchers concentrate on seeking out voices that are, for whatever reason, genuinely unheard – voices such as that of Henri Klieman, the author of *Flying Fur*, which challenged many now commonly held assumptions about the fur trade and animal rights activists. Jeremy Gibson comments significantly on the work of the Unit:

> The most important thing for me about those programmes is that it makes a better programme. You inform an audience in a much better way if you listen to an unmediated view because it hits them with a directness, it challenges them. They might not like it, they might not agree with it, but it's very important to hear something done in that way and I believe it excites an audience.[5]

While some of the fundamental principles might remain the same, Gibson's is a quite different rationale for access than the dull, earnest, political motivations stereotypically ascribed to advocates of the form. Here we have a senior producer not talking about the political necessity for access but arguing that access actually makes better TV!

This move towards the individual story-teller has taken a dramatic step further with *Video Diaries*, of which the Community Programme Unit has now completed three series. The first five experiments were broadcast in 1990, and the subsequent series of ten programmes appeared in 1991 and 1992. The Unit solicits and researches ideas from potential diarists with a compelling story to tell. Once chosen, the diarist is trained in the use of an S-VHS camera and packed off to shoot their story, with support from the Unit should it be needed. In this way the diarists are given not only editorial control but also control over the means of production. They return with anything up to 200 hours of material and attend all the edit sessions, from an initial assembly which is viewed and discussed at length to the offline and online edit processes.

The second series in 1991 was broadcast on BBC2 in primetime – 9.30 p.m. on Saturday night – and averaged 1.1m viewers with an audience appreciation rating of 73 (from a possible 100). The completed programmes run at around ninety minutes. An interesting piece of audience research for the series indicated that the programmes were actually gaining viewers through the programme; in other words, people were turning on, flicking through the channels and being 'grabbed' by *Video Diaries*. Subjects have included a piece by a Belfast author about his life in Northern Ireland; a professional wedding video-maker's account of the death of his mother-in-law; football fans on their way to Italy for the World Cup; exiles returning to South Africa; the photographer Jo Spence recording her fight with leukaemia; a convicted armed robber's account of life as a prisoner; and an account by photojournalist Nick Danziger about the aftermath of the war in Afghanistan.

The *Video Diaries* programmes have received major critical attention. Here, the critics agreed, was something genuinely new and fresh in the arid schedules of network TV. At least part of the fascination has to do with the aesthetics of what looks like home video in the public space of TV – a chance to see inside people's homes and lives at a level of intimacy no film crew, however sensitive, could ever match. Peter Keighron has argued that in *Video Diaries* we see 'video technology begin to interrogate the rules of documentary film making.... Now the fly is off the wall; the camera need no longer pretend to be a passive observer, but can accept the role of participant.'[6] Certainly this new wave of documentary film-making has been made possible by the camcorder, its aesthetic dependent on our tendency as viewers to interpret low resolution as veracity; the 'amateur video' tag seen with increasing frequency on TV newscasts signals subjectivity, but also immediacy and truth. Camcorders are having an impact similar to the one lightweight 16mm technology had in the 1960s.

A development of the *Video Diaries* concept has been the screening of two series of *Teenage Video Diaries* which, if anything, have been even more successful than their 'grown up' counterparts. Diarists have tackled their adolescent experiences of anorexia, boxing, life as a 'new age' traveller, and teenage rock-and-roll bands. Their familiarity with the lens, their combination of bravura performance and startling vulnerability have made compelling TV. Further developments are under way, possibly including old people's diaries and the formation of a 'citizens' archive' from which different programmes will be made. Jeremy Gibson comments:

> I doubt whether I will ever find excitement in television like I've got from this.... It's actually totally changed the availability of the means of production.... This isn't the end of the technology-led development – there are so many other areas of TV that could be refreshed by this.[7]

Rachel, a traveller,
BBC Video Diaries

Channel Four's major recent contribution to access TV has been *Free For All*, produced by the independent company Filmit using a format devised by Johnnie Turpie of Independents Birmingham and John Samson of Filmit. While the Community Programme Unit has concentrated on the single film, the major contribution of *Free For All* has been to develop a magazine format for access. Running at a commercial half hour at 9.00 p.m. on Thursdays, the first series ran for ten weeks in early 1991 with an average audience of one million, which compares favourably with the rest of Channel Four's current affairs output. *Free For All* researchers seek out authors for the programme, who then work on the story with a director. There is no studio presenter or link other than a graphic sequence. Sometimes the whole programme is given over to one story, at other times issues are given a short advertisement-style slot – each piece can be as long or as short as it needs to be within the format. This technique accentuates the effect of hearing an unmediated voice that 'appears' out of the airwaves.

Filmit are committed to the idea of building up a network of contributors and collaborators; they publicise their existence through community media and also give out Freefone numbers during the programme so that viewers can contribute stories and comments. They have also produced a four-page newspaper that provides back-up and contact information on the stories covered. Eileen Herlihy, the network co-ordinator, commented in a recent issue, 'Our programme is about local stories with national significance. We provide a platform for people to tell their side of the news.'[8] The same article reports that over 3,000 people contacted the Filmit office during the last series with ideas for features and feedback and comments. This response is reflected in the programme itself by the use of recordings from such calls over the closing credits. Filmit's commitment to building a campaigning network was reflected in the summer 1992 season of *Free For All*, which covered follow-ups to stories shown in the previous series. It recognises that a network of people involved in a social action process is a necessary correlative of an access programming practice, and as such places *Free For All* centrally in the issue-led tradition of access TV developed during the 1970s.

Each *Free For All* author is given a twelve-point statement of rights, which includes the following:

— to have their view, opinion, or story told in an unmediated way, in a form they choose and under their control.
— to appear in or present the programme if they so wish.
— to take joint responsibility with Filmit for the creative realisation of the item.
— to be involved in the 'offline' edit and to suggest improvements before the 'online' or final edit.[9]

The series has covered an array of topics and stories too large to describe here, though the list which follows gives some flavour of the territory: passenger safety on British Rail; a Sheffield campaign against water metering; Black perspectives on the Gulf War; soccer supporters' raw deal; campaigns against Primary Testing in schools; cheap labour in chain-stores and outworkers making Christmas crackers; low-flying jets over Welsh farms; student occupations; mysterious deaths at sea in Cornwall; the parental rights of unmarried fathers.

The programme seeks to respond to the prevailing news agenda. Rather than seeking out marginalised groups, it takes a lead from news stories of the day and attempts to find alternative cultural and political perspectives which remain untold in the usual run of current affairs reporting. This is another new departure for access television, which in the past would have found the mainstream news agenda largely irrelevant to its concerns.

As the author's charter above suggests, *Free For All* series editor John Samson places great store by building relationships with contributing authors:

You have a trusting relationship where people come to you and say, listen, this is actually an important issue and I know about it 'cause I'm experiencing it, and I want to say it unmediated, I don't want to say it through a journalist. I don't want to be a one-off article in a newspaper, I actually want to say it myself, the way that I want to say it, because I don't want a story about me by somebody else, I want a story by me. I want my story told.[10]

Like the Community Programme Unit, *Free For All* has moved away from political definitions of access principles to a more eclectic, hetero-dox position.

You can't pretend that all the working classes are somehow leftwing and need to be represented as such. You've actually got a real diversity of views and experience and that diversity of view and experience must, must be put onto the screen.[11]

Although the programme is issue-led, the subjects chosen challenge the orthodoxies of both liberal and establishment positions. Features on the rights of pit bull terrier owners, in support of soccer fans, or arguing for greater rights for unmarried fathers don't fit easily into any one identifiable ideological position.

What do the current practices of the Community Programme Unit and *Free For All* indicate about the condition of access TV in the UK? Both have emerged from the twenty-year tradition of access which is predicated on the principle of giving editorial control to non-professional broadcasters as an on-air corrective to systematic mis-representation or under-representation. However, the current models for this practice are a good deal more sophisticated than their previous incarnations, allowing access programming to go with the grain of the industry, producing programming which fits into prevailing cultural and economic forces in a number of ways.

Firstly, the concept of authored TV, the individual subjective point of view that leads a programme or feature, can be read as a response to the increasingly bland news and current affairs programming which had begun to dominate British screens by the end of the 1980s. Every government attack and censorship *cause célèbre* spawned a thousand examples of self-censorship; reporting became 'safer'. The individually authored programme, pioneered by the BBC Bristol *Byline* series, became an acceptable, 'personality-led' way of mounting contentious arguments. Equally, the collapse of the cosy certainties of leftwing traditions and the political emphasis on the individual rather than on class also underly the heterodox, iconoclastic stance that 'authored' programmes often take. *Open Space*, *Video Diaries* and *Free For All* have all adopted this individual-led programme model.

A second key element in the current condition of access TV concerns resources. The robust, positive enthusiasm for the form exhibited at both the Community Programme Unit and *Free For All* is based on an absolute commitment to give accessees the best: the best slots, the best equipment, the best people to work with. Indeed, *Free For All* compare their approach to their 'authors' with that of an advertising agency to a client. Producers are at pains to stress that current forms of access are not cheap to produce, and that their budgets are comparable to any other form of current affairs production, as are the slots in which they get transmitted. In other words, access demands to be seen not as the poor, marginalised relation of factual programming but as an equal partner.

Thirdly, the technological developments that have made *Video Diaries* and some of *Free For All* possible – in particular the increasing availability and quality of camcorders – are continually strengthening access programming. The range of people with access to the means of production is widening all the time, and viewers' perceptions of what is televisually acceptable are widening too. It is reported that there are now an estimated 14 million camcorders in the US, and a weekly network news magazine show, *I Witness Video*, is devoted to the news stories they record.[12] As the production technology penetrates our daily lives, our increasing familiarity with it can only serve to challenge further the monopoly of the TV professionals and the standards of 'objectivity' and balance which they have sought to uphold.

Finally, both the Community Programme Unit and *Free For All* take a pro-active role in setting up programmes. They don't sit back and wait for the request for airtime to come in, they go out and look for subject matter. They send out researchers looking for authors in ways indistinguishable from how current affairs journalists have traditionally searched out stories and sources.

How are we to assess the significance and value of these developments? In particular, how do we assess their political relevance? In both its production method and its programmes, access TV set itself the lofty task of challenging the power structures of mainstream TV. Its attempt to counter under-representation or misrepresentation set up the possibility of an alternative practice within broadcasting itself. How does the new, sophisticated access TV described above fit in with these aspirations?

There is a real political problem with the individually led programme as the dominant form of access TV. An individual can only stand for her or himself, unless they work very carefully to articulate some wider position. 'Authored' TV, though often very moving, is no substitute for thoroughly researched, well argued programmes about *issues*. The author-led programme can be dismissed because it is subjective; the diary form becomes merely another sub-genre of documentary rather than a far-reaching attempt to counter systematic misrepresentation.

Further, as a documentary genre the video diary engages the voyeuristic pleasures of the viewer with unique force. The complex process of private pain becoming public property in the domestic space of the living room delivers a *frisson* that is a long way from engaging our analytic faculties. Our fascination with revelations of child abuse or anorexia could be the flipside of our amused reaction to the painful pratfalls of *You've Been Framed!*

It is also necessary to consider who is making the choices about which stories and which individuals are to be given access. Since TV is run entirely without democratic structures, these choices are still in the hands of TV executives – mediacrats. While they may be sympathetic to the needs of the community, they alone are in the position of defining what those needs are. Such definitions will be subject to the individual vicissitudes of their personal histories, as well as the budget and ratings pressures which affect every TV programming decision. As an instance, video diarist Nick Danziger is a highly renowned international photographer who does not actually need the Community Programme Unit to provide a platform for his work. When pressed on this issue, Jeremy Gibson insisted that the diary idea was 'just too good' to limit to the kind of accessees one might previously have expected to work with Unit.[13]

Difficulties also cohere round the notion of the 'story', which is subject to a whole set of journalistic assumptions. These assumptions may have little or nothing to do with the material conditions of the subjects of a 'story', for whom injustice or pain does not come neatly packaged with a beginning, a middle and an end. A further, related, problem comes with the rate of turnover required to sustain the magazine-style, advertising agency access model. Accessees, or authors, are put through a high-speed practical media education process that must leave the professionals in a very powerful position in terms of the politics of representation. Doubtless, authors do challenge the ideas of the director, camera operator or editor, but the power relations generated by the position of media in society will remain inscribed in the production process unless a very lengthy period is devoted to rewriting them.

What we have witnessed with the current revival of access television is the naturalisation of the political project underlying its tradition within the market-led forces of contemporary TV. The current forms of access work because they provide commissioning editors with TV that is fresher and more immediate than anything the professionals could achieve. This is access TV as niche marketing.

However, the point here is that *all* TV is niche marketing in the current political and cultural context. Market-led TV is creating more distribution outlets, more channels, each with a smaller, more specific audience profile. The problem for traditional forms of access has been that this multiplicity of audiences makes it more difficult to determine who is unheard, who is misrepresented. The 'degree of misrepresentation' decreases as audience profiles become more and more specific, closer to many more sections of the community. It was easy to determine misrepresentation when TV denied difference by treating its entire audience as a homogeneous mass. TV today thrives on difference, replicating it, feeding from it. By its nature access is about responding to the demands and needs of the wider cultures we live in, so it is of course inevitable that the forms of access should change as they respond to the fragmentation described above. Attempts to impose a closed, historicised definition of what access TV 'should' be themselves derive from and belong to a cultural landscape that is fast disappearing.

These observations are in no way an attempt to justify the depoliticisation of access TV within the forces of the market. On the contrary. The rate of information production flowing from the burgeoning TV markets of the late twentieth century increases rather than decreases the need for challenging programmes and challenging production methods. More and more information produced by the same unrepresentative elites of mediacrats must be challenged if the so-called 'information society' is not to become a society of systematically produced ignorance. The models of access described above represent some ways in which this challenge can be mounted; there are others. Access producers must look to different emerging networks, from non-broadcast videogram distribution within interest group networks to the various slots available on local cable, satellite, and terrestrial channels. Each of these routes will have different economic, technical and political determinants and constraints.

The current models practised within British television offer *limited* windows for radical, challenging programming and as such are to be supported, despite the difficulties noted above. They demonstrate not only the public's continuing demand for access opportunities but also that such programming can make 'good TV'. It is to be hoped that new producers will emerge and use these footholds to maintain and strengthen the challenge of access TV.

NOTES

1. Professor Brian Groombridge, quoted in *Remote Control* (TV documentary transcript – London: Broadcast Support Services/Channel Four, 1990), p. 6.
2. Interview with the author (London, 1992).
3. Interview with the author (London, 1992).
4. Interview with the author (London, 1992).
5. Interview with the author (London, 1992).
6. Peter Keighron, 'Private Eyes', *New Statesman and Society*, 17 May 1991.
7. Interview with the author (London, 1992).
8. Eileen Herlihy, 'In Touch', *Free For All*, Spring 1992.
9. Filmit, 'The Author's Contract' (London, 1991).
10. Interview with the author (London, 1992).
11. Ibid.
12. Fenton Bailey, 'Neighbourhood Watch', *Television Week*, 17 September 1992.
13. Interview with the author (London, 1992).

RESISTANCE BY SATELLITE

The Gulf Crisis Project and the Deep Dish Satellite TV Network

Martin Lucas and Martha Wallner

Before the United States entered the Gulf War in 1991, the Bush Administration misled the American public about its intentions in various ways, most typically by suggesting that US and 'allied' troops were being sent to the Gulf solely to protect Saudi Arabia. The Fourth Estate abandoned its watchdog role for what amounted to boosterism, and Bush and Baker wheeled and dealed at the United Nations as huge numbers were mobilised for ill-explained goals. The media were full of images of Americans in the Saudi sands, but there were virtually no American voices asking hard questions about why this colossal and expensive call-up was taking place just as forty-odd years of Cold War were ending and a recession was tightening its grip on the economy. As Martin Lee and Norman Solomon put it, 'American journalism surrendered to the U.S. government long before Iraqi forces did on the battlefield.'[1]

In this thin and frantic atmosphere in a country glued to the screen, viewers were surprised to see on their televisions a series of programmes which gave clear evidence of a strong nationwide movement in opposition to the Gulf War, which was articulately questioning the Administration's goals and policies in the Middle East. This series, the *Gulf Crisis TV Project*, appeared on cable and broadcast TV in the days just before the war began in January 1991. It stood in stark relief against the babbling background of experts and pundits available on the networks. The *Gulf Project*, produced by a small independent group working on a shoestring budget, was seen by viewers across the USA and Canada, and in various forms in Japan, Australia, France and the UK, and became a focal point of grass-roots anti-war activism around the world.

176

What made it possible for media activists to counter the consolidated might of the information industry, and to gain timely access to TV in a jingoistic climate in a country where the press had failed in two previous conflicts to question the official options presented to the American public? And what made this possible in a situation where the media arts world is being squeezed both by economic recession and specific attacks on arts budgets and public television?

The answers lie on several fronts. Two are technological: the development of inexpensive home video cameras now in the hands of the American public in millions, and the commercial availability of satellite time on hundreds of leasable, relatively inexpensive channels. But these answers do not exist in isolation. Here we will explore what kind of human infrastructure we created to interact with these technologies. Camcorders and telecommunications satellites were a *sine qua non* of our efforts, but it is worth stressing that their high-tech appeal should not be allowed to overshadow the very important organising work that was critical in making them useful.

The media picture

The Gulf Crisis TV Project was organised in the same way that a connect-the-dots puzzle is filled in. Once we had made a plan connecting producers, organisers, journalists, public access and public television stations and viewers, a picture of US opposition to the war could emerge and a different model of media production and distribution also came into sharper focus. In some cases we were able to rely on connections that were the result of years of organisation and co-operation. In other cases new relationships were forged. Historically, government and industry in the US have resisted state support of non-commercial and electronic media. In this unfriendly climate, efforts to create alternatives to commercial media have resulted in a hodgepodge of media institutions, each with its own history and goals. An inventory of the institutional and technological resources with which the project had to work will aid an understanding of how it was accomplished.

The Public Broadcasting System (PBS). Despite opposition from the commercial media, space for non-commercial television has been reserved in most cities since the 1950s. The funding for these stations comes from a combination of local viewer subscriptions, shrinking state and federal funds, and increasingly through corporate underwriting. The member stations regularly downlink programming off the PBS satellite network. The bulk of this material, often repackaged British programming, comes from the big East Coast stations, though occasionally some PBS stations have demonstrated a willingness to air independently produced programming expressing controversial viewpoints critical of government policy. For the most part the stations are under-financed, very cautious in their programming policies, and extremely vulnerable to the political exigencies of the times.

Cable TV. In the late 1960s and early 1970s the development of portable video equipment signalled the possibility of video production independent of commercial media. During the same period, activists saw the introduction of cable television into communities across the country as an opportunity to organise for community access to the media. As cable operators negotiated with city governments for franchise agreements (contracts granting the cable company permission to dig up streets and lay cable), citizen committees were formed to pressure the city into demanding something in return from the cable companies, namely some sort of public access TV.

Public Access TV. In 1984 Congress underlined its support for public access in the Cable Franchise Policy and Communications Act, which upheld the right of cities to include provisions for public access in their contracts with cable operators. The Act recognised that public access channels are often the video equivalent of the speaker's soapbox or the electronic parallel to the printed leaflet: they provide groups and individuals who generally have not had access to the electronic media with the opportunity to become sources of information in the electronic market-place of ideas. The soapbox analogy underpinning public access has had contradictory repercussions. The enemies of access – large cable operators who resent having to provide a public service, and interest groups offended by access programming – have characterised the free speech on access as wacky, irresponsible and/or obscene. Supporters of access have been energetic in their response. They argue that access is one of the few places where free speech, guaranteed by the First Amendment of the US Constitution, is actually tolerated. Approximately 1,400 cable systems across the US have channels and, in many cases, equipment and training available for use by residents free of charge. Many of the producers who contributed to the *Gulf Crisis TV Project* were already using their local access facilities for the distribution and production of programmes on various grass-roots social issues.

Access stations generally programme locally produced material. Imported programming – programming from outside the local community via satellite or otherwise – makes up a small percentage of access fare. Many local cable networks in fact demand local sponsorship or production of all programmes. Access programmers who picked up the *Gulf Project*, for instance, did so on their own initiative, either because they appreciated more diversity on their channels or because they wanted to encourage more activist use of access.

Satellites and uplinks. Transponders on domestic satellites, owned by multi-national corporations, are relatively easy to rent at a reasonable cost, ranging from $250 to $800 per hour. Uplink services, which transmit the signal to the satellite, are available on the open market. A broker can shop for the uplink and the satellite time for you, or you can do it yourself once you know a few of the right questions to ask. Contrary to what many believe, tapes originating from home video formats, provided the signal quality is stable, can be transmitted by satellite without technical problems. Programming schedules can be listed in national magazines which reach an estimated 4 million home-dish owners, as well as institutional dish owners, like universities. Dishes with a price tag of under $1,000 are now proliferating.

Paper Tiger TV. Paper Tiger TV is a media collective who began producing programmes for public access cable in New York City in 1981. The shows set out to 'smash the myths of the information industry' by featuring critical 'readings' of various media products – newspapers, magazines, Hollywood films and TV – as well as offering sympathetic profiles of alternative media efforts.

The collective has very consciously tried to develop a model for low-budget production, and to share it with others through networking and aggressive national and international distribution of 200 of their programmes to access channels, museums, schools and community groups. The collective's work is done on an all-volunteer basis, except for two part-time distribution co-ordinators. The group has a fluid membership which expands and contracts on a project basis, and currently counts on some fifteen active members in New York and a similar number in San Francisco. Paper Tiger supports its work through distribution of tapes and through grants from the state and the occasional foundation, not to mention the sale of T-shirts, Tiger badges, books and many hours of volunteer labour.

Deep Dish TV. In 1985, Paper Tiger received a grant to distribute programming by satellite to public access centres around the country. The collective quickly expanded their original proposal for transmitting Paper Tiger shows into a plan to package and distribute the work of many other grass-roots video producers. The first series, transmitted in

1986, was designed to lay the foundation for an ongoing satellite network. The work of over a hundred producers was included in hour-long compilation programmes on themes such as militarism, labour, racism, and US policy in Central America. Clips were interspersed with 'segues' made by the Paper Tiger collective.

The success of the first series proved that there were at least 300 public access stations willing and able to downlink programming from a satellite, and that there were many producers willing to share their work with the network. By 1990, Deep Dish had grown into a national organisation, with a steering committee and three full-time staff (with medical benefits!). Every year the network distributes a spring and fall season, each consisting of one hour a week for thirteen consecutive weeks. Several different programming styles are used, including compilations co-ordinated by regional producers across the country, curated series, and tapes submitted in response to national solicitations. Past series have included *Green Screen: Grassroots Views of the Environmental Crisis, Will be Televised: Video Documents from Asia*, and *Behind Censorship: The Assault on Civil Liberties*. Deep Dish, funded by private foundations, state arts funds and individual contributions, provided the critical link between the *Gulf Project* and both a national audience and producers in all parts of the US.

Media arts centres. In many major cities in the United States there are facilities which make video equipment available to independent producers at subsidised rates. These centres also host public screenings of independent work and send out newsletters which reach local independent producers. Media arts centres were another important source of independent production for the *Gulf Crisis TV Project*.

Community radio. Across the US and Canada can be found a variety of small non-commercial stations. One group of these stations, the Pacifica Network, has a national news programme and programming syndicated via satellite. Pacifica stations are directly financed by listener contributions, giving them an independence cherished by listeners, whose numbers during the Gulf War swelled as they had during the Vietnam War. Pacifica provided analysis of the war and coverage of anti-war activities, including the *Gulf Crisis TV Project*.

Small publications. Another important component of the media picture is the variety of small newsletters put out by church groups, activist organisations, media groups, schools and others. These were critical connections to grass-roots constituencies interested in getting involved with the *Gulf Crisis Project*.

Connecting the dots

In August 1990, as bombers, troop transports and aircraft carriers were converging on the Gulf, links between the agencies we have described were still only a remote possibility. All we had was a critical sense of urgency and a feeling that the world was racing towards war while basic issues were not being addressed. At this stage 'we' were four people and a table in a corner of the already overcrowded Paper Tiger office. Our decision to go ahead was based on our lack of trust in the Administration's stated goals which, together with the large-scale mobilisation of military might by the US and Britain, led us to suspect that a major conflict was just around the corner. What could we reasonably expect to do?

On 28 September 1990, the National Coalition to End US Intervention in the Middle East held a big 'teach-in' in New York, which was taped by volunteers. At Paper Tiger we made a programme out of that material and sent it out. At the same time, other video groups were starting to send us tapes – The National Center for Defense Information, Labor Beat in Chicago, and more. When we put the list together with other information we had about upcoming anti-war activities, it was clear we had enough material to assemble some kind of series.

The first problem we faced was finding funding. Paper Tiger had a one-room office and an edit system. Deep Dish had a fax machine and a list of cable stations. We needed money for mailings, for more editing equipment, and of course we needed a camera. We came up with a modest budget ($25,000) and started floating proposals. By October, frenzied efforts had raised enough money to have one person working full-time. An initial sale of home video rights of our potential shows and some individual donations meant we could go ahead. Meanwhile, credit cards filled in the gaps. By November we got a larger foundation grant, small by independent documentary standards but enough to get four of us working.

The other big problem was time. The Deep Dish method depends on being able to elicit responses from independent producers around the country who must be told we are making a show, decide what to do, shoot and cut something and send it back to us – a process which normally takes several months. The people we were appealing to were video-makers connected with the hundreds of public access centres linked by Deep Dish TV. A separate grass-roots outreach was made to the large number of peace groups starting to mobilise in an attempt to get people involved on all levels from producing tapes to 'sponsoring' shows for their local cable station.

Uplinking and downlinking

Once we had decided to go ahead, we had to let people across the US know as soon as possible that the shows were coming. This meant naming the shows, booking satellite time well in advance, and letting station managers know when and how they could pick us up – all this with only a rough idea of what the shows would look like.

In consultation with Deep Dish, we decided to start with four shows. Getting 'good' time slots was an important priority, and getting them on the satellite channels which our downlinkers were accustomed to using limited our choices. But it was essential to be able to send out the shows on a schedule so that programmers and viewers could pick them up easily. Working through satellite brokers, Deep Dish finally booked the shows on to a satellite (the one used by the Playboy channel) so that each show would be fed twice, on 7 and 9 January 1991. Transmitting a show twice is more expensive but it was important to create as many opportunities as possible for stations with very small staffs to pick them up.

Putting a signal up – uplinking – is less than half the battle. Once we had satellite times we had two big outreach jobs to attend to. First, cable stations and dish owners needed to know the exact time of a feed and which satellite and which channel on the satellite (transponder) the programme would be on. We had a very short time to develop our publicity material, get it out to the access stations and do follow-up calls and mailings. Ensuring that people with dishes downlink to complete the information chain was a major effort.

The other part of the outreach was to the public, to get people to encourage their local stations to tape and run the shows. Stations without dishes would need extra encouragement to get them to 'bicycle' tapes from stations with dish facilities. Stations with programming restrictions needed to hear from local sponsors of the programming. Here links with local peace action groups were essential. A key moment was a massive meeting in New York of several thousand peace activists from around the country. The *Gulf Crisis TV Project* provided everyone attending with a packet of information describing how they could get involved, both as producers and as media activists lobbying local stations for more debate around the crisis in the Gulf. The links forged at this time were critical in expanding the scope of our efforts at every stage of production and distribution, and represented a new kind of relationship between media and peace activism.

Making the shows
As well as doing outreach, we had to get busy actually making the shows. We had four shows and we divided up into four groups of two. Each pair of co-ordinating producers would be responsible for one half-hour. A few other volunteers would help us log tapes. By 1 December, tapes were coming in by the dozen – 120 by our 15 December deadline. The biggest task was simply to keep track of the material and figure out who would use what.

Our office was full of people madly putting together outreach material, some sitting on the floor stuffing envelopes, someone else on the one phone trying to work out if a call was from a producer who could send us material, a station that could run the show, or a peace group that could use it. Tapes were coming in from practically every state in the country, and in practically every format. We transferred these from 8mm or VHS to 3/4″ and logged them for editing. Meanwhile we were producing more material of our own, running out to cover anti-war convocations or to interview key people with the one Hi-8 camera that producer Jen Lion had contributed for the duration.

The first series
Our first four shows were *War, Oil and Power*, which dealt with the interconnections between US energy and military policies; *Operation Dissidence*, which looked at how the war was sold to the American public; *Out of the Sandtrap*, which explored how a Middle East war fitted into US foreign policy in the post-Cold War period; and *Bring the Troops Home Now!*, which looked at grass-roots anti-war organising and resistance in the military. Since no single producer could possibly view all the material we had coming in, we depended on each other to pass along something that looked relevant for a particular show. Teach-ins, demos, interviews, theatre pieces, art videos, Public Service Announcements, all went into the logs on cards. Then there was the day we sat around and traded items from the hundreds of cards. 'Who is going to use the prayer meeting from the group in Fort Wayne?' 'Who wants oil well shots?' 'Did anyone ever send us footage of people chained to gas pumps?'

The material we received varied a great deal. We had short pieces produced by local cable stations where people at shopping malls and filling stations were interviewed on their feelings about the looming war. We had footage of prayer sessions, sit-ins at oil refineries, vigils, anti-war rallies, and civil disobedience. People sent entire town meetings (taped for local cable shows) where Gulf crisis options were being debated; they sent in rap videos and video art pieces. In many cases our initial solicitation elicited material, but often people would call us. For instance, we might get a call from Pennsylvania. 'We're having a vigil and a procession with a veterans for peace group. Is there anyway you can get a camera here? We are five hundred miles away and have only one camera.' – 'Well, it might be a little tough. Have you talked to your local cable station? Let me give you a couple of names.' At other times there would be no local cable station, in which case we would ask if anyone in the local peace group had a VHS camcorder. 'Just get a long shot that shows what town you're in. And a couple of short interviews, and send us the tape. Sure, we can broadcast it.'

While material from all over the country was coming in, we shot material of our own – dozens of interviews with progressive figures who were not showing up in the mainstream press, Vietnam veterans, economists, journalists, media critics – which helped round out the picture. We also taped agit-prop theatre and performance pieces, poetry, comedians, rallies, art videos. The result was a series of four fast-paced half-hours, an information collage quite unlike anything on TV. People like Dan Ellsberg, the Vietnam-era Pentagon employee turned anti-war activist, and the author Grace Paley were intercut with student leaders from Louisiana, soldiers resisting call-up orders in Hawaii, and Middle East scholars like Edward Said and Eqbal Ahmal. Viewers saw performance artists like Paul Zaloom and media critics like Laura Flanders from Pacifica radio and Jeff Cohen from Fairness and Accuracy in Reporting. They saw Los Angeles anti-war rockers and Bronx anti-war rappers – in short everyone the networks had not consulted.

While it is difficult to describe the *Gulf Project* to someone who hasn't seen the shows, an outline of the contents does suggest the richness and variety which we used deliberately to transcend the normal barriers between 'public affairs programming' or 'news' and other television forms. Since we had footage on every format from home video VHS to professional Betacam, the shows had a 'home-made' look, one that we encouraged with abrupt cuts and high-handed juxtapositions.

One viewer who saw the shows the night before the war started said he kept switching channels and coming back to the one programme that didn't look or sound like the rest of the material on the air waves. 'It was,' he said, 'like an explosion in my head!' As Janet Sorenson put it:

The Gulf Crisis TV Project, photos by Martin Lucas

It seems no accident that the tapes' montages of commentaries, demos, performances, concerts and speeches all move with a compelling rhythm. Certainly the atmosphere of the period influenced the lively sense of the tapes. This sense, coupled with scenes of direct action and angry commentary and with the fact that dates for marches and phone numbers for war resistance groups were often flashed on the screen, made for effective agitprop. *Just Say No* (1991), a tape documenting military resistance abroad, uses a rap soundtrack produced by soldiers in West Germany. Its visual pacing mimics the rhythm of disk-scratching, with certain images repeating in rapid fire sequence. Its broad appeal as something that comes close to resembling a music video is important for the function it serves – to alert soldiers to the possibility of resistance.[2]

The *Village Voice's* Amy Taubin suggested the shows 'appealed mainly to incipient teens rebelling against MTV.'[3] One of the shows' producers, Dee Dee Halleck, dubbed them 'America's Angriest Home Videos'. *The Gulf Crisis TV Project* programmes framed crucial questions that were not being asked by the mainstream press about the goals and purposes of what was shaping up to be the biggest US war since Vietnam, making it clear to any viewer that a large segment of the American public was not on board the war bandwagon, that the public was being manipulated by the Administration, and that people resented it. And they did it with a style that was oppositional but intimately televisual, however much the boundaries of conventional documentary or public affairs programming were broken. As *Newsday* writer Jonathan Mandel said, 'The video they make . . . does not employ what one could call sophisticated production techniques, and the various segments that make up the half-hour programme are dizzying in their difference of tone, subject, quality, format. But the message gets through.'[4]

Not only did the message get through, it did so, as Sorenson pointed out, in a way where style and content worked together to create a new kind of TV meaning:

Like a teach-in it happened in a public place, that is, the space of television. Anyone could wander into it clicking through the channels, as one might wander into a teach-in at the central square of a campus. The series made use of familiar TV conventions in its timing and flow, and even, occasionally, TV-style anchors, such as Laura Flanders' particularly effective introduction to *Operation Dissidence*.

186

Like a teach-in, it offered 'experts' – Noam Chomsky, Edward Said, Rabab Hadi, Judith Williamson, and Daniel Ellsberg. But also like a teach-in, the tapes afforded a balance between experts and an open-endedness which showed individuals, some politically active for the first time, voicing personal reservations and responses to the war.[5]

Where did it go?

The audio-visual home of both Paper Tiger and Deep Dish is public access cable television, an important viewing audience, but one usually counted in the tens or hundreds of thousands, not in the millions of the network ratings game. The *Gulf Crisis TV Project* was shown on cable in the US and Canada, but it was also broadcast on public television across the US, and, in a condensed version, in the UK and Australia as well.

Broadcasting the shows on the Public Broadcasting System meant a big increase in audience, and it is worth exploring this in some detail. PBS set up a satellite system in the late 1970s which was designed to link over 200 non-commercial stations located everywhere from San Juan, Puerto Rico to Anchorage, Alaska (and as far away as Guam, we later discovered) that make up the PBS network. Anyone with the money, which typically means Home Box Office or one of the other cable giants, can buy time on the PBS satellite. Buying time for what is called a 'soft feed' allows the user to provide material that local stations may take up. It also gives the user a chance to publicise the show to station managers and programming managers on the DACS system, an internal electronic mail system that PBS uses to alert local stations to their feeds. The trick is then to convince each individual station to tape and air your show. When we started the *Gulf Crisis TV Project*, we planned to use this system to increase viewing of our programmes. Several members of our group had previous satellite experience. Dee Dee Halleck had been one of the original media activists who lobbied to set up the access aspect of the system, while Martin Lucas had worked with documentary-maker Ilan Ziv during the 1982 Israeli invasion of Lebanon, putting together a one-hour special on that war which was picked up by several stations in the system.

Before we set up a soft feed, however, we talked with several stations about sponsoring our programmes. Any PBS station can sponsor a show to the system as a whole. In practice, the cost of producing programming means that usually only the larger stations, or groups of stations, actually do so. We were pleasantly surprised when we approached a young, innovative station in Philadelphia, WYBE. Programming manager John Vernille indicated that they were willing to sponsor the first four shows to the PBS system and work on the publicity to get stations to notice them. This meant our shows would have a 'hard feed'; the imprimatur of a PBS station meant the material would be looked at more seriously by other stations.

As soon as we could, we sent out a calendar with the dates, times, satellite name and transponder number for each of the first four shows. This meant that people in each local area could call their cable or public TV station with extremely specific information about how and when to downlink the shows. In areas where the stations might be reluctant to show the programming, outreach co-ordinator Cathy Scott organised 'phone zaps' whereby local viewers could call in and ask for the shows to be scheduled. The 'zaps' were not only useful in getting shows on the air, they were important in giving people in a local community a focal point for expressing their opposition to what was becoming a headlong rush to war.

Getting on PBS was a big boost for our work, but our core audience is and was the public access viewership which the Deep Dish Network reaches, and there our goal was not to 'capture viewers' but to encourage the widest possible dialogue and interaction. One important Deep Dish concept is the 'wraparound'. To every station we sent programme information we also sent a request for the national shows to be set in a context of local programming. Many cities responded by putting together panel discussions, call-in shows, live coverage of town meetings where the war was discussed. In Milwaukee, Wisconsin, the cable studio was going live with a group discussing ecology issues as the 'wraparound' for another Deep Dish show about the environment. They simply pulled out a monitor with CNN's war coverage into the studio and shifted their discussion to the war. In Burlington, Vermont, footage of the local Army Reservists being sent off to the Gulf became the most requested repeat in the history of the cable station.

Impact

Over thirty PBS stations from Anchorage, Alaska to San Juan, Puerto Rico aired the *Gulf Crisis TV Project* to an estimated 40 per cent of the PBS viewership. The largest PBS station, WNET in New York, ran the show three times in a week in the days just before the war began. In addition, hundreds of local cable stations ran the programme, some picking them up off the satellite, others by 'bicycling' the shows from stations with dishes. At the end of each half-hour we indicated the Deep Dish phone number. The phones rang round the clock for a week at our tiny New York office. While a few of our callers were furious, most were wildly enthusiastic, calling from as far away as California and Florida to tell us how important the shows were for them.

In Canada, Vision TV cable network, which links to some three million households, put aside two hours of its regular programming on 15 January to present the Gulf shows back to back. Vision Director of Programming Peter Fleming said, 'In light of concerns about the role played by the media in the unfolding of the entire crisis, it's the kind of programming we feel strongly compelled to present.'[6]

On Channel Four in Britain the four shows were condensed to one hour, dubbed *Hell, No, We Won't Go*, and run with a half-hour on UK anti-war activism. The effect of seeing the level of opposition in the US on British television – which was almost entirely wedded to the notion that America was monolithically behind the war – was electrifying. Channel Four's Alan Fountain suggested to us that the programme changed the tenor of the debate around the war in the UK.

In addition, some 2,000 copies of the show were distributed as home videos, winding up at rallies, at picnics, in living rooms, used by schools, peace groups, and so on.

The use of the *Gulf Crisis TV Project* tapes in Japan, as related by Tetsuo Kogawa, Japanese social critic and media activist, gives some idea of the creativity and imagination of users of the shows:

The Japanese people were told by US media that 90 per cent of the US population supported the war. We had no opportunity to evaluate this position.... Seeing the *Gulf Crisis TV Project* videos was a turning point for us. The timing was very good. Even the traditional left in Japan has suddenly become interested in using new technology: otherwise they cannot break through.

I circulated over thirty copies of the Gulf Crisis videos to key persons in various organisations and friends of mine in many locations throughout Japan. All of those who received the tape were very interested in the video and they either personally or with their organisations duplicated it and circulated it to other groups and individuals. So that one package of video made a loose network.

Each person and each organisation who received the video began to connect with each other. The act of duplication, transcription and translation became a means of organising: after they received the tape,

189

groups made copies and sent them to a new group. Many collaborated in making the transcriptions and translations and sending copies to those who received the video next. The complete text of the four programmes was entered into several computer networks, and became the basis for articles in newsletters and periodicals on the left.[7]

As the air war started in mid-January 1991, the mainstream press rallied round the flag. At the same time opposition to the war was building up steam. Project Co-ordinator Cathy Scott worked with Fairness and Accuracy in Reporting, a media watchdog group, and others to put together a demonstration on 30 January that took thousands of protesting people to the headquarters of the networks. Our success with the first series and our sense of outrage at the media-managed war made us feel it was critical to keep making shows.

The second series

For the first series we fed four shows as a block on the satellite, but for our second series we decided to adopt a weekly approach which we hoped would encourage programmers to pick us up on a regular rather than *ad hoc* basis.

The content of our first series had to a large extent been dictated by the material people sent us. For the second series we started by hammering out topics we felt were being dealt with by the mainstream press either poorly or not at all. These included issues of media censorship, racism, resistance in the military, Middle East geo-politics, economic issues surrounding the war, and, in an effort to do globally what we had done nationally, a show looking at the anti-war movement around the world. Having six shows meant we had room for more producers. We approached several people informally, based on the need we felt for increased representation from different racial and ethnic backgrounds. The group we ended up with consisted of over a dozen people, about half of whom had not worked with Deep Dish or Paper Tiger before, representing Latino, African-American, Caribbean, Asian and Middle Eastern backgrounds.

As producer Dee Dee Halleck noted, for the second series:

The goals were even bigger this time around as the situation of the real war going on added tremendous stress to everyone involved in the project. For the first series, we had been motivated with the urgent need to *stop* the war from happening. Once it had started with its inexorable pattern of destruction and violence, it was hard to feel any power to affect the outcome.[8]

The pressure of having to put out shows once a week was tremendous. We thought of ourselves as a collective, but without really acknowledging it we had moved into a situation of producing shows as individual producers without creating an effective framework for collective discussion of the content or direction of the shows.

Just getting us together was tough, and getting the shows out for the deadline was tougher. Our pairing of producers, intended to complement skills, worked well in some cases and very poorly in others. We now had a multi-cultural group, and issues of racism and sexism, from which we had assumed our larger goals would exempt us, came to the fore. As producer Dee Dee Halleck put it:

> The office was often chaotic and tense, but in spite of, or perhaps because of the difficult circumstances, there was a healthy autonomy given to the producers which resulted in shows that are very strong, often brilliant. More difficult were the personnel relations between show producers and among the larger group. It had been naive at best to assume that twelve headstrong creative people could be almost randomly paired together to make a television series in such a short time. It was even more naive to expect difficult racial and national tensions to be erased easily in a common project.[9]

But somehow, amid crises and problems, a series of shows came out. They looked more 'produced' than the first series, and the tone was one of anger, passion and deep commitment to political engagement. Our effort to give voice to the many communities opposed to the war was successful to the extent that viewers saw Arab-Americans, Latinos, Native Americans, African-Americans and protesters from Mexico to London to Amman stating a clear-cut case for an end to the Gulf War. As French media activist Nathalie Magnan noted: 'It's like the first series tried to be polite. In the second series they were saying, OK, guys, we tried to be polite and it didn't work. This time we're going to really give it to you.'[10]

For our second series, as for our first, we were counting on transmitting both to public access cable stations, via Deep Dish, and on PBS through WYBE, the Philadelphia station which had sponsored our first four shows. However, at the last possible moment, after our publicity had been distributed, WYBE pulled out. Programming manager John Vernille told us that the infant station was suddenly facing a licence challenge from the Federal Communications Commission on the technical grounds that their signal was interfering with that of an FM radio station. Since the FCC has the power to revoke a station's licence, they could not risk any other problems. This was early in February, and US forces were waging war in the air (and on the airwaves) with full ferocity. A 'rally round the flag' mentality had set in, and the climate that had allowed us access to the broadcast media had altered extensively.

Ultimately we soft-fed four of the shows, and a few PBS stations picked them up. But from 19 February, a show ran each week on public access cable. *News World Order* looked at media coverage of the war; *Manufacturing the Enemy* focused on the racism faced by Arab-Americans; *Global Dissent* brought together anti-war material from around the world; *Lines in the Sand* looked at US and European policy in the Middle East; *Just Say No!* dealt with resistance in the military; and *War on the Homefront* pinpointed the economic background of the war. The series ended with *Veterans for Peace*, a live feed with a telephone call-in produced by a veterans group in Boston.

The last three shows in the series came out after the war had ended. The loss of the PBS connection, along with the startling rapidity of the ground war, meant that the impact of the second half of the series was less than that of the first part. Nonetheless, we had succeeded in putting together an amazing amount of material in a very short time and getting it out to large numbers of people. In the months following the war the shows continued to go out to schools, universities, cable networks, festivals and media arts centres around the world.

Recent rulings by the Federal Communications Commission threaten to undermine public access cable. The FCC has ruled that local telephone companies may now provide video services directly to the home via phone lines. Previously only cable companies, under strict franchise agreements which included provisions for public access, were allowed to provide video services. The FCC has no plans to require that telephone companies provide public access to video 'dialtone' systems. The FCC is even considering adopting policies to allow cable companies and telephone companies to enter into joint ventures under which neither would be required to obtain a franchise. Present cable franchise agreements, some of which extend well into the 90s, must still be honoured, and telephone companies are not technologically ready to take immediate advantage of the government's green light. Despite this, the deregulatory fever, begun by Reagan and continued under the Bush administration, poses a huge long-term challenge to the public access movement.

With *The Gulf Crisis TV Project*, Deep Dish made its first intensive efforts to get PBS affiliates to downlink its programmes. Since that time, collaboration with the community-oriented PBS affiliate WYBE in Philadelphia has continued. Recently, WYBE presented another Deep Dish series on the PBS satellite. The series, *Behind Censorship: The Assault on Civil Liberties*, attempts to show the links between the issue of censorship in the arts and other restrictions of civil rights and liberties, and includes programmes on political prisoners, reproductive rights, and the struggle for self-determination in questions of language and culture by non-white people. Many PBS stations downlinked and broadcast the series.

The receptivity of these PBS programmers bodes well for the future programming offerings of the Independent Television Programming Service (ITVS), established in 1990. After several years of lobbying by an alliance of independent producers, the US Congress allocated a three-year budget of over US$20 million to fund a programming service which would supply PBS stations with programming that was independently produced. The first round of programming is still in the pipeline, and will be available for broadcast in early 1993. The reallocation for the next three years of funding is currently the target of conservatives like Senator Jesse Helms. Helms and his cohorts would prefer to eliminate federal support of public broadcasting altogether. Failing this, they will probably focus on the cancellation of further funding of ITVS. The real test will come when the first crop of programming is released. The controversy that is sure to arise will put the concept of independent programming in the limelight. Our hope is that the controversy can be used to expand support for innovative programming initiatives.

Finally, the international links formed by the *Gulf Crisis TV Project* are one of the more important, and as of now, one of the more difficult aspects of our effort to assess. Models of media vary widely from country to country. It is clear, however, that the proliferation of the profit-making 'American-style' model of television will continue to use new cable and satellite technologies to outflank older media under state control. At the same time, as the Gulf War made clear, the waning empires of the North will increasingly depend on international alliances to reinforce their hold on the world's strategic resources and to destabilise alternative centres of power.

Here the role of activist media in helping to forge a growing international grass-roots movement has become significant. A dioxin-producing chemical plant forced to leave Arkansas in 1990 by local citizens' action, for instance, was greeted on its arrival in Malaysia in 1991 by local environmentalists with a full range of information on the plant's deadly by-products. Increased threats to international peace and to the environment, hand in hand with a proliferation of commercial, entertainment-oriented broadcasting models, mean that the international connections formed by grass-roots media workers will become ever more critical.

NOTES

1. Martin Lee and Norman Solomon, *Unreliable Sources: A Guide to Detecting Bias in the News Media* (New York: Lyle Stuart, 1991), p. xxiii.
2. Janet Sorenson, 'The Missing Links: From Censorship to Access', *Afterimage* (Rochester, NY) vol. 19 no. 6, January 1992.
3. Amy Taubin, 'Talking Back to Television: the Gulf Crisis TV Project', *The Village Voice*, 5 March 1991.
4. Jonathan Mandel, 'Stay Tuned for America's Angriest Home Videos', *New York Newsday*, 25 February 1991.
5. Sorenson, 'The Missing Links'.
6. Peter Fleming, press release, Vision/TV, Toronto, 19 February 1991.
7. Tetsuo Kogawa, 'A Japanese Perspective on the Gulf War', unpublished interview with producers of the *Gulf Crisis TV Project*, February 1991.
8. Dee Dee Halleck, 'Chronology of the Gulf Crisis TV Project', unpublished article, August 1991.
9. Ibid.
10. Informal conversation, September 1991.